TEXT, THEORY, SPACE

Text, Theory, Space is an unprecedented, landmark text in post-colonial criticism and theory. This outstanding and timely collection focuses on two white settler societies, South Africa and Australia, and explores the meaning of 'The South' as an aesthetic, political, geographical and cultural space.

Arising from a conference sponsored by the University of London's School of Oriental and African Studies and Sir Robert Menzies Centre for Australian Studies, this collection draws on expansive disciplines, including literature, history, urban geography, politics and anthropology. Issues of claiming, naming and possessing land; national and personal boundaries; and questions of race, gender and nationalism are also explored.

Kate Darian-Smith is a lecturer in Australian Studies and Deputy Director at Sir Robert Menzies Centre for Australian Studies, University of London and is the author of *On the Home Front* and editor of *History and Memory in Twentieth-Century Australia*. **Liz Gunner** is a lecturer in African Literature at the School of Oriental and African Studies and is the editor of *The Journal of Southern African Studies*. **Sarah Nuttall** is a Research Fellow at the University of Cape Town and writes on South African literature.

TEXT, THEORY, SPACE

Land, literature and history in
South Africa and Australia

*Edited by Kate Darian-Smith,
Liz Gunner and Sarah Nuttall*

London and New York

First published 1996
by Routledge
11 New Fetter Lane, London EC4P 4EE

Simultaneously published in the USA and Canada
by Routledge
29 West 35th Street, New York, NY 10001

Routledge is an International Thomson Publishing company

© 1996 Kate Darian-Smith, Liz Gunner and Sarah Nuttall

Typeset in Baskerville by
Harper Phototypesetters Limited, Northampton
Printed in Great Britain by
TJ Press (Padstow) Ltd, Padstow, Cornwall

British Library Cataloguing in Publication Data
A catalogue record for this book is available from
the British Library

Library of Congress Cataloguing in Publication Data
A catalogue record for this book has been requested

ISBN 0–415–12407–7
ISBN 0–415–12408–5 (pbk)

To our mothers, Pam, Pearl, and Jean

CONTENTS

NOTES ON CONTRIBUTORS

Michelle Adler recently completed her PhD on South African women travel writers at the Institute of Commonwealth Studies, University of London, and is Lecturer in the Department of English at Rand Afrikaans University in Johannesburg. She is interested in women's writing of Empire, especially travel writing, and in African literature.

Tony Birch is completing a PhD in History at The University of Melbourne, but much prefers writing and publishing poetry, and cultivating vegetable gardens.

David Bunn is Professor in the Department of English at the University of the Western Cape. He has published on South African landscape and cultural studies, is a co-editor of the journal *Social Dynamics* and his book *Land Acts: Modernity, Representation and the Making of South African Space* is due out soon.

Paul Carter is a writer and historian, and is currently Senior Research Fellow at The Australian Centre, The University of Melbourne. His recent books include *Baroque Memories* (1994), *The Sound In-Between* (1992) and *Living in A New Country* (1992). His new title *The Lie of the Land* (1996) is published by Faber.

Kate Darian-Smith lectures in the Department of History and The Australian Centre at The University of Melbourne. Her publications include *On the Home Front: Melbourne in Wartime 1939–1945* (1990), as editor, *Captured Lives: Australian Captivity Narratives* (1992), and, as co-editor, *History and Memory in Twentieth-Century Australia* (1994).

Dorothy Driver has published widely on South African literature and is the editor of *Pauline Smith* (1983), in the McGraw-Hill casebook series. She has also compiled and introduced *Nadine Gordimer: A Bibliography* (1993). She is Associate Professor in the English Department at the University of Cape Town and is a leading critic on South African women writers.

Kerryn Goldsworthy is a Senior Lecturer in the English Department at Melbourne University. Well-known in the field of Australian Studies and in literary journalism, she is the editor of two anthologies of Australian short stories, and edited the national reviews journal *Australian Book Review* in 1986–7. Her collection of short stories *North of the Moonlight Sonata* was published in 1989. She is currently working on a full-length study of nineteenth-century Australian women's letters and diaries.

Liz Gunner is Senior Lecturer in the Department of African Languages and Cultures at the School of Oriental and African Studies. She has published articles on South African oral poetry, and a few short stories. Her publications include, *Musho! Zulu Popular Praises*, translated and co-edited with Mafika Gwala (1994) and as editor, *Politics and Performance in Southern African Theatre, Poetry and Song* (1994).

Nhlanhla Maake was Lecturer in Southern African Drama and Literature at the School of African and Oriental Studies until 1995 when he moved to the University of the Witwatersrand as Professor of African Languages. He has been an actor, has written articles on Sotho literature and South African theatre and language studies and is a prolific and successful novelist, writing in Sotho.

Rob Nixon is Associate Professor of English and Comparative Literature at Columbia University. He has written articles on contemporary South African politics and culture in journals such as *Transition* and *The Village Voice* and is the author of *London Calling: V.S. Naipaul, Postcolonial Mandarin* (1992) and *Homelands, Harlem and Hollywood: South African Culture and the World Beyond* (1994). He is currently writing a book on ostriches and ostrich farming in South Africa and North America.

Sarah Nuttall has recently completed her doctorate at Oxford University on reading practices amongst South African women and is Research Fellow in English at the University of Cape Town. She is currently working on a comparative study of South African and Australian fiction.

Abner Nyamende is Lecturer in African Literature at the University of Cape Town. His interests are in oral literature and literature written in indigenous South African languages, particularly Xhosa. He is currently working on a doctorate on the novelist Modikwe Dikobe.

Terence Ranger is Rhodes Professor of Race Relations at Oxford University. He has published numerous books and articles on African and particularly southern African history. His writings include *The Invention of Tradition*, co-edited with Eric Hobsbawm (1983), *Peasant Consciousness and Guerilla War* (1985), *Legitimacy and the State in Twentieth-Century Africa*, co-edited with Olufemi Vaughan, and *Dance and Society in Eastern Africa 1890-1970*.

Sue Rowley is Professor of Contemporary Australian Art History at The University of New South Wales College of Fine Arts. Her recent publications have included, as co-editor, the book *Debutante Nation: Feminism Contests the 1890s* (1993), and she also writes on craft theory and feminism in the visual arts.

Sophie Watson is Professor at the School of Policy Studies, University of Bristol. Her recent publications include, as editor, *Playing the State: Australian Feminist Interventions* (1990), and as co-editor, *Metropolis Now: Planning and the Urban in Contemporary Australia* (1994) and *Post-Modern Cities and Spaces* (1995)

Gillian Whitlock is Associate Professor in the Faculty of Humanities at Griffith University. Recently she co-edited the journal *Australian Canadian Studies* and the books *Australian and Canadian Literatures in English: Comparative Perspectives*, and *Re-Siting Queen's English*, among others. She has just completed editing a collection of contemporary Australian autobiographical writing, entitled *Autographs*, and is working on a study of post-colonial autobiography.

ACKNOWLEDGEMENTS

This book arose from a conference, 'Southern Spaces: Land, Representation and Identity in South African and Australian Literatures' organized by the School of African and Oriental Studies, and the Sir Robert Menzies Centre for Australian Studies at London University. We would particularly like to thank all those who participated in the conference and helped make it the stimulating and memorable event it undoubtedly was. We also wish to thank and acknowledge those who supported its organization in material and moral ways: Brian Matthews; Shula Marks; Jim Walter; Lawrence Harris; Louis Brenner; Graham Furniss; The British Academy; The Literature Board, Australia Council; The Aboriginal and Torres Strait Islander Arts Board, Australia Council; Kirsten McIntyre, Prue McKay, Sarah Dugdale, Anne Collett, Jackie Collis and staff at SOAS, the Menzies Centre and the Institute of Commonwealth Studies.

Talia Rodgers at Routledge has been encouraging from the very beginning and we are very grateful to her. Many thanks also to our friends and colleagues who gave us encouragement, support and lots of good ideas from the early stages of our planning: Peter Quartermaine, Lyn Innes, Angela Smith, Elleke Boehmer and Anne McClintock were particularly helpful. Our thanks also to Colin Gardner who acted as our messenger and mailbox at a crucial late stage of things when the three editors were separated by expanses of southern space. Mineke Schipper and Paul Gready read and commented on drafts of the introduction. Kai Easton, Scot Lerwill and Rachel Jenzen gave generously of their time in the final stages of the preparation of the manuscript and other time-absorbing details.

K.D-S., L.G., S.N.

INTRODUCTION

Kate Darian-Smith, Liz Gunner and Sarah Nuttall

Those of us who attended the 'Southern Spaces' conference in June 1993 were gathered in London, a metropolitan centre far from South Africa and Australia and yet historically and culturally connected to both places. It was a time of transition in South Africa, when the worst years of the struggle against apartheid, and the necessary isolation, were in the past and the structures of the new political order were being earnestly hammered into shape. In late 1992, the High Court of Australia had overturned the historical and judicial foundations of land ownership in Australia, recognizing that indigenous peoples had prior claim to lands colonized by the British; months later the Native Title Act would be passed. It seemed the appropriate moment, in this climate of momentous political change, to look again at the numerous features that united and separated South Africa and Australia. These two southern spaces, once part of the British Empire, had much in common: their similar latitudes, their arid, fragile interiors, and their shared settler myths of the 'empty land' and policies of white racial domination. Yet there were also divergences in the histories of colonization, the articulations of resistance to the imperial presence by the indigenous inhabitants, and the complex modernity and unitary nationhood of these two settler sites.

The 'Southern Spaces' conference was initially envisaged as one about literary production, but it soon became apparent that this was too narrow a conception. An interdisciplinary frame of interest emerged which brought together literary critics, writers, historians, urban planners and cultural geographers. The essays in this book all originated from that conference. As a collection, they demonstrate that in spite of the limited extent of any comparative examinations to date, the shared study of South African and Australian cultural and literary history is indeed a rich and intellectually rewarding one.

We have arranged the essays into three parts: 'Defining the South', 'Claiming Lands, Creating Identities, Making Nations', and 'Borders, Boundaries, Open Spaces'. While the titles of these sections indicate the thematic threads that tie the work of our contributors together, there are empirical and theoretical concerns that stretch across the sections and twine the essays together in alternative ways. This book, therefore, offers the reader a series of interlocking conversations that address the issues of land, space and cultural identity in South Africa and Australia, and open up new and exciting directions for further comparative scholarship. This introduction aims to provide an overview of the historical links between South Africa and Australia in the previous two centuries, and to tease out some of the questions raised by the essays in relation to contemporary debates and discussions about space, race, gender and imperialism.

TEXT, SPACE AND THE SOUTH

The notion of space as a multidimensional entity with social and cultural as well as territorial dimensions has been a prime concern in recent scholarship, particularly in the fields of post-colonial literatures and history, and social and cultural geography. Space has been linked to concepts of power, as in the writing of Michel Foucault, and there is a growing body of historical and literary criticism which deals with the peculiarities of colonial space and its relationship to, and representation through, the eye – and the pen – of the imperial beholder.[1] The complex interactions between space and power form the dominant, although variously expressed, theme of this collection. The four writers in the opening section introduce the colonial south in papers which address the underside of the colonizing psyche, landscape theory and practice, the liminality of the emigrant position, and the discursive formation of settler sites in the field of empire. Paul Carter gives a highly original and engaging reading of the fascination with the spirit world, and the irrational world of the imagination, amongst Victorian diarists and writers, some of whom travelled to South Africa and Australia. Within the stifling confines

2

of the Victorian domestic interior, Carter argues, the colonized world was being 'dreamed, theorized, modelled and re-enacted'. As the Victorian mind tried to ground itself in its role as the colonizer of 'new' lands, it was threatened with the abysses, cliffs, swamps and sands, not only of the southern lands it was colonizing, but of its own psyche. Swamps and sands, writes Carter, 'hovered ambiguously between the solid and the liquid, and were famously the source of miasmic spirits'. Thus, from the metropolis, the colonizers faced the possibility of sinking into the otherness of the 'spirit world', of becoming 'ungrounded' and experiencing a mirror-like autogenesis.

At the same time, on the peripheries of the British Empire, colonial space was being culturally 'grounded'; J. M. Coetzee's influential novel, *Foe*, (1986) can be usefully read as a critique of the 'founding' of colonial space.[2] W. J. T. Mitchell has pointed to the way in which landscape circulates as a medium of exchange, as 'a site of visual appropriation, a focus for the formation of identity'; the 'semiotic features' of landscape generate historical narratives.[3] In this sense, landscape is dynamic; it serves to create and naturalize the histories and identities inscribed upon it, and so simultaneously hides and makes evident social and historical formations. It is through the cultural processes of imagining, seeing, historicizing and remembering that space is transformed into place, and geographical territory into a culturally defined landscape. As Erica Carter and her co-authors have expressed it:

> It is not spaces which ground identifications but places. How then does space become place? By being named; as the flows of power and negotiation of social relations are rendered in the concrete form of architecture; and also, of course, by embodying the symbolic and imaginary investment of a population. Place is space to which meaning has been ascribed.[4]

The cultural contestations over naming and possessing the land, representing its landscape, and producing and defining a sense of place run through all the essays in this collection, and highlight the multiple and complex meanings attached to both land and place in South African and Australian colonial and post-colonial societies.

Any comparative approach to these issues has to confront the surprising fact that some of the influential academic scholarship in South Africa and Australia is little known in 'the other space'. This is true, for instance, of Bernard Smith's pathbreaking *European Vision and the South Pacific* (1960) and J. M. Coetzee's later but equally crucial *White Writing: the Culture of Letters in South Africa* (1989). Smith's and Coetzee's arguments not only concur in some respects but can also be seen as incremental. Smith points out that European ways of seeing the 'new worlds' of the South Pacific were culturally determined by European ways of knowing: 'European observers sought to come to grips with the realities of the Pacific by interpreting them in familiar terms.'[5] Thus the imperial perceptions of Pacific lands and peoples formed through the exploratory voyages of the late eighteenth and early nineteenth century both reflected and projected European philosophical, artistic and scientific knowledges. As Western scientific theories of biological evolution were transposed into social and political ideologies of imperial domination, this coincided with the predominance in nineteenth-century landscape painting of the 'typical landscape'. The pictorial composition of plant, animal and human components within their specific geographical and climatic sites provided aesthetic representations and symbols of each scenic type.

Smith's work on the South Pacific partially prefigures Edward Said's examination of the West's academic and imaginative construction of the East – the Orient – as 'Other'. Said, situating this emergent construction in the late eighteenth century, writes of 'Orientalism as a Western style for dominating, restructuring and having authority over the Orient'.[6] The link here between Eurocentric perceptions of the Orient and the imaging of the Pacific discussed by Bernard Smith is one of power – through imaging. In a different imperial context, Coetzee's discussion of European art and literature in South Africa from the mid-seventeenth to the twentieth centuries is also about Eurocentric visions which reduce the possibility of absorbing any scheme of seeing based on indigenous conceptual categories. Coetzee argues that twentieth-century white South African poets have adopted an antagonistic stance to African space:

> In all the poetry commemorating meetings with the silence and emptiness of Africa ... it is hard not to read a certain historical will to see as silent and empty a land that has been, if not full of human figures, not empty of them either.[7]

'The poetry of empty space', he continues, 'furthers the fiction of an empty land', and this observation can be applied equally to the white Australian literary tradition.

The myth of the 'empty' land can be seen not only as something willed in the imagination of the would-be possessor but, also, in its vastness, as potentially devouring and overwhelming. Anne McClintock has recently argued that British colonial maps, with their 'edges and blank spaces' filled with cannibals, mermaids and monsters, are vivid reminders of the contradictions of colonial discourse.[8] Maps embody both knowledge and possession but also a sense of the tenousness of such possession. As McClintock writes, 'The map is a liminal thing, associated with thresholds and marginal zones, burdened with dangerous powers.'[9]

In *The Road to Botany Bay* (1987), Paul Carter proposes spatial history – a 'prehistory of places, a history of roads, footprints, trails of dust and foaming waves' – as an alternative to histories of imperialism.[10] For Carter, space is a text upon which histories and cultures are inscribed and interpreted. He argues that the imperial landscape of Australia was created through the European naming and mapping of its geographical features by white explorers, administrators and settlers. The act of naming, and the names themselves, either blatantly ignored or subverted and incorporated pre-existing Aboriginal names and histories of the land. Thus competing or overlapping histories are either presenced or silenced through the cultural power of maps and place names.

Maps and globes also, of course, divided the world into two horizontal halves: the north and the south. From the northern, European perspective the southern hemisphere has been imbued with mysterious, unknowable qualities since classical times. The idea of a fantastical southern continent was present in the European imagination since Ptolemy, while Pliny believed there was 'always something new coming out of Africa'. Many of the essays in this collection consciously examine South Africa and Australia as southern settler societies, whose environments, indigenous peoples and thus historical experiences of colonialism were markedly different from imperial expansion in northern 'new worlds'. As Ross Gibson has argued, the South Land of Australia has been a 'duplicitous object' for the European and American north: a society that, over the last two centuries, has been viewed as primarily European but also understood as being exotic.[11] The lingering mystery still attached to the south during the nineteenth century is illustrated in Kerryn Goldsworthy's chapter, where she highlights the symbolic importance European immigrants attached to the crossing of the Equator. The entry into the southern hemisphere was observed in ritualized, carnivalesque forms by sailors and passengers alike.

Goldsworthy writes that the 'Equator implicitly becomes a metonym for the whole experience of emigration: the moment of crossing-the-line is the moment at which to enact the process of transformation.' For British subjects, the journey to the south involved not only a reorientation in spatial terms, but a shift in identity from European immigrant to colonial settler.

COLONIAL CONNECTIONS

While there is evidence from Great Zimbabwe of trade with Venice and China as early as the fourteenth century, it was not until the sixteenth century that European expansion began to reach into the southern hemisphere, and not until the late eighteenth century that the great southern voyages of 'discovery' were launched. Donald Denoon has suggested that the antipodean settler societies developed by Europe, including South Africa and Australia, shared geographical and historical characteristics that distinguished them from their northern neighbours in the tropics.[12] European colonization had initially concentrated on tropical territories that were densely populated by indigenous peoples, and could be transformed quickly into European merchant or plantation societies. In contrast, the indigenous populations of Southern Africa and Australia were relatively sparse, (the east coast of Southern Africa was an exception) and their lands were seen by Europeans, at least at first, as less suitable for intensive European-style agriculture. This meant, Denoon claims, that European settlements in southern temperate regions were intended to guard the edges of Empire and service imperial interests in the tropics. Cape Town was established by the Dutch East India Company during the eighteenth century as a port to assist Dutch ships en route to Java; the settlement of the penal colony at Botany Bay in 1788 provided an outpost from where the British could watch over their imperial interests in India and Asia.

From the early nineteenth century, however, the rise of Britain as the dominant imperial power and trading nation drew the Australian and (after the British occupation of the Cape in 1806) the South African colonies, into its imperial and international networks of capital, investment and trade. This provided a stimulus to agricultural, pastoral and manufacturing production. 'By the end of the century', writes Denoon:

> the settler societies had all felt the exhilaration of pulling in
> capital investment hand over fist, drawing migrants by the

thousands, laying railway tracks into the remotest interior, shovelling minerals furiously, harvesting grain by millions of tons, slaughtering thousands of stock, and enjoying per capita incomes that were the envy of the world.[13]

Land was cleared for agriculture, temperate grasslands turned over to intensive grazing and planting, European livestock was introduced with wool to become the critical common product (in Australasia there had previously been no hoofed animals). Native animals were hunted, sometimes to extinction, and mining dissected and cut open the earth. In southern Africa, as William Beinart has argued:

> the intensity of competition between settler and African communities over natural resources and the increasingly powerful hold of settlers over production and the instruments of state, ensured that any state attempt to regulate the environment became a deeply politicized issue.[14]

Physical contestation over land between imperial invaders and indigenous inhabitants was, in both South Africa and Australia, bound up with culturally different spatial concepts about the environment. In southern Africa, for instance, the colonial emphasis was on dividing land in accordance with models drawn from industrialized and capitalist Europe, so that there were separate areas with exclusive functions such as forestry, game reserves and farming. This clashed with African ideas of flexible land use and multi-purpose common land.[15] David Bunn's chapter discusses the imposition of two such interrelating spatial divisions in Natal: the sugar estate and the game reserve. Bunn shows how the sugar baron, William Campbell, after destroying the lush tropical flora around the Umgeni River to create sugar plantations, moved to the Transvaal bushveld. There he recreated at the Mala Mala game reserve both 'nature' and 'natural man' in an artificial hunting space, which admitted no freely operating hunters or farmers but only 'a narrow spectrum of docile, colourful subaltern personalities' and a quaint, colourful and invented ethnicity.

The Mala Mala reserve provides an example of how such conservation initiatives must be situated within broader political policies. As Beinart and Coates observe concerning South Africa's parks and reserves: 'Today's parks remain a powerful cultural statement fusing notions of nature and nation.'[16] Nor can all this be separated from the colonial discourse on race. The increasing dominance of Social

Darwinism and attitudes of white superiority by the middle of the nineteenth century meant that Africans were constructed as the unscientific over-exploiters of the environment, while in Australia Aborigines were falsely portrayed as nomads who failed to manage or harvest the land.[17]

During the nineteenth and twentieth centuries, the culture of British imperialism radiated outwards to what were conceived as the distant points of Empire, while those points in turn pressed back upon the centre in often unacknowledged and unrecognized ways.[18] The lands and peoples of South Africa and Australia, as well as those of other British possessions such as New Zealand, Canada and, of course, India, assumed a prominent role within the British imagination. These colonies featured as an often undifferentiated colonial backdrop in British popular culture; the adventures of Empire were variously told in publications like the *Boys Own Paper* and the genre of colonial romance. The new societies of South Africa and Australia provided imaginative spaces for the playing out of fantasies – particularly male fantasies – born from the social and geographical constrictions of old Europe.

The world of Empire with its white hunters and obsequious blacks, ambiguously savage and exotic, became the stage for numerous Empire novels, the most famous being H. Rider Haggard's *King Solomon's Mines* (1885) set in 'Kekuanaland', a thinly disguised northern Zululand.[19] Similar romances were produced from within the colonial spaces themselves; there were, for instance, distinctive Australian romances which allowed play for the colonial, and again usually male, imagination.[20] Just as Africa was seen as a 'heart of darkness', the Australian centre was seen as a dark, unknowable void. Indeed, until the mid-nineteenth century, European exploration in Australia was preoccupied with discovering an inland lake or sea. By the 1880s and 1890s, a number of bizarre stories with echoes of Haggard appeared, telling of lost white civilizations and treasures in the heart of Australia. They were, though, far from simply derivative, as the image of the empty centre, and the threatening bush, had force as a constant, nervous theme in white Australian culture. This sense of deep insecurity and alienation from the Australian environment, and the melancholia induced by the bush, is reflected some in Australian settler literature and art, and is discussed in Sue Rowley's chapter on madness and the bush in Australian fiction. 'Taming the land' in Australia, as well as in South Africa, involved not only the technicalities of agriculture, mining and suchlike, but making links between identity and the environment.

The fluidity of culture, capital and people between Britain and its colonies, and between the colonies themselves, had implications for the formation of government policies across the Empire. Imperial administrators often moved from one colony to the other, leaving their names, or those of their wives, scattered arbitrarily over 'undomesticated' territories geographically distant from each other. Sir George Grey, for instance, (1812–98) was the Governor of South Australia, New Zealand (twice) and the Cape Colony; Sir Frederick Broome (1842–96) farmed in New Zealand and held senior government posts in Natal and Mauritius before being appointed governor of Western Australia in 1883. Civil and military employees were accompanied by their families as they served throughout the Empire. The observations of life in South Africa and Western Australia by Broome's wife, Lady Mary Anne Barker, are examined in Gillian Whitlock's chapter, where she fascinatingly highlights the voice of the sharply observing women who wrote themselves into a particular colonial history and, as in Barker's case, made important connections between places within the Empire. It was, however, male colonial administrators who interpreted, changed and carried out policy; they brought political, social and racial ideas learnt from experience in one colonial situation to another and adapted these – sometimes radically – in response to localized conditions.

It was not only colonial officials and their families who took new ideas and impressions with them as they travelled throughout the British world. Indentured labourers from India were brought to South Africa from the 1860s, and were to have a significant effect on that country's social and political history. Furthermore, the lure of land, gold, business interest, and adventure that had attracted European immigrants to the Australasian or southern African colonies in the first place, also stimulated the intra-colonial migration of white settlers between these two southern parts of the Empire. Economic depression in eastern Australia during the 1890s resulted in increased emigration from the Australian colonies to New Zealand, Paraguay or South Africa.[21] And other bonds within the British Empire were forged by imperial loyalty. The Anglo-Boer war of 1899–1902 brought more than 16,000 Australian 'Bushmen' to South Africa to fight in British and colonial contingents.[22] Many Australian soldiers chose to remain in South Africa, working mainly in the Witwatersrand gold mines. These immigrants brought with them a tradition of Australian trade unionism, and often racist ideas towards Asian and African labour which were significant in the early development of the South African union movement and Labour Party.

Immigration within the 'southern British world' decreased during the twentieth century due to economic factors – although by the 1970s and 1980s Australia had become a favoured destination for white South African immigrants. Nonetheless, the experience of Pearl Adams, mother of one of the editors, was not unique. Pearl was born in England in 1910, migrated to Australia on the S.S. *Demosthenes* with her mother in 1925, married and lived in Ceylon, then moved to South Africa and finally returned to England in the early 1970s. Her experiences included key moments in the national memory of each country: she was present at the opening of Sydney Harbour Bridge and, as the train passed through the little border town she lived in in South Africa, was part of the team that provided 'refreshments for the troops' during the Second World War. There was, therefore, the dispersal of men and women whose lives held vivid experiences of both places. But as immigration between South Africa and Australia decreased in the early twentieth century, these decades also saw the rise of different forms of colonial nationalisms, the growth of black African nationalism, and the emergence of different forms of settler identification with the land, in these two settler societies.[23]

MEMORY, SPACE AND NATION

[There is] an elaborate frame through which our adult eyes survey the landscape ... Before it can ever be a repose for the senses, landscape is the work of the mind. Its scenery is built up as much from strata of memory as from layers of rock.

Simon Schama, *Landscape and Memory*

The way in which discordant memories or slipping 'frames' accommodate each other plays a crucial part in the emergence of any sense of a unitary national culture. In the Australian and South African contexts, Simon Schama's words on landscape, cited above, need to be read alongside an awareness of the presence of conflicting or at least overlaid memories in the make-up of 'the nation'.[24] As Schama also notes, national identity 'would lose much of its ferocious enchantment without the mystique of a particular landscape tradition, its topography, mapped, elaborated and enriched as a homeland'.[25]

10

The example of Bruce Beresford's 1980 Australian film about the Anglo-Boer war, *Breaker Morant*, in which the South Australian landscape is substituted for that of the eastern Transvaal (now part of the renamed province of Mpumalanga), points to a striking 'double vision' and a shared imperial history. The terrain of the South Australian outback may appear (at least from a distance) to be similar to the South African veld, but it does not hold the deep memory of the Anglo-Boer war that the actual place does. There are *cultural* differences in terms of landscape and memory between the two regions.

Moreover, within the two regions the inhabitants, white and black, very frequently have contrasting and conflicting memories of the same place. This constitutes, however, far more than the co-existence of dissonant memories; it points to quite different percep-tions of the land itself. Liz Gunner's chapter highlights the different memories – and languages – that are used in staking out a sense of belonging to land, and to place. Her chapter deals with a theme that surfaces continually in this collection: the journey, and the possession and dispossession of the land. In Nguni and Sotho oral poetry of the early nineteenth century, a sense of belonging is established through multiple references to place. It is not a settled poetry, but one turning on restless movement, skirmishes, conquests. This is a reminder that the state of 'migrancy' seen by Homi Bhabha as a phenomenon of the post-colonial moment and the metropolitan centres of America and Europe, is also embedded, as Aijaz Ahmad has claimed, in much older histories.[26]

Sue Rowley's chapter also discusses the spatial metaphor of the journey and makes the important point that emergent nationalisms turn constantly for the confirmation of identity to reified imaginings of the land, or in Schama's sense, a 'homeland'. Rowley demon-strates how nationalist Australian bush mythology of the 1890s 'represents national landscapes through a specific and limited ex-perience of the land', and how the journey towards nationhood infuses the narratives of explorers, pioneers and bushmen with the potency of the quest.

These issues of memories of the land and national identity are also brought out in Sarah Nuttall's essay on the recent South African novels by Elleke Boehmer and Damon Galgut. The South African writing Nuttall discusses mocks and undercuts the established discourses around the land; and like Rowley, Nuttall teases out the interconnections between gendered representations of land and nationalism. She puts before the reader the alternative literary

11

strategies that Boehmer and Galgut adopt in the landscapes and characters they create. Both authors dislocate the old connections of gender, power and land in their presentations of an anti-hero and anti-heroine in the unbounded spaces of the Namibian desert and the flat western hinterland of southern Africa. Both fictions also point to the need to rethink images of the land in the uncertain times of new nationalisms and national boundaries.

THE RACIALIZING AND GENDERING OF SPACE

In the public sphere of state policy, it is in the area of race relations that the distinctions and similarities between South Africa and Australia emerge most clearly. The final section of this introduction turns to the interactions between race, gender and power in the definitions and representations of these southern lands. Both countries share some common historical and cultural features in the ways that space has been racialized and sexualized, although the extremities of the policies of apartheid resulted in unique spatial configurations within South African society.

The British invasion and possession of the Australian continent was based on the (British) legal dictum of *terra nullius:* that the land was uninhabited, empty of people. From the late eighteenth century, indigenous populations of Australia were driven from their lands, defeated in bloody frontier warfare, and killed by the spread of European diseases. Estimates of Aboriginal populations in 1788 range between 750,000 and 3 million, but in any case had fallen to only 50,000 by 1900. In South Africa, apart from the southwest of the country, the far greater indigenous population meant that white settlers were always outnumbered by Africans. On the east coast, the defiant Xhosa resisted thrust upon thrust of settler intrusion and were pushed, with difficulty, further north during a number of frontier wars.[27] In the early decades of the nineteenth century, Dutch hunters and trekboers moved northwards from the Cape Colony, by this time a British possession, and became the major agents of settler expansion.[28] The settlers wreaked havoc and destruction on indigenous African societies, which were themselves in a state of great flux during what was known as the 'mfecane'.[29] The image of the embattled Boer laager – the wagons tied together in a circle as protection from the attacking regiments of black warriors – became a standard emblem of emergent Afrikaner nationalism from the late nineteenth century onwards.[30] But in numerical terms what was to become, particularly after the National Party election victory in 1948, an entrenched white hegemony always remained a minority which never exceeded more than 21 per cent of the total population, and by the 1990s accounted for only 14 per cent.

Governments in both South Africa and Australia institutionalized policies of racial segregation and discrimination from the nineteenth century onwards. To keep Australia 'for the white man', in the words of the slogan of the influential *Bulletin* magazine, the first legislation passed by the new Federal parliament of 1901 was the Immigration Restriction Act, popularly known as the White Australia Policy. When the four South African colonies formed the Union of South Africa in 1910, the new constitution gave the white minority a monopoly of political representation. Australian Prime Minister Andrew Fisher, who visited South Africa at this time, noted the difference between the two settler colonies. Because of the size of the black African population, Fisher believed that South Africa could never 'become, in the Australian sense, a white man's country. It must always be a black man's country, ruled over by an aristocracy of white labour.'[31] In Australia, however, such an 'aristocracy' had ruled over 62,000 Melanesian indentured labourers on the Queensland sugar plantations until 1904, and persisted on the remote pastoral stations of northern Australia, with their unpaid Aboriginal workforce, until the 1960s. Nonetheless, by the early twentieth century Australian society was almost entirely of Anglo-Celtic origin (this was to alter due to immigration towards the century's close). The indigenous minority were subjected to policies of racial exclusion, segregation and control.

South Africa was, indeed, a 'black man's country' – and the gendering of the epithet is also, of course, of great significance. The management of race relations and the maintenance of white supremacy in the interests of capitalist expansion were central to South African state power. This meant that all residential, commercial, agricultural and industrial space was racially determined and controlled. An exhibition of documents at the University of the Witwatersrand during 1994 powerfully demonstrated the extent to which space in South Africa in the apartheid era was linked not only to race but to language. Maps of the Johannesburg urban area, maps of locations (apartheid-era sites for African urban living), municipal documents, photographs and recorded testimonies were placed on view. A typical letter, written in the register of officialese, from the

Johannesburg Municipal Council Locations Department to the Director of Native Labour referred to 'Segregation: Native Urban Areas Act of 1923':

> I send you herewith for your information and necessary action, a list of natives who have left together with a list of those who have taken up accommodation at the Western Native Township, Wemmer Native Barracks, Salisbury and Jubilee Compound.

The names that followed show the standard brutal erasure of black African identities: Dixon 340,141; Johannes 1,430,259; Jim 1,132,091 and so on.[32] The Exhibition notes pointed out how urban planning thus utilized the lines of the map as a technical means of politically defining space.[33] Cemeteries were segregated; spaces for sleeping could be withdrawn at the stroke of a bureaucratic pen wielded by the white hostel superintendent; passes both curtailed and allowed physical movement.[34] South African writers, such as those in the *Drum* magazine group of the 1950s and early 1960s, have lampooned, documented and satirized what they saw as spatial madness. Yet simultaneously, black locations and townships such as Soweto became places that sustained distinctive African cultural identities, and were the sites of vigorous resistance to the apartheid state.

Two of the chapters in this book, those by Abner Nyamende and Dorothy Driver, discuss the writing that arose from the black experience of racialized urban space. Driver analyses the writings in *Drum* magazine during the 1950s and examines the ways that rural African patriarchal structures were reconstructed in new, urban formations and the pivotal space that was accorded to the representation of the African woman in these negotiations. She explores spatial gender configurations and defines a moment when a different African space, a different relationship between the rural past and urban present, and between blacks and whites, opened up in *Drum*, only to be closed over again in later years.

Abner Nyamende's reading of Modikwe Dikobe's novel *The Marabi Dance*, like Driver's paper, is also concerned with identities divided between the legacies of a rural past and a harsh urban present. It focuses on the way each space, particularly for a black woman, implied a starkly different identity. Nyamende explores the questions raised by Dikobe concerning the tensions caused by the fact that recently urbanized blacks had been severed from their rural heritage, and were unable to own the lands they 'belonged to' in either the rural or urban space.

Rob Nixon's chapter on the author Bessie Head explores the division between rural and urban identities in apartheid South Africa, and tackles the configuration of woman, land and nation from another perspective. Head adopted a southern African identity which was based on a rural transnationalism. These 'southern spaces', Nixon argues, offset Head's estrangement from national and Pan-Africanist movements, and her writing reflected and recreated regenerative traditions of cultural syncretism. In this way, Head's work opens up the possibility of a southern African literature, a literary space that is more than the sum of the region's national literatures, but is connected across national borders.

In Australia, space and land ownership were also prescribed in terms of race and power. Dispossessed of their traditional lands during the nineteenth century, Aborigines were driven to missions and reserves. White institutions and officials regulated all facets of their lives, including physical movement. Under the policy of assimilation, the long-term practice of removing Aboriginal children from their mothers and sending them to state institutions to be trained as domestic servants and labourers provided a particularly insidious form of spatial and social control. The racial segregation of residential space and public services was a feature of Australian country towns, and was highlighted in the 'Freedom Rides' by political activists throughout New South Wales during the 1960s. In 1967, Aborigines and Torres Strait Islanders were granted the rights of citizenship, and subsequent anti-discrimination legislation has technically removed racial segregation. In addition, various legislation culminating in the Native Title Act of 1993 has also recognized some indigenous claims to land. Nonetheless, the disproportionate number of Aborigines who are incarcerated in Australian gaols or are unemployed suggests that space – both in Australia and South Africa – now needs to be conceptualized in terms of social justice and access to the political structures and institutions of the state.

Many of the chapters in this collection examine the contestations between indigenous and European populations over the naming, ownership and symbolic currency of land in South Africa and Australia. Nhlanhla Maake examines the imagery of national flags and anthems in the 'old' and 'new' South Africa, and the names given to South African cities and black townships. He reminds us of the competing claims to the land and nation expressed through the imperial languages of English and Afrikaans as well as through African languages.

Terence Ranger examines the production of competing symbols and myths of two very different sacred spaces, comparing two 'rocky icons' in Australia and southern Africa: Uluru (Ayers Rock) and the Matopos. In both cases foreign, European names have been imposed on these landforms. Ranger finds parallels in the colonial histories of South Africa and Australia, and suggests that the concept of transcontinental 'southern spaces' within the sphere of British imperialism and white domination can provide a useful analytical framework. However, Ranger argues, the points of difference which emerge in a study of the present negotiations over the ownership and identity of the two sacred places of Uluru and the Matopos also mark the historical and cultural difference inherent in Australia and southern African society and academic discourse.

The chapter by Tony Birch, like that by Nhlanhla Maake, foregrounds the importance of names and the contestations surrounding these items of crucial symbolic capital. He discusses the controversy surrounding the restoration of the Aboriginal name 'Gariwerd' to the Grampians National Park in Victoria in recent years. Birch examines the arguments mounted by white opponents to the name restoration, and hence the recognition of a prior and continuing Aboriginal presence in the region, and the subsequent decision by government and tourist authorities to reverse the name change. Birch reflects on the naming practices of the nineteenth-century surveyor and explorer of the region, Major Thomas Mitchell, to demonstrate the relationship, referred to earlier in this introduction, between possessing and naming land.

Space – and place – in South Africa and Australia were, and are, not only racialized but also gendered, and this emerges as a consistent theme across many of the essays in this book. Just as the politics of identity and difference are gendered, so too are the institutional and private practices that socially constitute space. Recent feminist analyses are challenging the universalist dichotomy between private (women's) and public (men's) spaces by arguing that such clear distinctions ignore the significance of race and class.[35] Feminist scholarship has also emphasized the gendered perceptions of the imperial beholder, and the complicity of European women in the broader project of European colonialism.[36] Sara Mills, for instance, has argued that the production and reception of women's travel writing during the height of the British Empire was constructed through the shifting discourses of gender and race in the metropolitan and colonial spheres.[37]

The observations of nineteenth-century European women travellers are examined in Kerryn Goldsworthy's analytically bold study of the shipboard experiences of female emigrants to Australia, in Gillian Whitlock's examination of Lady Barker's responses to Natal and Western Australia from her privileged position as a senior colonial official's wife, and in Michelle Adler's chapter on the differing South African experiences of British writers Florence Dixie and Sarah Heckford. Adler looks at the cultural and literary spaces which opened up for such colonial women travellers, and reveals the tensions implicit in their engagement with Empire and masculine narrative conventions. The spaces that were opened up for them remained marginal and, interestingly, Adler shows that their portrayals of Africa and African society centred on the theme of possession and dispossession of the landscape.

White women like Lady Barker, Florence Dixie and Sarah Heckford were signifiers of European civilization in the settler colonies. They were also, as McClintock suggests, 'boundary' figures and thus ambiguous markers of colonial identity.[38] The 'ferocious enchantment' and cultural ambiguity attached to the colonial white woman is suggested in Kate Darian-Smith's chapter in this collection on the transgressions – in terms of sex and racial purity – of 'captivity' narratives in the Australian context. The myth of the white woman 'captured' by non-white peoples was deeply connected to a sense of both danger and security in the white settler mentality. Darian-Smith's study of the (lost) white woman of Gippsland during the 1840s argues that she became 'the symbolic wife or daughter of every white settler, an idealized representative of European womanhood in a hostile land'. She shows how a counter-narrative of racial integration and inter-racial sexuality plays upon and disturbs white cultural expectations, and undercuts the dominant account of woman, mother and nation.

Sophie Watson's chapter 'Spaces of the "Other"' examines the spatial ramifications of multiculturalism in contemporary Australian society. This is the only essay in this collection which introduces a new cultural dimension into the social jostlings over space: that of the various non-dominant migrant communities that exist in South Africa, and to a far greater extent, in modern Australia. Watson describes how, in the ethnically diverse suburbs of western Sydney, recent immigrant communities compete with longer-term Anglo-

Celtic residents for recognition and territory. She notes how cultural differences can be perceived by the dominant society as either exotic or threatening, and cites the example of the Vietnamese community at Cabramatta which was initially viewed by dominant Australian society as a cultural threat, and then as an exotic place, attracting tourists and generating income.

Every chapter in this book has constituted itself around inter-locking, and sometimes contesting, notions of space and place; around colonial discourses and post-colonial theories; and around a variety of cultural texts produced in Australia and South Africa, as well as in metropolitan centres. The ideas and concepts raised here about land, literature and history in South Africa and Australia will, we hope, provide sufficient energy and impetus for a rich new body of comparative work: this is something that both southern spaces, and the field of post-colonial studies, undoubtedly deserve.

NOTES

1 For instance, see Peter Hulme, *Colonial Encounters: Europe and the Native Caribbean 1492–1797*, London and New York, Routledge, 1986; Stephen Greenblatt, *Marvellous Possessions: The Wonder of the New World*, Oxford, Clarendon Press, 1991; Mary Louise Pratt, *Imperial Eyes: Travel Writing and Transculturation*, London and New York, Routledge, 1992; and for a recent and perceptive survey of post-colonial literature see Elleke Boehmer, *Colonial and Post-colonial Writing: Migrant Metaphors*, Oxford, Oxford University Press, 1995.

2 Herman Wittenberg, 'Space and Narrative in J. M. Coetzee's *Foe*', unpublished paper, Association of University English Teachers of South Africa Conference, Pietermaritzburg, July 1995.

3 W. J. T. Mitchell (ed.), *Landscape and Power*, Chicago and London, Chicago University Press, 1994, pp. 2, 17.

4 Erica Carter, James Donald and Judith Squires (eds.), *Space and Place: Theories of Identity and Location*, London, Lawrence & Wishart, 1993, p. xii.

5 Bernard Smith, *European Vision and the South Pacific*, Melbourne, Oxford University Press, first edn. 1960, 2nd edn. 1985, p. 5; see also Bernard Smith, *Imaging the Pacific: In the Wake of the Cook Voyages*, Melbourne, Melbourne University Press, 1992. For an overview of Smith's work see Peter Beilharz, 'Bernard Smith: Imaging the Antipodes', in *Thesis Eleven* no. 38, 1994, pp. 93-103.

6 Edward Said, *Orientalism: Western Conceptions of the Orient*, London, Penguin, first pub. 1978; 1991, p. 3.

7 J. M. Coetzee, *White Writing: The Culture of Letters in South Africa*, Massachusetts, Yale University Press, 1989, Chapter 9.

8 Anne McClintock, *Imperial Leather, Race, Gender and Sexuality in the Colonial Contest*, London and New York, Routledge, 1995, p. 27.

18

9 McClintock, *Imperial Leather*, p. 28.

10 Paul Carter, *The Road to Botany Bay: An Essay in Spatial History*, London, Faber & Faber, 1987, p. xxi.

11 Ross Gibson, *South of the West: Postcolonialism and the Narrative Construction of Australia*, Bloomington, Indiana University Press, 1992, pp. ix–xii.

12 Donald Denoon, *Settler Capitalism: The Dynamics of Dependent Development in the Southern Hemisphere*, Oxford, Clarendon Press, 1983.

13 Denoon, *Settler Capitalism*, p. 4.

14 William Beinart, 'Introduction: the politics of colonial conservation in Herschel', in *Journal of Southern African Studies*, vol. 15, no. 2, 1989, p. 147; See also William Beinart and Peter Coates, *Environment and History: the Taming of Nature in the United States of America and South Africa*, London and New York, Routledge, 1995.

15 Beinart, 'Introduction', pp. 158–9.

16 Beinart and Coates, *Environment and History*, p. 90.

17 For other relevant works on land use and conservation see Geoffrey Bolton, *Spoils and Spoilers: A History of Australians Shaping their Environment*, 2nd edn., Sydney, Allen & Unwin, 1992; William J. Lines, *Taming the Great South Land: A History of the Conquest of Nature in Australia*, Sydney, Allen & Unwin, 1991; David Anderson and Richard Grove (eds), *Conservation in Africa: Peoples, Policies and Practice*, Cambridge, Cambridge University Press, 1987; Richard Grove, *Green Imperialism*, Cambridge, Cambridge University Press, 1994.

18 Edward Said, *Culture and Imperialism*, London, Chatto & Windus, 1993.

19 Stephen Gray, *Southern African Literature: An Introduction*, Cape Town, David Philip, 1979; Martin Hall, 'The Legend of the Lost City; or, The Man with Golden Balls', *Journal of Southern African Studies*, vol. 21, no. 2, 1995, pp. 179–9.

20 See, for instance, John Docker, *The Nervous Nineties: Australian Cultural Life in the 1890s*, Melbourne, Oxford University Press, 1991; Robert Dixon, *Writing the Colonial Frontier: Race, Gender and Nation in Anglo-Australian Popular Fiction, 1875–1914*, Cambridge, Cambridge University Press, 1995.

21 Brian Kennedy, *A Tale of Two Mining Cities: Johannesburg and Broken Hill 1885–1925*, Melbourne, Melbourne University Press, 1984.

22 Bill Gammage, 'The Crucible: The Establishment of the Anzac Tradition 1899–1918', in Michael McKernan and Margaret Browne (eds), *Australia: Two Decades of War and Peace*, Canberra, Australian War Memorial/Allen & Unwin, 1988, pp. 147–66.

23 See John Eddy and Deryck Schreuder (eds), *The Rise of Colonial Nationalism: Australia, New Zealand, Canada and South Africa First Assert Their Nationalities 1880–1914*, Sydney, Allen & Unwin, 1988.

24 Simon Schama, *Landscape and Memory*, London and New York, Harper Collins, 1995, pp. 6–7.

25 Schama, *Landscape and Memory*, p. 15.

26 Homi K. Bhabha, *The Location of Culture*, London and New York, Routledge, 1994; Aijaz Ahmad, *In Theory: Classes, Nations, Literatures*, London, Verso, 1992.

27 See Richard Elphick and Herman Giliomee (eds), *The Shaping of South*

African Society, 1652–1820, Cape Town, Longman Penguin and London, Longman, 1979.

28 Beinart and Coates, *Environment and History*, p. 12.

29 See J. D. Omer-Cooper, *The Zulu Aftermath*, London, 1966; and, for a revisionist approach, C. A. Hamilton, 'The Character and Objects of Chaka: A Reconsideration of the Making of Chaka as "Mfecane Motor" ', *Journal of African History*, vol. 33, 1992.

30 For Afrikaner symbolism see McClintock, *Imperial Leather*.

31 Andrew Fisher, in *Age*, 29 Dec. 1910, quoted in Kennedy, *Tale of Two Mining Cities*, p. 4.

32 From notes taken by Liz Gunner at the Gertrude Posel Exhibition on 'Language, Power and Space' , University of the Witwatersrand, 14 July 1994. See also P. Bonner, P. Delius and D. Posel (eds), *Apartheid's Genesis*, Johannesburg, Ravan and Witwatersrand University Press, 1993.

33 'Language, Space and Power', Exhibition Notes.

34 For a powerful denunciation of control of space in an African's life see Athol Fugard, John Kani and Winston Ntshona's play, *Sizwe Banzi is Dead* in Athol Fugard, *Statements: Three Plays*, Oxford, Oxford University Press, 1974.

35 For a comprehensive overview of feminist scholarship in relation to space, see Alison Blunt and Gillian Rose, 'Introduction', in Alison Blunt and Gillian Rose (eds), *Writing Women and Space: Colonial and Post-colonial Geographies*, New York and London, The Guildford Press, 1994, pp. 1–28; Jenny Robinson, '(Dis)locating Historical Narrative: Writing, Space and Gender in South African Social History', *South African Historical Journal*, vol. 30, May 1994, pp. 144–57.

36 See, for instance, Nupur Chadhuri and Margaret Strobel (eds), *Western Women and Imperialism: Complicity and Resistance*, Bloomington, Indiana University Press, 1992.

37 Sara Mills, *Discourses of Difference: An Analysis of Women's Travel Writing and Colonialism*, London and New York, Routledge, 1991.

38 McClintock, *Imperial Leather*, Chapter 1.

Part I

DEFINING THE SOUTH

1

TURNING THE TABLES – OR, GROUNDING POST-COLONIALISM

Paul Carter

If the true is what is grounded, then the ground is not true, nor yet false.

Ludwig Wittgenstein, *On Certainty*[1]

At the end of my *The Lie of the Land*, reflecting on the difficulties that attend negotiations between colonizing and colonized peoples, even where common interests have apparently been identified, some questions are posed: 'We could do worse than begin by reflecting on the mechanism of the negotiating table and the model of communication it implies. What does the polished, horizontal surface hoisted off the ground signify? What history of violence does its pretence of smoothness, its equalisation of places, conceal? We could do worse than ask: when did we in the West leave the ground?'[2] Even this brief extract gives some indication of that book's argument, and there is no reason to repeat it here. Rather than recapitulate the proposition that a new, possibly post-colonial polity depends on evolving a different poetics of exchange, it might be useful here to ground as it were that last seemingly rhetorical flourish.

Perhaps we are to take it literally. Edwardian writer, Richard Church, reports in his autobiography that as an asthmatic, somewhat imaginative child he possessed the power of self-levitation, being capable when emotional and psychological need required to raise himself off the ground and steer about the picture-rails, bumping against cornices like a party balloon; this gift survived well into puberty.[3] Perhaps there is a Freudian explanation for these

23

flights of fancy in late Victorian households. How common were they? Why in our own day are these experiences of flying only confessed to in dreams? The gloomy, over-furnished interiors of suburban London frame Church's little theatre of the double as eccentric: but perhaps in flying, in gently nosing about the idling air, he felt reconnected to his soul. Perhaps an intuition that floorboards and linoleum were mask-grounds under which another ground suffocated contributed to his difficulty in breathing. Another thought: when did rubber balloons first become part of childhood's fantasy vocabulary? What flights of fancy are sublimated in their coloured clouds? What listlessness, what ground deprivation, is mirrored there?

The domestic interior's theatrical floors, planar, rectangular, have as their architectural corollary upright doorways and squared-off windows. A morality of posture is implied, as the definition of self-possession is erectness of carriage, directness of gait. Steps and stair-cases are not out of place, they help to notate this planar environment: they make concrete the digitization of movement, its arithmetic divorce from the dance. The tedium of floors, their forgetfulness! To occupy their ground is to be 'off' the ground: to be 'off' the ground, alive to the fluid mechanics of the air's transport, may be to be grounded – not only in the privately therapeutic way Church experienced. To stand erect, proud, to walk in straight lines – the ordinary counterpoise of left and right assimilated to the monotony of the perambulating wheel – externalizes a sense of paranoia, fear that the ground is hostile, conspires to trip and stumble.

These domestic musings appear to have little to do with the mundane drama of colonization. But what is the object of the colonist's 'first step'? It is to mark a line in the ground, to open a clearing, to remove obstacles.[4] The *reductio ad absurdum* of this theatricalization of the ground – its transformation into the *tabula rasa* of space which, by virtue of its palpable emptiness, licenses the colonist's usurpation of it – occurs in the seventeenth-century writer Gabriel de Foigny's utopian fable of the Great Southern Land: on asking the inhabitants of this *tabula rasa* country where the mountains are, he is told that they have all been flattened.[5] But to stay with Victorian England: the intimate history of lost grounds is cognate with the history of imperialism. Domestic interiors reproduced the interiors of exotic countries; they were populated with sub-rational beings – spirit doubles, unruly children, illnesses and unhappinesses, that, as Edmund Gosse's childhood portrait poignantly reminds us, had to be confronted and exorcized.

The Victorian table was not only the place where the eight-year-old Gosse leaned over the shallow pan of sea-water, investigating the minute surface for novel forms of life – an activity whose satisfaction consisted, it seems, in its resemblance to the boy's persistent fantasy of amphibious release: 'My great desire was to walk out over the sea as far as I could, and then lie flat on it, face downwards, and peer into the depths.'[6] The table had another side. Perhaps the very blandness of its upper surface promoted nausea, disequilibrium, a fear of what might lie concealed underneath. Not by chance did the spirit visitants to the seance first make their presence known by rapping the underside of the table. More generally, the mournful sideboards and wardrobes of those times were the medium's essential décor. Without their gloomy photographic recesses, their locks and sliding doors, their false bottoms and surprising mirrors, where would the 'Aladdins' and 'Gypsies' be summoned from, where disappear to?

Those summoned to materialize themselves were various: recently departed relatives, historical figures; and, more libidinally appealing, instances of the primitive – carelessly arranged nursing mothers, diamante-bedecked Indian slaves, ebony-burnished warriors. These pre-televisual domestic charades, with their repertoire of disembodied hands, overturning goblets and discarded garments, gave the participants a sensation of getting in contact with what was missing from their lives, the unconscious, say.[7] But contact was, as in the colonial situation, inquisitorial, one-sided. The medium and her helpers put the questions, as conquistadors, missionaries and government officals did: spirits, like natives, were endlessly being asked their names, as if their existence were in doubt. Those who were credible were those who knew best how to act the role assigned to them, and could discover amazing coincidences between their experiences, their memories, interests and range of acquaintance, and those of their questioners. If called upon to materialize themselves, they had to imitate other expectations: to know how to slip through curtains, how to trim the lamp, to throw a shadow on a frosted pane. Like circus performers, conjured to occupy the debatable land between being and non-being, they needed to mimic the spiritualists' melodramatic imaginary if they were to ring true.

The phrase 'debatable land', from an early map of the Port Phillip region in what was to become Victoria, Australia, once furnished me with a chapter title and a theme: land without a name can still be talked about, it provides an in-between zone, an invitation to dialogue.[8] It suggests that frontier rhetoric is only one way of conceptualizing land rights and their protection; in Aboriginal cultures liminal areas where neighbouring peoples can negotiate across difference, can as the case demands exchange and incorporate each other's cultural practices, are vital to maintaining peaceful relations. But what of the West? In this culture, with its in-between zones where the ground has yet to be named, the notion of the enclosed seem to have been internalized, transferred from the physical to the psychic realm. Two books published around 1870, said to be amongst the most convincing in demonstrating the reality of psychic phenomena rejoice in the titles *Footfalls on the Boundary of Another World* and *The Debatable Land between this World and the Next.*[9]

In a chapter of his life-story called 'Psychical', the author of *King Solomon's Mines*, Rider Haggard, records a number of 'dream-pictures' that seem to him to have had telepathic origins. Among these is a series of 'tableaux' apparently recapitulating the history of humankind from its humblest beginnings 'in the mouth of a cavern', to the pomp and decadence of an Egyptian palace. Rider Haggard wonders whether these are proof of 'Racial memories of events that had happened to forefathers' – an instance, it seems, of Haeckel's biological theory of ontogeny recapitulating phylogeny occurring in the psychic realm. These dioramic dream tableaux have a suggestive bearing on Rider Haggard's 'fictions of empire' as his romances have been called, but their interest here lies in the sequel: when Rider Haggard described them to Sir Oliver Lodge, a man who regarded the 'etheric medium' as equally amenable to radio and spirit communication, the latter remarked disappointingly, that he could make nothing of them as 'he lacked imagination'.[10]

The men who, in the second half of the nineteenth century, interested themselves in mesmerism, in spiritualism, in the occult, in the workings of the unconscious, prided themselves on their lack of imagination. They stood firmly on the parquet floor of Positivism, interested in obtaining the indisputable facts. They declined to be taken in, made it a point of honour not to be overtaken by any form of sympathetic identification. Their position was not even fully 'scientific' in the sense of implying the furnishing of provisional theories. They preferred to see with a child's eyes, without prejudice or the blinkers of premature rationalization. The puppet 'others' thus conjured up, with their hidden wires, their sub-vocal clatter, their dismal repertoire of circus-tricks, reflected – were the mimics –

of this emotional (and spiritual) infantilism. These men so keen to step over the border into the country of the unconscious seemed indifferent to the emotional and aesthetic poverty of the living environment they normally inhabited. Gosse's father took the Bible in its literal sense. His faith might have been 'fanatical' but there was nothing 'mystical' about it; rather, it displayed 'a rigid and iconoclastic literalness'. He was, his son writes, 'devoid of sympathetic imagination'.[11]

But to return from the shrouded Elysium of the table's underworld – jungle, wigwam and cavern to generations of children hiding behind its ankle-long table-cloth – to the upper-world of its polished, walnut-veneer. Trying to enter that debatable land of the spirit, inhabited by ghosts, by doubles, by homeless spirits and echoes, these Victorians, and their Bostonian counterparts, were self-styled anthropologists of the mind. Commenting on the Kurnai belief that their sorcerer or Birraark could communicate with ghosts, that his own ancestral ghosts visited him in dreams, A. W. Howitt, in 1880, commented, 'We should be loth to reproach him with superstition when we reflect upon the extraordinary resemblance between the proceedings of the Birraark and the proceedings even now taking place in the midst of our highest civilization at 'spirit seances'.[12] Popular writers like Andrew Lang assumed a continuity between 'savage spiritualism', 'ancient spiritualism' and contemporary psychic research.[13]

The penumbral gloom of late Victorian interiors was cultivated. The table by the window on which resided specimens neatly labelled, letters and magnifying glass, might come into its own when the light streamed in. But in the evening, with the curtains drawn, another light dawned. It was in the underworld of night, whether electrically-illuminated or protoplasmically punctuated by gas lamps, with its vestal flames cultured in alb-shaped columns of dusky glass, that one could read reports from the colony; or bring one's correspondence up to date. But between these two realms, which technology had made mimics of each other, the heavy furniture, the piano, the writing-desk, the bell-jar with its feathered relics of some tropical paradise, the Japanese screen – these belonged to debatable land. They could go either way: into the light or into the dark. An intimate history of the table would suggest there were more sides to it than one; the shadow it cast was quite as telling as the surface it provided.

That the debatable land of the mind might resemble the crepuscular hour of a middle-class Victorian household would not have surprised Schopenhauer, who glossed the processes of falling asleep and dreaming thus: as the brain draws the curtain on external sensations, so it becomes aware of the 'inner nerve-centre of organic life' – a transition comparable to a 'candle that begins to shine when the evening twilight comes'.[14] The mind is not a *tabula rasa*: it receives external impressions, but it also projects its own images; images and impressions may bear some relationship to each other but, as the nature of dreams demonstrates, the organic life of the mind is a magic lantern capable of generating and projecting its own wonderful worlds – 'we see ourselves in strange and even impossible situations.'[15] Only when the subject is dead to the external world 'can the dream occur, just as the pictures of a magic lantern can appear only after the lights of the room have been extinguished'.[16] And the power of projection onto that mental screen is nothing other than what the Scots call 'second sight'.[17] So, by steps, Schopenhauer could demonstrate the reality of 'spirit seeing', and the phenomena of animal magnetism, magic, sympathetic cures, ghosts and visions of all kinds, even though they had no counterpart in external reality.

The middle-class Victorian domestic interior was *una sacra rappresentazione* of the Victorian mind, of its unconscious as well as conscious 'operations', and even of the debatable land in-between these realms, where psychic and physical phenomena ambiguously, sometimes promiscuously, mimicked one another. This structural symmetry is clear, and it anticipates more intimately the resemblance between Freud's mental architecture and the typically tripartite Viennese town-house. But our point is different: that, and to return to the adolescent Richard Church, these domestic dramas, these projections of unconscious desire, repressed a deeper anxiety – one which their troupes of ghosts and levitating tables mimicked but could neither name nor assuage – the anxiety of groundlessness.

Further, we can give this anxiety a historical name and a local habitation: colonialism. Colonialism's *raison d'être* was the eradication of differences – the smoothing away, say, of folded grounds (cultural, spiritual as well as topographical). But without the 'other' of its own construction – the primitive, the irrational, even the puzzlingly factual – colonialism had no reason to be, no place it could call its own. Colonialism was continually pulling the carpet from under its own feet. Without the baffingly fertile Moluccas, and its proliferation of insect look-alikes, Wallace would have had no theory of evolution to propound; without the unenclosed horizons of South Africa, Rider Haggard would have had no basis for his romances. But destruction was incipient in their imaginative transference: dissolving the ground of difference, these men found they had nowhere to stand.

Gosse's father specialized in the marine biology of the littoral zone; the Devon shoreline was his little frontier: 'We burst in, he used to say, where no one had ever thought of intruding before.' But the sequel was dismal: 'The fairy paradise has been violated, the exquisite product of centuries of natural selection has been crushed under the rough paw of well-meaning, idle-minded curiosity ... my Father ... had by the popularity of his books acquired direct responsibility for a calamity that he never anticipated.'[18] Rider Haggard and Wallace, though politically divergent, both devoted much of their own post-colonial energies to domestic land reform; while their recommendations were superficially different, they identified the same fundamental problem: how in a period of organized population displacement, not least to the colonies, to ground Englishmen locally. And at home, as in the British colonies, the symptom of groundlessness was the same: the disappearance of unenclosed, still debatable land.

The problem was even subtler: to revive a regime of small-holdings, as Rider Haggard desired to see, meant, in effect, returning the larger farms created by a century of Enclosure Acts to an earlier condition. It meant the active encouragement of local difference, even in a sense a return to the picturesquely primitive. It is as if to arrest the 'ominous migration of the blood and sinew of the race' and 'to keep folk in the country' England must be recolonized rationally, learning from the colonial experience overseas.[19] In pursuit of individual ownership Wallace went further, wishing to see the land nationalized. But again this regrounding of the rural proletariat, which had been colonized and thrown off its land by the larger landowners, contained the seeds of its own destruction: against the pseudo-selection of the land manipulated by powerful interests, Wallace recommended a system of 'natural selection', in which the survival of the fittest small-holders guaranteed the productivity of the land.[20] But his own logic dictated that this must lead to 'progress', to a marked population increase and, if a Malthusian apocalypse was to be deferred, to the clearing and cultivation of every last acre of 'jungle' in order to accommodate this newly enfranchised and vigorous citizenry.

Like Rider Haggard, Wallace conceived of this process as a going-back to origins, one whose appeal was as much emotional as political: comparing the arithmetically colonized landscape of the United States unfavourably with the ungridded and irregular lie of the English rural scene, Wallace wrote warmly of 'The slow development of agriculture and of settlement which renders our country picturesque and beautiful; the narrow winding lanes, following the contours of the ground; the ever-varying size of the enclosures, and their naturally curved boundaries.'[21] There were, it seems, enclosures and Enclosures: the former corresponded to the landscape of his early childhood, the latter to early manhood when, as a surveyor's assistant, he had actively assisted in the land enclosure process. But pre-Enclosure enclosures, though less rigidly ruled, were not 'grounded': protected by property laws, they inscribed a history of division. Wallace's sympathetic identification was an act of affiliation rather than filiation, reflecting the vulnerability he felt in not being able to identify his own genealogy, to ground himself differently.

Glossing the passage from *The Lie of the Land* in this way may not enable us to fix the date when our ungrounding commenced, but it helps define its historical meaning. To be groundless was to masquerade as being everywhere: the colonial mind was a citizen of the entire intellectual world, atopic, occupying the transcendental plain of its own reason. By the same token it was surrounded on every side by abysses and cliffs or, more insidiously, by swamps or sands that hovered ambiguously between the solid and the liquid, and were famously the source of miasmatic spirits. Essentially, to be ungrounded was to lose touch with one's human and physical surroundings; it was to become an echoing shell, an antenna eye. It was to experience the nightmare of autogenesis, the realm of mirrors. No wonder that in these unnatural circumstances men and women were overwhelmed by a nostalgia for the 'other' which, being unable to confess as a condition of their daily coming into being, was sublimated into the realm of the spiritual.

In this way, producing their psychic rabbits out of the medium magician's hat, they could simultaneously admit their existential anxiety and perpetuate the myth of phoenix-like self production. Everywhere the West colonized it found disturbing evidence of ghosts; of magic rituals, totemic superstitions; of sorcerers who could fly. These reports were eagerly studied – witness the prolific and widely influential labours of Edward Tylor or J. G. Frazer – but the West, or at least north European nineteenth-century intellectuals, could not admit that anything lay outside its ken. It was as if in order to rationalize these ethnographic data it had to shift them into the realm of its own collective psychic experience, and retrospectively to discover within its own unconscious (a department of knowledge especially opened to deal with the new information) precedents for what was now being reported. The West had already gone through this; what spiritualism represented was a sympathetic revisiting of the early psychic history of the Aryan people, designed to substantiate, to ground the ideology of autogenetic progress.

To return to the table – which was never merely passive and, at least after 1853,[22] given to turning of its own accord, stamping its feet and hospitably harbouring a veritable host of spirits predominantly of the species *spiritus percutiens*. In triangulating between the European discovery of the Unconscious, the cathexis of historical experience it symbolized, and the facts of colonization which constituted the core experience of the 'Other' thus conveniently internalized and once again projected as a collective self-discovery, table-turning also has its place. The conditions necessary for its animation depended on overcoming an inhibition which was as much scientific as emotional, and which involved the earnest taxonomist and tabulator in a contradiction: without a sympathetic identification with the subject of his enquiry, how was the student of knowledge to gain a purchase on the world? How enter in to it? Evidently he had to go beyond himself. But by what means? How, without sacrificing his autonomy of viewpoint and judgement, was he to place himself inside the phenomena he wished to study, and so comprehend their reason? And then, if he went beyond himself, daring to 'participate' in the life of the other, how was he to retain self-consciousness?

Holding hands was a practical answer: the chain of touching people seated round the table signified the resolution of this paradox. Puzzled by Plato's concept of the Forms, Parmenides wanted to know whether they were One or Many; was a Form present in the class of objects formed in its likeness? If so, had it suffered self-division? If not, was it really transcendent? The concept of methexis or participation proposed by Plato was intriguing, but mystical rather than logical.[23] But in north London parlours methexis was regularly achieved as the players round the table became simultaneously one and many, in the process achieving a breakthrough into a higher, or perhaps lower, realm of knowledge, one that had previously been confined to the underworld of the unconscious.

Again these scientifically-licensed excursions into a realm where the intangible became tangible – not perhaps without a certain erotic frisson – had a context: they seemed to gloss, if not anticipate, late Victorian speculations about the origins of religion. The rings of studious, nervously perspiring men and women crouched about the percussive table were a slowed-down parody of those chains of dancing maenads, the handmaidens of Dionysus, whose erotic figures beat the ground, making physically present the primitive 'group soul'. In the name of science they took part in a group-experience which not only recapitulated the beginnings of Western art and drama before the autochthonous *genii loci* were colonized, Olympianized and individuated as migratory cult-heroes: it found its contemporary counterpart in the totemic ceremonies of the Aranda of central Australia.[24] Or, better, they engaged in a thoroughly post-modern pastiche of these things – with this rider: that the pastiche was probably unconscious.

In more ways than one the off-the-ground table inscribes, shapes and writes the other history of colonialism – that shadow narrative of domestic spaces where the colonized world was being dreamed, theorized, modelled and re-enacted. An enlarged account along these lines might be a useful corrective to Gaston Bachelard's wonderfully poetic evocations of similar spaces in France: for the histories these rooms contained were not only cosmic but colonial, fateful in a more than individual sense. If they raised the solitary dreamer up, so that he could seem to be a visitor to a distant planet, they also dragged him down with their collection of lengthening shadows and airless retreats. Their physical enclosure mirrored – doubled and legitimated – his own ideological and historical enclosure. But these facts did not find their significance in the unconscious; they were not to be grounded in a new pseudo-archaeology of the mind. They had entirely historical provenances, in the economy of imperialism – an economy that shared with capitalism a mystification of its own ground, the roots of its authority and power in colonialism.

Wherever the colonizers advanced, they were mainly interested in hearing themselves speak; the mirrors they handed over were a deception, beguiling the time until reinforcements landed. Even in the bush the newcomers looked through windows and imagined doors. The pioneer ethnographer no sooner collected his native informants than he quickly put up his other camera, the collapsible writing table, and began writing: sheet by sheet, surface after surface, he covered and removed – but the table, magically, did not seem sensibly diminished.[25] The colonial explorers and writers had, from the point of view of those they colonized, no need to indulge in facile trickery: it was not necessary to make tables leap and tremble. The tables were turned merely by the act of writing all this down, substituting another ground for the one they one-sidedly occupied – and, in the process, pretending the square of light did not cast a shadow – and that the shadow, the soul of the shadow, needed that native ground to dwell in.

These intimate preoccupations may seem to have little to do with the politics of the negotiating table; and it is true, to amplify further the connections is a task well beyond the scope of this essay. Nor have we mentioned the materials themselves: the provenances of those timbers, the trapped and mutilated dryads undoubtedly inhabiting them. But even these remarks, although little more than a speculative footnote, are suggestive.[26] The phenomenon of talking tables suggests a guilty conscience. One would like to know what they want to upset, why they sulkily revolt against the doctrine of the level playing-field. Why are they always trying to escape? And into what dimension? But one thing is clear: in those negotiations intended to mark the transition from colonial to post-colonial consensuses, the common ground signified by the table cannot be taken for granted. Off the ground, it reminds us that the ground is not given.

NOTES

1 Ludwig Wittgenstein, *On Certainty*, Oxford, Oxford University Press, 1969, p. 28.
2 Paul Carter, *The Lie of the Land*, London, Faber & Faber, 1996, p. 365.
3 Richard Church, *Over the Bridge*, London, Reprint Society, 1956, pp. 191–2.
4 See for example the quotations from predominantly First Fleet sources collected in a catalogue of an exhibition at the Museum of Sydney, *Fleeting Encounters: Pictures and Chronicles of the First Fleet*, Sydney, Historic Houses Trust of New South Wales, 1995, pp. 78–89.
5 Gabriel de Foigny, *The Southern Land, Known*, trans. D. Fausett, Syracuse, N.Y., Syracuse University Press, 1995, p. 40.
6 Edmund Gosse, *Father and Son*, London, Penguin, 1982, p. 73.
7 These seance phenomena are taken mainly from Alfred Russel Wallace, *My Life*, London, George Bell & Sons, 1905, vol. 2, chapters XXXV–XXXVII, and from Andrew Lang, *Cock Lane and Common-Sense*, London, Longmans, Green & Co, 1894, *passim*.
8 See my T*he Road to Botany Bay*, London, Faber & Faber, 1987, chapter 5.
9 Both books by Robert Dale Owen. See Wallace, *My Life*, vol. 2, p. 294.
10 H. Rider Haggard, *The Days of My Life*, London, Longmans, Green & Co., 1926, vol. 2, pp. 168–71.

11 Gosse, *Father and Son*, p. 50.
12 L. Fison and A. W. Howitt, *Kamilaroi and Kurnai*, Melbourne, George Robertson, 1880, p. 256.
13 See Wallace, *My Life*, vol. 2, chapters XXXV–XXXVII and Lang, *Cock Lane and Common-Sense*.
14 A. Schopenhauer, 'Essay on Spirit Seeing' in *Parerga and Paralipomena*, trans. by E. F. J. Payne, Oxford, Clarendon Press, 1974, vol. 1, p. 235.
15 Schopenhauer, 'Essay on Spirit Seeing', p. 231.
16 Schopenhauer, 'Essay on Spirit Seeing', p. 232.
17 Schopenhauer, 'Essay on Spirit Seeing', p. 238.
18 Gosse, *Father and Son*, p. 97.
19 H. Rider Haggard, *Rural England*, London, Longmans, Green & Co, 1906, vol. 2, p. 546ff.
20 Alfred Russel Wallace, *Land Nationalisation: Its Necessity and Its Aims*, London, Trubner & Co, 1882, passim. Also Wallace, *My Life*, vol. 2, chapter XXXIV.
21 Wallace, *My Life*, vol. 2, pp. 191–2.
22 The table-turning craze was said to be at its height between 1853 and 1860. See Lang, *Cock Lane and Common-Sense*, p. 332.
23 The term methexis is discussed by F. M. Cornford in *From Religion to Philosophy*, New York, Harper & Brothers, 1957, p. 254 and in *Plato and Parmenides*, London, Kegan Paul, Trench & Trubner, 1939, p. 84ff. Jane Harrison makes a connection between Platonic methexis and the poetics of Aranda initiation ceremonies in *Themis*, London, Merlin Press, 1963 (originally pub. 1911), p. 125. These connections are elaborated in my *The Lie of the Land*.
24 See Harrison, *Themis*, especially chapters IX and X. Of course these relationships were not linear. What Spencer and Gillen thought they saw and described in central Australia was in part a product of what Frazer wanted them to see: the primitivism of Aranda ritual was Evolutionism's necessary other. On the feedback loop between Frazer and Spencer and Gillen, see S. E. Hyman, *The Tangled Bank*, New York, Athenaeum, 1974, p. 222ff. T. G. H. Strehlow effectively dismisses the primitivism myth in his *Introduction to Songs of Central Australia*, Sydney, Angus & Robertson, 1971, p. 20ff.
25 Photographs of cross-legged native informants facing the ethnographer at his makeshift table abound. The implications of not granting an audience in this way, and being willing to communicate at the same height, more or less on a common ground, are explored by John Mack, *Emile Torday and the Art of the Congo 1900–1909*, London, British Museum Publications, n.d., pp.50–1, where sharply contrasting images of Torday and the German anthropologist Frobenius are tellingly juxtaposed.
26 The term 'ground' is itself highly ethnocentric in its connotations, and one object of *The Lie of the Land* is to reconceive the term in ways that avoid the usual Western associations of foundedness, stasis and origin.

BIBLIOGRAPHY

Carter, P., *The Lie of the Land*, London, Faber & Faber, 1996.

——, *The Road to Botany Bay*, London, Faber & Faber, 1987.

Cornford, F. M., *From Religion to Philosophy*, New York, Harper & Brothers,1957.

——, *Plato and Parmenides*, London, Kegan Paul, Trench & Trubner, 1939.

Church, R., *Over the Bridge*, London, Reprint Society, 1956.

de Foigny, G., *The Southern Land, Known*, trans. D. Fausett, Syracuse, N.Y., Syracuse University Press, 1995.

Fison, L. and Howitt, A. W., *Kamilaroi and Kurnai*, Melbourne, George Robertson, 1880.

Fleeting Encounters: Pictures and Chronicles of the First Fleet, Sydney, Historic Houses Trust of New South Wales, 1995.

Gosse, E., *Father and Son*, London, Penguin, 1982 (originally pub. 1907).

Haggard, H. Rider, *Rural England*, London, Longmans, Green & Co., 1906, vol. 2.

——, *The Days of My Life*, London, Longmans, Green & Co., 1926, vol. 2.

Harrison, J., *Themis*, London, Merlin Press, 1963 (originally pub. 1911).

Hyman, S. E., *The Tangled Bank*, New York, Athenaeum, 1974.

Lang, A., *Cock Lane and Common-Sense*, London, Longmans, Green & Co., 1894.

Mack, J., *Emile Torday and the Art of the Congo 1900–1909*, London, British Museum Publications, n.d..

Schopenhauer, A., 'Essay on Spirit Seeing' in *Parerga and Paralipomena*, trans. by E. F. J. Payne, Oxford, Clarendon Press, 1974, vol. 1.

Strehlow, T. G. H., *Introduction to Songs of Central Australia*, Sydney, Angus & Robertson, 1971.

Wallace, A. R., *Land Nationalisation: Its Necessity and Its Aims*, London, Trubner & Co, 1882.

——, *My Life*, London, George Bell & Sons, 1905, vol. 2.

Wittgenstein, L., *On Certainty*, Oxford, Oxford University Press, 1969.

2

COMPARATIVE BARBARISM
Game reserves, sugar plantations, and the modernization of South African landscape[1]

David Bunn

> There is one more thing that I intend to devote myself to, and that is the total exclusion of all foreigners from Zu-Vendis. . . . I am convinced of the sacred duty that rests upon me of preserving to this, on the whole, upright and generous-hearted people *the blessings of comparative barbarism.*
>
> Sir Henry Curtis in H. Rider Haggard's *Alan Quatermain*

THE OUT-OF-DOORS MAN

The official history of the Natal Mounted Rifles contains an obituary for William Alfred ('Wac') Campbell, uncle to the well-known South African poet Roy Campbell, in which it is stated, almost apologetically, that despite the fact that he was educated at Hilton College and Cambridge, and spent most of his life as Managing Director of Natal Estates Limited he was, 'nevertheless, essentially *an out-of-doors man*' (my emphasis).[2] This essay seeks to examine the meaning of that qualifying phrase.

In the late nineteenth and early twentieth centuries, there was an increasing perception that industrial capitalism, and its harbinger, the commodity form, had produced a crisis of *value*. In Huxley's *Brave New World*, the grotesquely developed, yet still recognizably Fordist economy of the future, has displaced genuine communal value outwards into a debased last refuge, the 'Savage Reservation' ringed by high voltage fences. Writing in 1932, Huxley first had in mind a contrast between the totalitarian, late Fordist city and that 'savage', sequestered space. By the time he completed the post-war preface to the novel, however, the Reservation had come to represent a viable alternative, a place where new forms of social democracy could be imagined.[3]

This chapter explores the emergence of such notions of enclaved, 'primitive' space – the space of the 'Reserve' – as an imaginary repository of value forms lost in the process of modernization. It tells the story of two places, a bushveld game reserve named Mala Mala and an industrial work site in the Natal sugar belt.

Boys in the bush

At first glance primitivist or expressionist trends in South African landscape painting appear to be determined by internal squabbles or European fashions, and to have little in common with the rhetoric of industrial modernization. Yet central to both constituencies, is the idea of the enclaved, tribal domain, in which a different, pre-capitalist mode of social organization and temporality exists.

A convenient point at which the two rhetorics intersect is in the figure of the painter Strat Caldecott. Shortly after his return from Paris, Caldecott was offered the opportunity to accompany a South African Railways tour to the Sabi Game Reserve, with the proviso that he would then write a series of articles popularizing the cause of a new National Park.[4] His two-month stay with the legendary warden Stevenson-Hamilton in what was to become the Kruger National Park was completely transformative for the painter, and from then on 'there was no single man in South Africa who worked as strenuously and successfully for the cause of wildlife preservation in the mid-continent.'[5] Thus began a series of commissions Caldecott undertook for South African Railways and Harbours (SAR&H).

During this period, as has frequently been pointed out, a new sense of national identity was stirring among whites in South Africa.'[6] Caldecott's brief career straddles some of the most important controversies over white national identity and race solidarity between English and Afrikaans speakers, many of which centred on the deployment of nature as a public symbol: the National Parks question, which raged until the creation of the Kruger National Park and the National Parks Board of Trustees in 1926; the choosing of an appropriate design for a South African national flag; and the SAR&H campaign to expand international tourism by popularizing a notion of bushveld safari in its magazine and in motion pictures shot on location in the Transvaal. There was thus a tremendous appetite among whites for images of the lowveld in the 1920s. Moreover in this decade, South African Railways and Harbours played a crucial role in advancing the idea that visually starved white urban populations needed a compensatory experience of the rural. As it popularized the notion of the renewing 'short break', SAR&H also encouraged the idea that it was possible to dip into primitive locales and refresh oneself. Two entirely contradictory maps of ethnically conceived space came about: that of railway tourism for whites, emphasizing the picturesque experience of tribal domains; and that of state labour organization, which attempted to prevent African urban populations from becoming settled, by holding them in segregated Native Locations, or by enforcing migrancy to and from rural Reserves.

In 1926, the Kruger National Park emerged into this contradictory understanding of space. The existence of a new national reserve solved the problem of the need for a zone of 'primitive' space and time that was non-contradictory, that did not remind obviously of exploited labour – it was a game reserve, not a 'native reserve' – and which could be twinned with the modernizing space of Johannesburg. Within easy reach of the city, according to one 1929 SAR&H publicity brochure, there was the potential for a renewing encounter with archaic time:

> Consequently, a man may leave Johannesburg one evening and reach Pretorius Kop [the only tourist accommodation in the Reserve] on the afternoon of the following day. And as lions may often be heard roaring there . . . it would be true to say that the city of Johannesburg, which sparkles with its myriad lights . . . in the long chain of gold mines, is within twenty four hours of the natural habitat of the lion which seeks his prey . . . even as he did when Southern Africa was the Bushman's undisputed hunting ground.[7]

Two forms of temporal organization are juxtaposed in this description: the lights of the proto-modern city burn all night long, extending pleasure and shift work far into the dark; within a day's drive, however, the Kruger National Park offers an intense, managed experience of pre-historical time and Nature.

Throughout the 1920s and 1930s, the idea of compensatory enclaved and conserved natural domains played a key role in the discourse of modernity, but this rhetoric took little account of the catastrophe of African land loss in the same period. Recent South African work on the origins, systematic functioning, and moral economy of twentieth-century labour control (by historians like Dunbar Moodie, William Worger, Patrick Harries, Keith Breckenridge, Jonathan Crush, and others), has been focused on the emergence of the closed compound system. Resistance and surveillance on the Natal sugar plantations is less well understood than discipline in the closed compounds of the Rand. Down on plantations like Natal Estates, the brutal indentured labour system of the previous decades had been replaced by a less obvious type of exploitation in the form of mills which were, according to Lincoln, 'centralised, capitalised, technologically sophisticated, and dependent on free labour'.[8] Labour control and reproduction of the conditions of production were effected spatially, as well as ideologically, by the form of the *sugar village*, an integrated system that combined worker management, crop and machinery surveillance, and ostentatious displays of landowning benevolence. Prominent on all the estates was the sugar baron's mansion, advertising itself as a site of cultural value with a specifically nostalgic set of architectural allusions to British landed estates.[9] The mansion, in other words, had a centrifugal effect in terms of the symbolic geography of the estate: it was perceived to radiate paternal control to surrounding areas, especially 'tribal' areas, a process vividly epitomized in the naming of Kwamashu ('the place of Marshall', the township outside Durban) after William's father.

Natal Estates was one of the most progressive farms in the region, playing a key role in experimenting with new varieties of cane and modernizing its production process through the introduction of the 'double carbonation method'. Persisting within this technologically sophisticated context, however, was an older, colonial labour logic: according to one account, small Indian boys were required to squat in a line outside the administration offices at Mount Edgecombe, to act as runners when summoned by a rough call of 'Boy!' from inside. The Sirdar system of field supervisors was also employed. All in all, while the Natal plantations were modernizing, many of them still looked and felt like British colonial outposts. Yet by 1920 most Natal sugarmills had adopted the international rhetoric of industrial progressivism, and for this they relied heavily on references to 'nature'. Illovo Sugar Estates, in 1925, describes itself situated within pleasant surrounds where the difference between indigenous bush and cane is elided:

The estate is situated in delightful country. A mile or two before the factory is reached, having ascended a high hill, a vast expanse of glorious country greets the eye. . . . To the north, west and south, an undulating country with hills in the distance . . . unfolds itself in all its pristine glory, while the Illovo river winds its serpentine course through miles and miles of cane fields. There is cane everywhere.[10]

Here we come upon the rhetoric of the picturesque. This is the eye of the landowner, the 'improver' of estates in the eighteenth-century mould, the privileged viewer that the landscape 'greets' and for whom it 'unfolds'.[11] The Illovo River becomes a serpentine rill, as well as establishing a syntactical order to the unfolding of detail, so that our view concludes by widening into an abstract idea of 'cane everywhere'. But the manipulation of 'nature' for specific prop-aganda effects was a widely accepted doctrine in the 1920s. A partisan sugar-baron audience heaped great praise on the Association's first propaganda film:

The interest [is] sustained by a story based upon the savage conditions of the country when Chaka's hordes held sway. A fine herd of elephants . . . and hippo in their natural habitat concentrate interest upon the country and its conditions before the Sugar Industry came into being to rescue it from its primaeval wilderness.[12]

Triumphalist claims about 'improvement' make up much of the Sugar Association's rhetoric in the 1920s. Not only is propaganda on behalf of this destructive form of monocropping advanced through references to the manipulation of nature, but, when dealing with the problem of labour, it stages itself *as distinct from* employment practices on the Transvaal gold mines. In complete disregard for the industrial nature of their practices, sugar barons of the period clung ten-aciously to the idea of themselves as farmers, unlike the 'capitalist' mine bosses to the North.[13]

Thus the improvement of the sugar estate is justified as a philan-thropic act; like the eighteenth- and nineteenth-century gentry they mime, plantation owners come to talk of their labour force in terms of family units rather than unmarried wage labourers. Dr Park Ross, Official Health Officer for the Union, found a ready audience when trying to convince owners of the necessity for new model housing units to combat malaria. Married labourers, he suggests in this transcript, are a more stable commodity:

> The man who comes with a wife to settle on a place, a respectable type if given a suitable house – something that is really comfortable, especially if it has a hard floor – finds that his good lady takes a fancy to the premises. Her demands for the amenities of the beginnings of civilization gradually increase, and so the poor devil has to work his lifetime out to satisfy her demands, and you don't have to drag the territories through with recruiters, as your man is tied to you by a force more potent than even the tax collectors in the Native areas. (*Laughter*)[14]

By encouraging the gendered asymmetry between production, reproduction, and consumption, sugar estates hoped to tie workers down with newly benevolent conditions of employment. Crucial to this strategy is the invention of the labourer's family as a supervised unit within the space of the estate.

What is extraordinarily interesting about the William Campbell case, is the clarity with which it demonstrates how the development of ideology, linked to particular productive needs, requires an increasingly complex delineation of sites and spaces.[15] In the form of the sugar baron's mansion, the grid plan of the plantations and irrigation systems, the displacement of married quarters across the sugar village, we see evidence not only of totalizing control masquerading as landed paternalism, but also of the simple 'regionalization' of space into different symbolic zones occupied by different classes.[16] However, even though industrial capitalism draws on images of nature and landscape paradigms when it presents utopian images of development, it also destroys nature and elides the difference between country and city, peasant and wage labourer. It should not surprise us, then, when we find manufacturers *going elsewhere* for their images of nature, and this is precisely what William Campbell did. Even though he was the owner of a vast tract of land inscribed with the symbolism of the landowner's improving hand, Wac concluded in the early 1920s that what he really wanted was an unspoiled slice of Transvaal bushveld. To this effect, in 1927, the year after he was appointed as the Natal representative on the new National Parks Board of Trustees, he bought a number of farms adjoining the new Kruger National Park and consolidated them into one spectacular small reserve: Mala Mala.

'The mountain which is not pointed at'

South African agriculture was in its most intense period of capitalization in the 1920s, the period associated with modernist self-critique in Europe. To put it another way: South Africa in 1920 recapitulates, with differences, the landscape aesthetics and property relations of nineteenth-century Britain. Game reserves are in a sense to agrarian labour pools what the reformed picturesque estate was to the nineteenth-century English village.

Finally, it comes down to a question of value. In classical Marxism, the production of surplus value depends on the manipulation of labour time, and failing that, through increased efficiency in the production process. Marx of course believed that this became more difficult to achieve, because of the tendency of the rate of profit to fall. Thus two destructive elements enter the equation: the instituting of alienated social structures; and the destruction of the natural environment.[17] 'Nature', in South Africa, becomes significantly problematized at a time when agriculture is modernizing, when it is reducing the eco-environment to an exchange value and hastening the destruction of sharecropping and the smallholder's sustained utilization of resources. Ironically, despite claims of improvement, an increase in profit at Natal Estates is thus associated with the exhaustion of Nature as a site of value (the pristine bush replaced by a monotonous sea of cane), and the destruction of 'natural' bonds of fealty between peasant labourers and their lords coincides with the commoditization of tropical labour in Natal.

There was a critical point at which modernizing agrarian capitalism in Natal visibly began to destroy that 'natural' environment fast becoming a valued tourist commodity amongst the white population, and it is not surprising to find a compensatory logic in which value comes increasingly to reside in those landscape features that appear to predate these effects. Try as they might, landowners like Campbell would have found it near impossible to speak without contradiction about an African workforce imbued with tribal grace and driven by feudal loyalty alone. Paradoxically, it is only by maintaining enclaved domains like game reserves, in which older regimental hierarchies apparently persist, where guests are free to wander, and Nature uncorrupted offers itself up for consumption by select tourists, that these contradictions may be managed. Mala Mala in the Transvaal thus became, as it were, the conscience of Natal Estates. It is there that landscape aesthetics worked to return

Nature to the domain of use value, and labourers, apparently
released from their proletarian role, became costumed and
uniformed tribal subjects, once again involved in picturesque labour.

How did Campbell's private game reserve compensate for the
ruined scenery of Natal Estates? Perhaps Mala Mala is best thought
of as a kind of allegory. Like all allegories, its symbolic form is organized in relation to another syntax, one that is not immediately
obvious but transparent to a certain class of viewer. As a ruling class,
English-speaking landowner, Campbell fashioned his game park into
a bounded space that dramatized the principle of *custodianship*, an
archaic eighteenth-century ideal of benevolent proprietorship that
also mimicked aristocratic attitudes towards the distribution of estate
surpluses and the management, by picturesque labourers, of
proscribed game. Custodianship is also a strongly compensatory
mechanism: there was a sort of feudal paternalism instituted at
Campbell's lowveld reserve which compensated for the modernization of labour relations at Natal Estates. Typically this paternalism
was also displayed in elaborate hunting expeditions to the Transvaal:
'a cattle truck was loaded at Mount Edgecombe with provisions: half
a dozen gun dogs, eight horses, eighteen servants (headed by Wac's
faithful Mhlaba), tents, saddles, food and cooking equipment.'[18]
Rattray reports Wac's admission that he 'bought the farms as a
shooting box', but that he claimed also to be an 'ardent Game
protectionist and not a Biltong Hunter'.[19] So while Campbell thinks
of Mala Mala as a 'conserved' area, his custodianship consists not in
refraining from the hunt – indeed he believes in the therapeutic
effects of shooting – but in having the wisdom to discriminate, cull,
redistribute surplus game, and provide regular specimens for
Transvaal and Natal museums.[20]

Mala Mala was an enclaved space in which particular values and
allegiances were dramatized so as to reinforce certain class, race, and
gender asymmetries. We have already heard about Campbell's
yearly caravan to the Transvaal with a select contingent of Natal
servants. When considering this symbolic trek, it is as well not to
forget the wider context of class conflict and ethnic rivalry amongst
Zulus in the Natal region. Given the increasing militancy and
frequent strikes initiated by the fledgling Industrial and Commercial
Workers' Union (ICU) in Natal, reaction from a complex Zulu
ethnic movement (frequently with direct affiliation to Solomon ka
Dinizulu, grandson of the Zulu monarch) constituted what Shula
Marks calls 'a bulwark against radical change – a bulwark as much

for the African intelligentsia as for the white ideologues of segregation'.[21] Because of their close ties with ethnic traditionalism, landowners like Campbell were integrally involved in the encouragement of Zulu nationalism.

Moreover, people like William Alfred Campbell imagined *themselves* part of a tribal community. Nostalgia for the class semiotics of the British aristocracy became propped upon a fantasy of being a white Zulu chief, and supporting the threatened power of the *amakhosi*. Those whites who knew Campbell frequently remarked on the ease with which 'among the Africans in his service he assumed the role of the tribal head'. One anecdote recalls him 'smoking a cigar and flicking the ash back over his shoulder where it was caught in a brass bowl held by a patient Zulu';[22] others frequently allude to the Zulu name conferred upon him: *Ntaba-Kayi-Konjwa* [*sic*] ('The Mountain which is not pointed at').[23] Authorized biographers refer to the fact that he inherited the title 'Councillor to the AmaQadi tribe' from his father, and Durban papers regularly record his involvement in Zulu regal affairs. As Shula Marks and Caroline Hamilton have shown, the annals of colonial Natal are strewn with episodes in which Zulu nationalism is propped upon the authority of 'progressive' white colonial officials, even those at the top of the hierarchy like Shepstone, who had royal Zulu authority bestowed upon them. What makes this case even more interesting, perhaps, is that like Rider Haggard's Sir Henry Curtis, Campbell believed absolutely in his ability to study, master, and conserve the Zulu past. People like him feared that the pageantry of the Zulu past (which they imagined, essentially, in terms of regimental warfare) was in danger of being undermined by proletarianization, and saw themselves as crucial custodians of a dying heroic tradition. One of the most remarkable stories to come out of the Campbell archives concerns the installation of Mzonjani Ngcobo as head of the Qadi clan in 1957. Officials of the Department of Native Affairs stayed away from the affair, feeling 'that it was desirable to preserve the tribe's privacy and dignity', but Campbell was invited to play a key role. Perhaps the oddest moment in the ceremony, according to newspaper reports, is Campbell's showing the assembled masses 'two Zulu relics, the great bracelet of ivory worn by Shaka and the hand-carved stool on which Dinizulu, the last king of the Zulus, sat when in council'. Despite the 'great cry of wonder' from the ranks, Campbell then went on to explain that these items would not be returned, but stored in a new museum to be named after his father

Sir Marshall Campbell, 'trusted advisor not only to the Qadi but to many other Zulu tribes'.[24]

When Campbell established the 'Mashu Museum', his ethnographic collection in Durban (attached to the Killie Campbell African library), the sugar baron set in place the last element of a complicated mechanism for narrating and regulating his version of the Zulu tribal past. As custodian of Zulu memorabilia, and preserver of tribal traditions, Wac now had a museum that would combat the effects of modernization by providing a means of returning the true past to the people. Similarly, in Mala Mala this 'friend of the Natives' had invented a space which maintained a fiction of pre-modern, feudal affiliation. These articulated spaces, the sugar plantation, the Reserve, and various museums, between which people and tribal artifacts were shuttled, amount to a complex material means by which fictions about archaic, primitive nature were sustained and disseminated in the public domain. Like picturesque landscapes generally, in which the representation of work is displaced by images of rural repose or contented peasant types, Mala Mala only acknowledges the presence of a strictly defined typology of labourers. Africans fall into a series of conventional categories including game guards (one of Campbell's first acts on purchasing the farms was to send badges for a 'native game guard' up to the Transvaal), trackers, gun bearers, and a narrow spectrum of docile, colourful subaltern personalities, including Mala Mala's chief icon, the imported tracker 'Mhlaba'.

Appropriate ethnic subjects were constantly being created at Mala Mala, so as to populate that imaginary space as though with actors on a stage. Consider the following curious example:

> There was a procedure following the shooting of a lion which was traditional and adhered to throughout Wac's time at Mala Mala. A cry, the 'Campbell cry' – '*ngaulana*', was uttered by Wac whenever a leopard or a lion was shot (no lesser beast warranted it). This cry it is said was the war-cry of an old Zulu regiment, and . . . [it] was permitted to be used by the trackers as they brought the lion carcass back to camp on the back of the specially-adapted jeep. Guests in the camp would hear the cry, followed by the Shangaan 'lion song' as the procession crossed the river.[25]

In recent years, historians interested in the production of Zulu ethnic identity have often been confronted by indignant informants who insist on the unchanging nature of the tradition. The case of the lion song at Mala Mala is an intriguing one, precisely because it shows how complicated the agency of colonial officials may be as conduits for invented traditions. Another version of the same story is given by a visitor during the War:

> Bringing a lion into camp is a real thrill for it is ceremonious. As soon as the shooting is over the native hunters shout 'Ngoulon' which is the Zulu name given to the Campbell family some eighty years ago. It is a victory cry and it is passed along the mysterious 'vine' system of the natives, so that by the time we reached the camp every man, woman and child was already waiting at the entrance of the camp area, which is encircled by a high reed-type fence, to sing the 'Lion Song'. And how they sing it![26]

Thus the 'lion song' has nothing necessarily to do with lions, the Transvaal bushveld, or Shangaan ritual. Rather, it has its origins in the complicated relationship between Wac's grandfather and his plantation employees, a memory that is then conserved, so to speak, in the colonial archive, and offered up to different communities – Shangaan in this case – in the next generation, to reaffirm their feudal trust. But why should Shangaan families have participated so enthusiastically in this silly performance? Clearly their lives and livelihood depended on pleasing a powerful employer. Even more crucially, however, it is obvious that by 1945 Mala Mala and other private reserves had so altered the ecosocial environment of the lowveld that peasant families had become dependent on the protection of white hunters. 'It is easy to understand why they put so much fervour into their song', Janule remarks, for 'the natives cannot possess a gun, and . . . when lion are infrequently hunted they become bold and not only kill the native's cattle but attach [sic] the natives themselves'.[27]

Mala Mala uses a form of landscape pragmatics that naturalizes certain types of ethnic identification: it creates 'subalternities', in the older Gramscian and Bengali Marxist sense of that word. Trackers, game guards, cooks, waiters, gun bearers, inhabit positions and wear fantastical uniforms that advertise the pseudo-regimental code of authority imposed by a class of white capitalist managers like Wac Campbell. Existing for the pleasure of another, these actors perform roles whose ontological emphasis is towards the other's system of meaning.[28] Furthermore, while this symbolization speaks about patriarchal authority over the safari world, it is even more helpful to see the landscape of Mala Mala as a context in which a variety of uneasily collaborating *masculinities* are performed. Just as 'femininity' at Natal Estates or Mala Mala consisted in various practices, so discourses anchored by these different institutions produce masculinities, coming together in phallocratic alliances.

Until recently, conservation historians like Mackenzie encouraged the view that the bloody slaughter of the colonial hunt was propelled by the same logic that eventually allowed a transition to game reserves.[29] Nonetheless, the masculine associations of the game reserve world are perhaps less straightforward than this suggests. Men following the hunt or directing game reserves between the wars were frequently involved in ostentatious displays of masculine prowess, but their self-identification frequently depended in complicated ways on male alliances across ethnic and class divides. Thus headmen or boss boys on Natal plantations are not too dissimilar from the picturesque Shangaan trackers celebrated by the conservative rhetoric at Mala Mala. For the landowner himself, the staging of Zulu or Shangaan maleness provides a dramatic context in which the dreary logic of the Natal Estates boardroom is shed, and more authentic, more directly masculine affinities between executives and their younger protégés are rehearsed. The bond between trackers and hunters becomes a model for 'instinctual' loyalties elsewhere.

There is, furthermore, a crucial link between identity and movement. In a sense, Campbell's faithful servant Mhlaba epitomizes what I am speaking about: his is an identity dependent on a 'shuttling' between two spaces, primitive bushveld retreat and sugar mansion. It cannot exist outside of that spatio-temporal process. Similarly, the young white executives 'lionized' in Campbell's private reserve are in a sense raised up into the officer class by being transported north out of modernity into an experience of deep, archaic time.

As a form of landscape, the bounded space of Mala Mala is inscribed with the interests of a narrowly conceived public, ideally comprising types such as the royal guest and the faithful company executive. Throughout his career, Campbell, like many of the Natal sugar barons, appears to have maintained sycophantic ties with the British aristocracy, at one point hosting South Africa's Governor General with Princess Alice on a memorable Mala Mala safari, and acting as personal guide for the Royal Family on their 1947 visit to the Kruger National Park.

Within the demarcated zone that constituted Campbell's vision of the bushveld, two particular sites helped to reinforce class and race attitudes by reduplicating certain types of spatial organization. First, the camp itself imposed a series of *outward looking* diorama-like views on the surroundings, framed images of wildlife in its pristine, tranquil abode. Part of the same system of manufactured views, but this time turned *inward*, was the area known as 'the boma'. A number of evocative photographs of this locale still exist. One of them shows the structure in its original simplicity, a screen of branches surrounding rattan chairs for guests, each coupled with a rough table made from paraffin tin packing crates. The logic of this space entails not only an affected rusticity – like a film set, in fact – but it also clearly embodies attitudes towards male homosociality: drinking and eating, with the visible traffic of servants backlit by firelight making up a sort of performance. The division of symbolic space is confirmed in another picture, taken some twenty years later, where the original look of the packing case tables has been reduplicated. Now, however, with the addition of human figures, a semicircle of prominent guests turned towards the camera, the function of this space is far clearer: it marks the extension, into the bushveld, of the boardroom, with its potential for the transmission of gender asymmetries, labour classification, and executive retraining radically enhanced. Completely unlike disseminated, modernist forms of control, it is a return to a form of spectacle that concentrates the gaze of the young executive and the older partners on the figure of the managing director.

Despite the presence of a single woman in the picture of the campfire semi-circle, the Mala Mala camp area was a form of hegemonic male space structured according to a gendered logic that is also visible in the attitudes towards wives and servants at Natal Estates. It is, in fact, an extreme example of the apparently gendered separation of spheres. Above all, it was a place of 'Nature', of simple, rugged contrasts: 'Nobody has lived', claimed one doggerel writer in the camp journal of 1956, 'who has not seen and heard the dawn / At Mala Mala. Each new day is born . . . divorced entirely from the violence of the previous night (E.J.C.S. 2).[30] In the archaic, instinctual relations of predator and prey, night and day, is rehearsed an older form of value that is rejuvenating for the alienated visitor.

Now that Natal Estates has long been absorbed into the Hulett's monopoly, Mala Mala has become a millionaire's playground, and lowveld reserves brace themselves against the demands of land redistribution; that triangular exchange between plantation, estate and museum that took up so much of Campbell's life has fallen away. Substantial in his influence at the time, Wac Campbell's legacy is far less clear than that of his sister or nephew. More than most, however, Campbell epitomized the principle by which landscape aesthetics come to mediate between articulated spaces, and it is the collapse of that *system* that has finally made a ghost of him.

NOTES

1 An earlier version of this article deals extensively with landscape aesthetics in modernist South African poetry and painting. See my 'Relocations: Landscape Theory, South African Landscape Practice, and the Transmission of Political Value', *Pretexts*, 4.2 (Summer 1993), pp. 44–67
2 Eric Goetzsche, *Rough But Ready: An Official History of the Natal Mounted Rifles*, Durban, Interprint, n.d., p. 346.
3 Aldous Huxley, *Brave New World*, St Alban's, Panther, 1977, p. 8.
4 J. du P. Scholtz, *Strat Caldecott, 1886–1929*, Cape Town, A. A. Balkema, 1970, pp. 12–13.
5 Stephenson-Hamilton, quoted in Scholtz, *Strat Caldecott*, p. 13.
6 Isabel Hofmeyer, 'Building a Nation From Words: Afrikaans Language, Literature and Ethnic Identity', in Shula Marks and Stanley Trapido (eds), *The Politics of Race, Class, and Nationalism in Twentieth-Century South Africa*, London, Longman, 1987, pp. 95–123.
7 Hedley Chilvers, *The Seven Wonders of Southern Africa*, Johannesburg, SAR&H, 1929, p. 245.
8 Mervyn Lincoln, 'The Culture of the South African Sugarmill: the Impress of the Sugarocracy', Unpublished doctoral dissertation, University of Cape Town, 1985, p. 1.
9 Lincoln, 'Sugarmill', p. 93.
10 *Sugar Journal Annual* 1925, p. 86.
11 See John Barrell's study of James Thomson, in *The Idea of Landscape and the Sense of Place*, Cambridge, Cambridge University Press, 1972.
12 *South African Sugar Journal*, 30 April 1930, p. 227.
13 Lincoln, 'Sugarmill', p. 111.
14 *South African Sugar Journal* 1925, p. 216.
15 See Edward Soja, *Postmodern Geographies*, London, Verso, 1989, pp. 183–9.
16 'Regionalization' is Anthony Giddens' extremely useful term for the symbolic division of locales. See his 'Time, Space, and Regionalization', in Derek Gregory and John Urry, eds, *Social Relations and Spatial Structures*, London, Macmillan, 1985, pp. 265–95.
17 See Moishe Postone, *Time, Labour, Social Domination*, Chicago, University of Chicago Press, 1993, p. 311.
18 Rattray, Gillian, *To Everything Its Season: Mala Mala, The Story of a Game Reserve*, Johannesburg, Jonathan Ball, 1986, p. 86.

19 Rattray, *To Everything Its Season*, p. 86. 'Biltong' is dried venison, once the staple of migratory South African hunters and farmers.
20 See Shirley Brooks, 'Save the Game: Conservationist Discourse in Early Twentieth-Century Natal', Unpublished paper, South African Economic History Conference, 1992.
21 Shula Marks, 'Patriotism, Patriarchy and Purity: Natal and the Politics of Zulu Ethnic Consciousness', in Leroy Vail, (ed.), *The Creation of Tribalism in South Africa*, Berkeley, University of California Press, 1989, p. 217.
22 Both quotations are from Norman Herd's, *Killie's Africa*, Pietermaritzburg, Blue Crane Books, 1982, p. 156.
23 Herd, *Killie's Africa*, p. 156.
24 Quotations from Justice Alexander, 'War Dances and Christian Blessings at Installation of Qadi Chief', *South African Panorama* 1.7 (1957), p. 23.
25 Rattray, *To Everything Its Season*, p. 102.
26 M. H. Janule, 'Huntin' and shootin' at Mala Mala', typescript, Killie Campbell Africana Library Manuscript Collection (MS JAN 2.092), p. 7.
27 Janule, 'Huntin' and shootin' ', pp. 7–8.
28 Robert Young, *White Mythologies: Writing, History and the West*, London, Routledge, 1990, p. 164.
29 John M. Mackenzie, *The Empire of Nature: Hunting, Conservation and British Imperialism*, Manchester, Manchester University Press, 1988.
30 "E.J.C.S." (pseudonym), 'Mala Mala', typescript manuscript, p. 2. I am grateful to Belinda Eisenhauer of the Durban Natural History museum for making this available to me.

BIBLIOGRAPHY

Barrell, J., *The Idea of Landscape and the Sense of Place*, Cambridge, Cambridge University Press, 1972.

Berman, E., *Art and Artists of South Africa*, Cape Town and Rotterdam, A. A. Balkema, 1983.

Bradford, H., *The Industrial and Commercial Worker's Union of South Africa in the South African Countryside, 1924–1930*, Massachusetts, Yale University Press, 1988.

Brooks, S., 'Save the Game: Conservationist Discourse in Early Twentieth-Century Natal', Unpublished paper, South African Economic History Conference, 1992.

Chilvers, H., *The Seven Wonders of Southern Africa*, Johannesburg, SAR&H, 1929.

Giddens, A., 'Time, Space, and Regionalisation', in Gregory, D., and Urry, J., (eds), *Social Relations and Spatial Structures*, London, Macmillan, 1985.

Goetzsche, E., *Rough But Ready: An Official History of the Natal Mounted Rifles*, Durban, Interprint, n.d.

Herd, N., *Killie's Africa*, Pietermaritzburg, Blue Crane Books, 1982.

Hofmeyer, I., 'Building a Nation From Words: Afrikaans Language,

Literature and Ethnic Identity', in Marks, S. and Trapido, S. (eds), *The Politics of Race, Class, and Nationalism in Twentieth-Century South Africa*, London, Longman, 1987, pp. 95–123.

Huxley, A., *Brave New World*, St Alban's, Panther, 1977 (originally pub. 1932), p. 8.

Lincoln, M., 'The Culture of the South African Sugarmill: the Impress of the Sugarocracy', Unpublished doctoral dissertation, University of Cape Town, 1985.

Marks, S., 'Patriotism, Patriarchy and Purity: Natal and the Politics of Zulu Ethnic Consciousness', in Vail, L., (ed.), *The Creation of Tribalism in South Africa*, Berkeley, University of California Press, 1989.

Mackenzie, J. M., *The Empire of Nature: Hunting, Conservation and British Imperialism*, Manchester, Manchester University Press, 1988.

Postone, M., *Time, Labour, Social Domination*, Chicago, University of Chicago Press, 1993.

Ranger, T., 'Gendering the Zimbabwean Landscape', *Southern African Review of Books*, 1993.

Rattray, Gillian, *To Everything Its Season: Mala Mala, The Story of a Game Reserve*, Johannesburg, Jonathan Ball, 1986.

Scholtz, J. du P., *Strat Caldecott, 1886–1929*, Cape Town, A. A. Balkema, 1970, pp. 12–13.

Soja, E., *Postmodern Geographies*, London, Verso, 1989.

Tosh, J., 'What Should Historians do with Masculinity?', *History Workshop* 38 (Autumn 1994), p. 192.

Vawda, S., Padayachee, S. and Tichmann, P., 'From Indentured Labourers to Industrial Proletariat: the Formation of An Indian Industrial Working Class, 1910–1950', Unpublished conference paper, Annual Conference of South African Anthropologists, September 1985, University of Natal, pp. 7–8.

3

THE VOYAGE SOUTH
Writing immigration

Kerryn Goldsworthy

This study of shipboard diaries and letters written by nineteenth-century British emigrants to Australia uses ideas of liminality from anthropological and psychoanalytic theory as a way of thinking about the experience of emigration, and about the effects that experience had on the emigrants' sense of their own identity. As Mary Douglas writes in *Purity and Danger*:

> all margins are dangerous. If they are pulled this way or that the shape of fundamental experience is altered. Any structure of ideas is vulnerable at its margins.[1]

There is a sense in which both a nation and a person can be called a structure of ideas; and an emigrant is someone in whose life those vulnerable margins have suddenly begun to shift, to yield, to stretch, or to disappear. From the coastlines of their countries and the barriers of class, right down to the skin of their bodies and the limits of the family, the boundaries of people's lives begin to change from the moment they decide to leave. And an emigrant is not only a being in transition, but a transitional being; to be an emigrant is not just to be on the border, but to be the border itself.

In the course of the nineteenth century, British ideas about Australia remained ambiguous and self-contradictory. This is reflected in what were probably the most widely known represent-ations in Britain of colonial Australia: in Dickens' *David Copperfield* (1850), Australia features as the place to which the 'ruined' Little Em'ly is sent to start a new life, while in *Great Expectations* (1861) it is the place from which the convict Magwitch so dangerously returns, and the source of Pip's poisoned inheritance. Although the last convict ship to Australia arrived in 1868, Australia's very negative initial status as a place of prison and exile soon developed as a counterweight the kind of attitude expressed by free emigrant Sarah Davenport as early as 1841: 'as maney poeple leving home fro new south wales and Port philip sent gloing accounts of the country . . . we was all in good hopes that we was coming to beeter our selves [*sic*].'[2]

In those 'good hopes', hundreds of thousands of emigrants in the nineteenth century made the voyage under sail from Britain to Australia. Using the letters and journals that some of them wrote on the way, this chapter reads that journey as a ritual process, a process of negotiating boundaries, borders and margins on three levels: the Trip, the Ship, and the Body.

THE TRIP

By the time a ship full of emigrants had lost sight of land, two important things had happened to them: they had become an isolated community, and they had begun to learn at first hand the literal meaning of the expression 'all in the same boat'. There was one new and absolute boundary in their lives – the visible line of the deck-rail – but a number of old boundaries had begun to collapse.

For while the efforts that were made to keep the classes and sexes separate on board ship were prodigious and sometimes ludicrous, and while many of the trials of shipboard life were indescribably worse for the steerage passengers than for anybody else, the very condition of being at sea and bound for Australia was in some ways a radical equalizer. All of the emigrating passengers had new and unfamiliar things in common: their destination, their physical vulnerability, their lack of spatial freedom, their knowledge that their lives were in someone else's hands, and, most importantly, their psychic and physical condition as emigrants.

Victor Turner, in *The Ritual Process*, defines two related anthropological concepts he calls liminality and *communitas*:

The attributes of liminality or of liminal personae ('threshold people') are necessarily ambiguous, since this condition and these persons elude or slip through the network of classifications that normally locate states and positions in cultural space.

54

Liminal entities are neither here nor there; they are betwixt and between the positions assigned and arrayed by law, custom, convention, and ceremonial ... Liminal entities, such as neophytes in initiation or puberty rites, may be represented as possessing nothing ... It is as though they are being reduced or ground down to a uniform condition to be fashioned anew and endowed with additional powers to enable them to cope with their new station in life ... What is interesting about liminal phenomena ... is the blend they offer of lowliness and sacredness, of homogeneity and comradeship. We are presented ... with a 'moment in and out of time', and in and out of secular social structure, which reveals ... some recognition ... of a generalized social bond.[3]

Turner goes on to attach the term *communitas* to this concept of a non-hierarchical liminal group in the grip of ritual; and I want to argue that to some degree at least, this description fits the condition of a boatload of emigrants while at sea. They were liminal beings, literally neither here nor there. They were in a condition of virtual captivity and enforced passivity that equates with the idea of being 'stripped'. They were suspended between a number of apparent, but by definition illusory, binary oppositions: emigrant and immigrant, north and south, the known and the unknown, the old life and the new. They were undergoing a ritual process of transformation, and their living conditions at sea resembled rites of initiation: ritualistic, equalizing, physically testing and – perhaps most of all – conducive to self-examination and self-reflexivity.

Journal-writing, for the literate, became the main focus of this last activity. The very act of transforming shipboard experience into language was a form of meditation on that experience; and the act of writing itself became, for some, an important daily ritual. A number of emigrant diarists made their daily entries under amazing physical conditions: in the dark, in the wet, at a forty-five degree angle to the deck, in between bouts of seasickness, and sometimes all of those things at once. 'I wish particularly to impress upon your minds the advantage and amusement to be derived from keeping a journal of the occurrences each day,' wrote William Kingston in *The Emigrant Voyager's Manual* of 1850. 'If the weather is very bad, and you cannot have the ink-bottle out, write it up in pencil.'[4]

What they frequently wrote up, however, was the fact that nothing much had happened. Anna Cook, in a journal-letter addressed to her mother, wrote in 1883, 'I wish every day you were here, although I should not like you to come in a sailing vessel – it is too long for anyone without children. I hear all the women say the time hangs so heavily on their hands – they have nothing to do.'[5] Fifty-five years earlier, in Sarah Docker's shipboard journal of 1828, the phrase 'nothing particular has occurred' is repeated like a refrain.[6]

This is the 'amplification of absence' discussed by Paul Carter in *The Road to Botany Bay*: the paradoxical use of language to turn nothingness itself into a point of interest, and to repel boredom by writing about it and thus reaffirming the self in the midst of all this nothingness. 'Absence,' says Carter of Augustus Gregory's 1858 exploration diary, 'becomes a metaphor expressive of his own presence.'[7] This is the case not only with diarists' assertions that 'nothing has happened' but also with another negatively framed and even more frequently occurring phrase. When these diarists say 'Words cannot describe . . .', as they often do, they are usually talking about one of three things: the view, or a particularly bad storm, or the death of a child. 'The sea looks magnificent, it is impossible to describe it', wrote Anne Gratton aboard the *Conway* in 1858.[8] Fanny Davis, on the same trip, described the effects of a storm: 'The people were all very much frightened . . . The scene was one that cannot be described.'[9] Twenty years earlier, Sarah Brunskill had written of the shipboard deaths of her two children: 'No words can express with truth the pain and agony of the heart.'[10]

They all go on, of course, to utter, express and describe at some length. But what is interesting, for my purposes, about these outbreaks of paralepsis is that they are almost always prompted by some aspect of the sublime – extremes of beauty, terror, or grief – and what this frequently produces is a kind of discursive two-step: the initial assertion that no form of language is equal to the task of representation is often followed by a shift into the discourse of the sacred, in the form of psalms, hymns, scriptural allusions, biblical syntax and various appeals to the Almighty. Women whose children had died almost never wrote about it without some reference to the will of God. Fanny Davis, still describing the same storm, wrote 'I don't know how it was that I was not at all frightened, but I felt that there was One able to calm the tempest and it seemed as if somebody whispered "Fear not, for I am with thee; be not dismayed for I am thy God." '[11] And two different women, confronted with the task of describing what they could see from the deck, resorted to a near-identical discursive strategy. First there is Anna Cook's description of the sunset: 'a deep golden colour spreads over the whole sky, tipped with bright gold and red. "Jerusalem the Golden", the hymn, seems to describe it a little, and that only gives a very faint idea.'[12] The following year, in 1884, Sarah Harrison's diary entry for 4 May reads 'Today the sea is like a great shining lake . . . It very often reminds me of the silver river that flows by the Throne of God and I very often sing [that hymn] while sitting on the side and looking over.'[13]

What all of these women are doing, very sensibly, is dealing with hitherto unknown extremes of feeling by recourse to familiar sacred texts and rituals of hymn-singing and prayer. New experiences are absorbed and assimilated one by one, each granted the status of ritual and each contributing to the process of transforming identity.

There is a strong contrast between these gentle and gradual nego-tiations of change and the sailors' shipboard ceremonies performed in the name of 'crossing the line'. The equator, as a line which is both imaginary and charged with significance, seems to be – like most hard boundaries and territorial markers – a particularly dangerous margin. One horrified diarist called Robert Poynter describes the line-crossing ceremony as 'foolish' 'cruel', 'grotesque' and 'brutal', and revealingly remarks that '[the] Captain seemed to have no power over his crew.'[14] This Bacchic and Bakhtinian outbreak of chaos among the sailors is contained by ritual and is therefore only temporary, but Poynter stays miffed with the Captain for nearly a week.

On Anna Cook's ship *Scottish Hero*, the passengers invent an equa-torial ritual of their own, in which the emigrant's best hopes are acted out:

> two of [the single men] dressed up and walked up and down the deck representing old and new England, one in the Bush with his pockets full of money, the other at home starving, and [his] pockets hanging [inside out].[15]

Here the equator implicitly becomes a metonym for the whole ex-perience of emigration; the moment of crossing-the-line is the moment at which to enact the process of transformation, like casting magic spells at midnight.

THE SHIP

In his recently published book *Mr Bligh's Bad Language*, a brilliant study of Captain William Bligh and the mutiny on the *Bounty*, Australian historian Greg Dening meditates on the meaning of shipboard space: on the ways in which it is constructed, divided and named, and on the way those things symbolize power relations and confer authority. 'Space and the language used to describe it make a ship,' says Dening. 'Space was inseparable from the authority it displayed and the relationships it involved.'[16] Thus, on the emigrant ships, words like 'cabin' and 'steerage' are not only used to refer to places on the ship, but also function as adjectives describing the passengers. A passenger named William Johnstone, who was 'cabin' and therefore qualified to disport himself at leisure on the poop deck, described in his 1841 journal the fate of steerage emigrants who had inadvertently crossed the territorial barriers:

> some of them had mounted on the Poop, from whence they were most unceremoniously expelled by the Captain, who commanded them never to have the impudence to shew their faces there again.[17]

'Cabin and intermediate passengers,' writes Don Charlwood in *The Long Farewell*, 'did not usually regard themselves as emigrants . . . To them an emigrant was not one who left his own country to settle in another, but one who was financially assisted to do so.'[18] This radical slippage of meaning in a perfectly ordinary word is an example of what Greg Dening means about language; the socio-historical context temporarily redefined the word 'emigrant' as the name of a piece of space.

Divisions of shipboard space were radically different, however, on the ships used in the scheme of emigration developed by Caroline Chisholm in 1850, which Charlwood describes thus:

> She refused to accept the prevailing lack of privacy; . . . the rigid segregation of single males and females, which involved separation from members of their own families; . . . the contrasting conditions of the classes. She aimed to have the family as the basic unit of emigration. She envisaged families paying small amounts into a co-operative organization toward their own fares . . . She had chartered the [ship] *Slains Castle* and had it fitted out to her specifications. There was no division into classes. Instead of long rows of open bunks between

decks, she devised small cabins of varying sizes [depending on the size of the group].[19]

So, on Chisholm's ships, the only demarcation line distinguishing between the passengers was that of family membership; and even that line was breached by the passengers' voluntary pledge: 'We pledge ourselves as Christian fathers and heads of families to exercise parental control and guardianship over all orphans and friendless females proceeding with family groups. To protect them as our children and allow them to share the same claims as our daughters.'[20]

The values and the rhetoric of the patriarchal family are here invoked in an oath which is potentially threatening to it, in the strongly worded promise to treat those who are not family exactly as though they were. Here, in a move which brought the group of passengers on any Chisholm ship very close to Turner's idea of *communitas*, the family itself is made 'vulnerable at its margins'; through the medium of language sanctified by a solemn ritual pledge, the family is admitting at its borders a class of liminal beings who both do and do not belong.

All but the Chisholm ships, however, had class-based and money-determined divisions of passenger space. Steerage accommodation, the space that came to be signified by the word 'emigrant', was largely open space, where the only solid partitions between passengers were made on the basis of marital status and sex. In a diagram of steerage accommodation on the *St Vincent*, which was typical, the divisions are between married people, single males and single females.[21] Space was minimal and privacy nonexistent. 'By night,' writes Don Charlwood in *The Long Farewell*,

> the teeming married quarters must have blessed the screen of background groans from the ship's timbers as they argued, wept, urinated, broke wind, copulated, snored, vomited, prayed, or cried out in dreams . . . It was their only screen.[22]

There was no respite from other people's bodies, and no effective containment of one's own. It was an environment in which the very boundaries of identity began to collapse.

THE BODY

Many of the shipboard diaries are understandably preoccupied with the immediate physical circumstances, and a great deal of space is given to the discussion of food and clothes. On a trip which is by definition altering the terms and conditions of identity, it makes perfect sense that some anxieties would manifest themselves, even in the comparative comfort of cabin class, as a preoccupation with what covers the body and what nourishes it.

Clothing itself is a particularly porous and mutable liminal phenomenon. It both is and is not the body, a kind of outer skin, a layer of the body's boundary. Clothing mediates between the body and the world, acting as both signal and disguise. It is also one of the clearest markers of identity, but on board ship where no new clothes were to be had for the duration, this convention broke down as garments were recycled and reassigned. 'I have cut up Emm's red shawl to make [the baby] another frock,' wrote Anna Cook to her mother, 'and . . . I have cut up baby's grey frock that was made out of your dress [to make Bernard] another pair [of trousers].'[23]

Like almost everything else on board ship, clothing was subject to unique conditions. Keeping it clean was impossible, especially if you were seasick. There was a ritual exchange of dirty clothes for clean once a month when passengers' baggage was brought up out of the hold for the purpose. Sometimes this held a few nasty surprises, as Fanny Davis's diary unsympathetically records:

> in one [family's] box a bottle of jam had burst and spoiled a new dress . . . and can anyone pity them if people will be so careless as to pack jam and clothes together.[24]

The packing of jam and clothes together, and the inevitable result, provides a vivid symbol for the general derangement of bodily needs, bodily functions and bodily boundaries that shipboard conditions tended to produce. The paragraph by Mary Douglas from which I quoted at the beginning of this chapter continues like this:

> Any structure of ideas is vulnerable at its margins. We should expect the orifices of the body to symbolise its specially vulnerable points. Matter issuing from them is marginal stuff of the most obvious kind. . . . blood, milk, urine, faeces or tears by simply issuing forth have traversed the boundary of the body.[25]

In assembling her theory of 'abjection', Julia Kristeva adds to this list, as a kind of logical conclusion, the corpse itself, the body after death. Her argument is, in part, that psychic health inheres in a clear sense of one's own subjectivity and its boundaries, as manifest in what she calls 'one's clean and proper body'. So, she argues, our horror at bodily waste and corpses is a response to their marginal nature: such matter is stuff that exists at the boundaries of the self, obscuring our sense of exactly where those boundaries are.[26] 'A dead body,' writes Helen Garner, 'makes perfect sense of itself, in no language but its own . . . It has presence. And yet it is no longer a person.'[27]

Normally the boundaries of identity are marked off by a clear knowledge of difference: bodily wastes are of, but other to, the self; so are clothes; so too are dead bodies, including those of one's own children. But shipboard conditions sometimes made this knowledge hard to hold on to. One diarist recorded glimpsing a pair of female feet covered in what he took at first for boots but proved to be a thick coating of grime and dirt. Another described the horror of his fellow-passengers on discovering one of their number, clearly desperate for a receptacle, being sick into his own food dish. While these things are funny in a Hogarthian sort of way, the real breakdown of identity they represent is taken to its logical conclusion in a brief shipboard journal entry from a Scottish bootmaker called Thomas Small on 6 June, 1863:

> A child died at 8 o'c. & the father passed us with the little corpse in his arms going to put it out at one of the portholes on the quiet.[28]

What was once a person has become a corpse, and a corpse has become rubbish to be expelled like waste from the body of the ship.

This was originally going to be an essay about women's writing and women's bodies, about written accounts of maternity and childbirth at sea. I was going to quote Kristeva on the subject of childbirth as the ultimate threshold, what she calls 'flayed identity . . . the height of bloodshed and life, [the] scorching moment of hesitation between inside and outside, ego and other, life and death, horror and beauty'.[29] But Sarah Docker, travelling on the Adams in 1828 and making her diary entry for 27 June was altogether less poetic and more informative.[30] She gives no previous hint of her pregnant state, so the announcement comes as a complete surprise. The voyage south transformed Sarah Docker's identity in more ways than one, turning her not only into an emigrant but also into a mother – an event which seems to have been transformative in itself, though it seems like a fairly drastic cure even for seasickness. 'Nothing particular occurred during the week,' she wrote. 'I still continued very [sea]sick and became so weak that I could scarcely sit up. About 6 o'clock this morning I felt very unwell and had the

Doctor and Mrs Davies called up, and a little after six Mary-Jane
was born . . . After my confinement I was never the least sick . . . [I]
looked so well that the Captain said he should scarcely have known
me for the same person.'

NOTES

1 Mary Douglas, *Purity and Danger: An Analysis of the Concepts of Pollution and Taboo*, London, Routledge, 1991, p. 121.
2 Lucy Frost, *No Place for a Nervous Lady: Voices From the Australian Bush*, Melbourne, McPhee Gribble/Penguin, 1984, p. 239.
3 Victor Turner, *The Ritual Process: Structure and Anti-Structure*, Chicago, Aldine, 1969, pp. 95–7.
4 Don Charlwood, *The Long Farewell*, Melbourne, Penguin, 1993, p. 193.
5 Frost, *No Place for a Nervous Lady*, p. 27.
6 MS 9115–21, La Trobe Collection, State Library of Victoria: Journal of Sarah Docker.
7 Paul Carter, *The Road to Botany Bay: An Essay in Spatial History*, London, Faber & Faber, 1987, p. 78.
8 MS 9367, La Trobe Collection, State Library of Victoria: Journal of Anne Gratton.
9 Charlwood, *The Long Farewell*, p. 254.
10 Patricia Clarke and Dale Spender (eds), *Life Lines: Australian Women's Letter and Diaries 1788 to 1840*, Sydney, Allen & Unwin, 1992, p. 59.
11 Charlwood, *The Long Farewell*, p. 255.
12 Frost, *No Place for a Nervous Lady*, p. 22.
13 MS 11831, La Trobe Collection, State Library of Victoria: Journal of Sarah Harrison.
14 Charlwood, *The Long Farewell*, pp. 205-6.
15 Frost, *No Place for a Nervous Lady*, p. 22.
16 Greg Dening, *Mr Bligh's Bad Language: Passion, Power and Theatre on the Bounty*, Cambridge, Cambridge University Press/Canto, 1994, p. 19.
17 Charlwood, *The Long Farewell*, p. 110.
18 Charlwood, *The Long Farewell*, p. 92.
19 Charlwood, *The Long Farewell*, p. 111.
20 Charlwood, *The Long Farewell*, p. 112.
21 See Charlwood, *The Long Farewell*, p. 98.
22 Charlwood, *The Long Farewell*, p. 103.
23 Frost, *No Place for a Nervous Lady*, p. 24.
24 Charlwood, *The Long Farewell*, p. 258.
25 Douglas, *Purity and Danger*, p. 121.
26 Julia Kristeva, *Powers of Horror: An Essay on Abjection*, New York, Columbia University Press, 1982, p. 4.
27 Helen Garner, 'The Last Remains', in *The Age Saturday Extra* (Melbourne), 16 May 1992, pp. 1, 4.
28 Charlwood, *The Long Farewell*, p. 166.
29 Kristeva, *Powers of Horror*, p. 155.
30 Charlwood, *The Long Farewell*, p. 159.

BIBLIOGRAPHY

Carter, Paul, *The Road to Botany Bay*, London, Faber & Faber, 1987.

Charlwood, Don, *The Long Farewell*, Melbourne, Penguin, 1993.

Clarke, Patricia and Spender, Lynne (eds), *Life Lines: Australian Women's Letters and Diaries 1788 to 1840*, Sydney, Allen & Unwin, 1992.

Dening, Greg, *Mr Bligh's Bad Language: Passion, Power and Theatre on the Bounty*, Cambridge, Cambridge University Press/Canto, 1994.

Douglas, Mary, *Purity and Danger: An Analysis of the Concepts of Pollution and Taboo*, London, Routledge, 1991.

Frost, Lucy, *No Place for a Nervous Lady: Voices From the Australian Bush*, Melbourne, McPhee Gribble/Penguin, 1984.

Kristeva, Julia, *Powers of Horror: An Essay on Abjection*, New York, Columbia University Press, 1982.

Turner, Victor, *The Ritual Process: Structure and Anti-Structure*, Chicago, Aldine, 1969.

4

A 'WHITE-SOULED STATE'
Across the 'South' with Lady Barker

Gillian Whitlock

What does it mean to read 'across' Australian and South African texts? One can search databases, 'surf the Net', send research assistants to hunt and gather and still reap relatively little in the way of cross-national comparisons of these two literatures. Australian and New Zealand comparisons are slightly more common, with Ian Reid's book *Fiction and the Great Depression* the most outstanding example of intra-Commonwealth comparative reading. Of Australia and Canada there is more to be said: a recent collection of essays includes a bibliography of some fifty articles; a substantial comparative study, *Tradition in Exile*, was published in 1962, and Terry Goldie's book, *Fear and Temptation: The Image of the Indigene in Canadian, Australian and New Zealand Literature* stands alone as an ambitious comparative study of settler/invader literatures.[1]

The absence of comparative perspectives on the southern settler states is worthy of comment, given the recent surge in post-colonial studies. As Edward Said has recently argued, the rethinking and reformulating of historical experiences which had once been based on the geographical separation of peoples is critical to post-colonial studies.[2] Yet in the context of the British Empire and its residue, little attention has been paid to the settler states/invader territories of Canada, South Africa and Australasia, although the 'white Dominions' were collectively important to imperialist thinking in Britain in the late nineteenth century. The work of US, British and subaltern post-colonial studies has focused on decolonization, particularly in the Third World. Although the earlier tradition of

Commonwealth literary studies which emerged in the 1960s began with a comparative bent,[3] as Anna Rutherford has argued the nation was at the centre of this criticism, which (like post-colonialism) was intimately connected to processes of decolonization and Third World nationalism.[4]

The political strategies which insist that post-colonial and Commonwealth canons focus on writings from the Third World and black writing from South Africa, Australia and Canada, and the attention given to the 'writing back' to Empire, are not to be cast aside lightly. Literary texts have had a critical role to play in the liberation movements in the former colonies of European imperialism. How do settler colonies figure in this? Tim Brennan argues that the field of the post-colonial must be 'the literature not of the 'colonies' but of the 'colonized':

[Writers such as] Nadine Gordimer or John Coetzee of South Africa, along with others from the white Commonwealth countries, while clearly playing [a] mediating role [between colonizer and colonized], are probably better placed in some category of the European novel of Empire because of their compromised positions of segregated privilege within colonial settler states. They are too much like the fictional 'us' of the so-called mainstream, on the inside looking out.[5]

As writers and critics who write from settler spaces, we may choose to resist the binarism of 'Europe and its Others' which organizes Brennan's argument, and insist on the strategic necessity of formulating 'the literature of the colonies'. Post-colonial readings of 'white writing' in settler states need to be informed by approaches which articulate an ambivalent relation to Empire, and the position of white settlers as being both colonized by metropolitan societies, and, in their turn, brutally colonizing indigenous peoples. If, as Sara Mills argues, each colonial relation develops narrative and descriptive techniques and a range of colonialist practices particular to its setting and history,[6] the question remains as to whether there are discursive frameworks which characterize writing from these settler/invader spaces, what these might be, and how these may be analyzed.

Alan Lawson uses the concept of 'Second-world' to devise a discursive framework and a reading strategy for writings grounded in post-colonial cultures peculiar to settler societies.[7] He takes up Homi Bhabha's point that 'the colonial presence is always ambivalent, split between its appearance as original and authoritative and

66

its articulation as repetition and difference' to argue that particular kinds of doubleness seem to be 'distinctively Second-world', and are one way of thematizing the 'second-ness of their worlds'. Stephen Slemon also acknowledges the 'middle ground' of the settler states, stating that the ambivalence of literary resistance is the 'always already' condition of Second-world settler and post-colonial writings:

> For in the white literatures of Australia, or New Zealand, or Canada, anti-colonialist resistance has never been directed at an object or discursive structure which can been seen as purely external to the self. The Second-world writer, the second-world text, that is, have always been complicit in colonialism's territorial appropriation of land, and voice, and agency, and this has been their inescapable condition even at those moments when they have promulgated their most strident and most spectacular figures of post-colonial resistance.[8]

For Lawson and Slemon, the inclusion of settler sites into post-colonial criticism is a necessary development, emphasizing the historical specificity of literary resistance and ambivalence in places 'where First-world post-colonial theory has so far forgotten to look.'

Other critics note the difficulties of using a 'settler' template to organize readings of South African writing. Christy Collis examines the usefulness of the 'Second-world' concept for South Africa, pointing out that the 'familiar question marks of Canadian and Australian settler discourses' are less apparent: 'The central question taken up by many South African critics and writers is most often not the non-essentialist, post-colonial one of "where is here" . . . but instead the polemical "which side are you on?" '[9] The unique polarization and institutionalization of class and racial politics, and of apartheid and resistance, in South Africa have led some critics to argue that discourses of post-colonialism are inappropriately applied to literature written by whites. The hold of the post-colonial label on 'white writing' in the South African context is a particularly uneasy one.[10]

The debate over territorial access to post-colonial taxonomies is a matter of concern for those of us who approach South African writing now, from the 'outside', with a comparative perspective and/or with the discourses of post-colonial criticism as tools. This book, the conference which was its genesis, and other recent academic initiatives are harbingers of what is to come: a rapidly growing body of work on South Africa across an international community of scholars. On one hand the gains are obvious: for example, South African writings may remind Australians of the importance of the construction of whiteness in their own historical and cultural context. In the white supremacist settler societies, where ideologies of whiteness have been taken as given, critiques of the 'making' of whiteness are now emerging. J. M. Coetzee's concept of 'white writing', for all its specificity about Afrikaner culture, provides a useful framework for thinking about writing in Australia and in New Zealand.[11] Recently Mudrooroo Narogin has argued that African writing is potentially a comparative reference for Black Australian writing.[12]

But what do we, as outsiders, bring to South Africa? The danger is that we become raiders of the 'lost ark', turning to the 'new' South Africa to prove what we already know, seeking (and finding) evidence which justifies theories produced elsewhere. In a consideration of various approaches to comparative literary studies in settler societies, Robert Wilson stresses that textual analysis resides uneasily within contextual investigation: 'Place two objects together, Canadian pears and Australian papayas, say, and the possibilities for comparison will appear to be endless. Most of these will be adventitious and arbitrary.'[13] Ingenuity needs to be replaced (or at least supplemented) with the 'weight of positive, concrete and precisely historical connections', with what is playfully described as 'a fly's eye':

> Seeing with a fly's eye requires that the individual facets focus clearly and that they are functionally co-ordinated. A co-ordinated set of perspectives, constituting a compound structure for analysis and explanation, works effectively in proportion to the extent that its principles of structuration make sense, are arguable and coherent . . . What does seem to work . . . is a perspective explicitly grounded in either the socio-cultural history of the two (or more) national literatures . . . in a recognizable theoretical model . . . Given a conceptual archive with sufficient depth and sophistication (a bit of self-awareness added to its arsenal of propositions), then it may be possible eventually to construct the innovative compound structures necessary for comparative perspectives in Commonwealth literature.[14]

At its best, this 'fly's eye' will come alongside national studies of South African writing to observe not only what is distinctive, but also what it might share with other sites as a facet of larger cross-national formations. In the case of post-colonial readings this larger form-ation, or imagined community, will be generated as a legacy of Empire, of processes of colonization and decolonization.

Clearly various interpretations of settler sites as a particular type of contact zone need to be sharpened in the light of the criticisms which surround the attempts to incorporate South Africa into comparative post-colonial frameworks. In my view we have a licence to proceed, but with caution. To avoid the 'adventitious and arb-itrary', three points need to guide our analysis. Firstly, post-colonial critics will need to examine representations of and from South Africa with a view to ongoing formulations of post-colonial interpretation, a practice which will be strategic and contingent, perpetually in a process of transformation. Secondly, comparative approaches will need to proceed along the lines of precisely tuned socio-historical analyses, sceptical of interpellations in terms of fixed subject pos-itions, mentalities and relations. Finally, texts themselves need to be read in terms of the mesh of institutions which determine the production, circulation and reception of literary and other writings. Post-colonial critics in particular can ill-afford expressive views of authorship and text, in which literature floats free of social and cultural determinants and individual texts speciously resolve deeply embedded contradiction and resistance. The South African instance can serve as a kind of 'limit' case, a reminder of how what gets read or viewed or heard, by whom, where and when are vital, politically important components of a post-colonial analysis.[15]

What follows is an attempt to sketch one articulation of settler sites as a contact zone; one discursive formation which brought them together in the field of Empire. What is suggested is not a fixed or transhistorical set of relationships. To the contrary I would argue that the comparison needs to be contingent and modest in its claims.

THE DOMESTICATION OF THE 'SOUTH'

In a pioneering essay, Dorothy Driver examined the production of female identities in South African colonial history. Taking up Mannoni's point that 'the father's absolute authority . . . is [to be] exercised through the agency of the mother', Driver argued that frontierswomen in South Africa were used by the patriarchal and imperialist system to reproduce the crucial dichotomies of culture and nature, civilized and uncivilized, masculinity and femininity, rationality and irrationality.[16] Driver's analysis draws on post-

Lacanian concepts of the symbolic order to examine the ideological determinants of the role of settler women in the British colonies.

As Anna Davin comments from a different perspective, good motherhood was an essential component in Victorian ideologies of racial health and purity. Mothering was connected to the wealth of the Empire and the fitness of the British race, with particular concern for the propagation of the race in the white settler colonies.[17] Although the emergence of feminism and the 'new woman' produced competing conceptions of femininity, domesticity remained critical to conceptions of Englishness, although Englishwomen were increasingly defined not by their nationality, but by their race. Immigration propaganda emphasized the white woman's 'civilizing mission' in the African and Australian colonies. From the 1880s, when British imperialist sentiment peaked, the numbers of women immigrating to the colonies grew substantially. Their role was to carry British ideals abroad, and to preserve, and reproduce, the British race throughout the Empire – to be, in ideological terms, invincible, and global, agents of civilization.[18] So, for example, in 1902, one of a series of articles on 'The Needs of South Africa' claimed that:

> The emigration of women to South Africa has become a question of national importance. If that country is in the future to become one of the great self-governing colonies of the British Empire, warm in sympathy and attachment to the mother country, it must be peopled with loyal British women as well as British men.[19]

Australian feminist historians have demonstrated that in Australia the notions of motherhood, race and settler locale seem to reach a critical conjunction at the end of the nineteenth century. Patricia Grimshaw et al. argue that femininity and masculinity are contested domains which are crucially linked to ideas of race and nationality. Their analysis positions the concept of mothering as crucial to the identity, and social empowerment, of settler women. The valorization of motherhood at the Federation of the Australian colonies in 1901 served different political causes: the labour movement, the women's movement, the temperance movement, and nationalists and imperialists:

> Concern for preserving white society and for fostering white motherhood, were key motives seeking to integrate colonies

within which otherwise so much contestation was evident between classes and people of differing religious persuasions and geographical areas.[20]

The first act of the new Commonwealth of Australia was restricting non-white immigration so that 'Australia's spaces would be filled instead by pure white babies.'[21]

The articulations of feminine domesticity and white racial purity in South Africa and Australia served to draw the settler sites of the 'South' together in a particular relationship to metropolitan Britain and the Empire. The proliferation of familial metaphors, with Britain as the 'Mother Countries', was deliberate. What defined the settler sites in opposition to other colonial enterprises in British India and Africa was that *racial* process of filiation and the desire to 'reproduce' – in terms of culture and population – the British race abroad. This 'reproduction' led to specific settler anxieties about race, gender and sexuality.

This domestication of the 'South' is, I would argue, one way in which settler sites were ideologically 'produced' as a particular type of contact zone. A post-colonial (as distinct from feminist, psycho-analytic and other approaches) analysis of this ideology emphasizes colonial relationships within the framework of Empire. Post-colonial analysis must resist the temptation to seek transhistorical and trans-cultural explanations of the specific formulation of gender, race and nationality in white settler spaces; it must examine the discursive production, reproduction and power of colonial ideology in various texts – both literary and non-fiction, including conduct manuals and cookery books. How was this ideology resisted and subverted? Under what conditions, by who and for whom did it circulate? It is at this point that we can move on to the Lady who will inhabit the remainder of this chapter.

A LADY'S INFLUENCE

A lady's influence out here appears to be very great, and capable of indefinite expansion. She represents refinement and culture (in Mr Arnold's sense of the words), and her footsteps on a new soil such as this should be marked by a trail of light.

Lady Barker, *Station Life in New Zealand*[22]

The intrepid colonial matriarch Lady Barker (Broome) wrote and edited a series of writings which are a prime resource for thinking about the 'South' and its evocation as part of Greater Britain during the late Victorian period. Barker was uniquely placed to speculate about colonial matters. She was born Mary Anne Stewart in Jamaica in 1831, and joined her first husband, Sir George Barker, in India after the Mutiny. Upon his death in 1861, she returned to England, and later sailed with her second husband, Frederick Broome, to New Zealand. Her letters 'home' were published as *Station Life in New Zealand* (1870). Returning to England, Lady Barker published eight books, and served as Lady Superintendent of the new National School of Cookery. In 1875 Frederick Broome was appointed Colonial Secretary to Natal, and Lady Barker followed him there with their two young sons, Guy and Louis. Her year in Natal was the basis of *A Year's Housekeeping in South Africa* (1880). She then accompanied Broome to Mauritius, and to Western Australia in 1883 when he became governor of the colony. Her recollections of the Australian years were published as *Letters to Guy* (1885).

Barker's writings strung together colonies of the 'South': New Zealand, Natal, Western Australia. Her version of daily life in southern spaces appeared during a period when accounts of British imperialism in the southern hemisphere were critical to how British identity was perceived both at home and abroad. Barker's accounts were directed to a metropolitan English readership, and were reprinted in the 1880s and distributed throughout the Empire by the Macmillan Colonial Library as an authoritative depiction of colonial experiences.[23] In *A Year's Housekeeping in South Africa* and *Letters to Guy* we find the articulation of the colonies of the 'South' as places where concepts of femininity, race and class came together to produce a generation which promulgated what Barker called 'the white-souled state'.

In 1904, some seven years before her death, Barker wrote *Colonial Memories*. She concluded with a description of the 'white-souled state' which women of her class and generation had cultivated: 'we were trained to be unselfish, and certainly we were obedient and docile'.[24] This docility seems odd when compared to her pleasure in *Station Life* at dressing in mannish attire, having her hair cropped like a boy's, and openly savouring physical pleasures; or when contrasted with the gendered role reversal in the Natal letters, where Frederick Broome 'never ceases pining for his papers and arm chair' and Lady Barker organizes expeditions to the 'Bush'.[25] When it suited her, Barker took advantage of opportunities to take up 'masculine' behaviours and dress in the colonies.

Barker's comment in her memoirs makes more sense when examined in the context in which it was written: London, 1902. At this time, several events, including federation in Australia and the Anglo-Boer War in South Africa, and the growing influence of eugenics, intensified anxiety about the future of the white race in Britain and abroad. Barker's retrospective comments on the 'white-souled state' emerge at a moment of crisis in thinking about Britishness and Empire. Her self-conscious reference to 'training', to a generational identity and, one is inclined to suggest, to the *performance* of a particular subject position are particularly interesting, and infer a clear sense of her place-in-time.

Barker's letters from the 'South' were published alongside several other key British texts on household management which stressed the importance of cleanliness, discipline, regulation, and the importance of the household to the nation. Isabella Beeton's *Book of Household Management* (1861) claimed that, 'As with the Commander of an Army or the leader of any enterprise, so it is with the mistress of a house.'[26] This alliance of military and domestic force would assume particular power in the colonies; indeed, colonial experience was a vital component of its formation. The notes on nursing written by Barker's contemporary, Florence Nightingale, brought together domestic and military narratives, and deployed a domestic ideal to support Britain's imperial designs in India and the expansion of state administrative control over the poor at home.[27] Lady Barker was herself an expert on domestic management, as the first Lady Superintendent of the National School of Cookery. In *Colonial Memories* she professed 'deep amazement' at her appointment, for 'I never cared in the least what I ate as long as it was "neat and clean".' Yet the curriculum she introduced, with its training in neatness and cleanliness as much as in preparing food, suggests why she was an appropriate director in an age when cooking, like other forms of domestic economy, was part of the social apparatus which regulated middle-class values and sensibilities.

For both Barker and Nightingale, experience in colonial spaces was critical in establishing their regimes of order and discipline. This reminds us of Mary Louise Pratt's concept of 'transculturation', whereby modes of conduct and representation are received and appropriated by groups on the periphery, but then exported back to the centre in various and altered ways. Europe was constructed from the outside in, as much as from the inside out.[28] Traffic between the imperial centres and the colonies was two-way: ideas of domestic order and hygiene which were taught to the English population were in part produced overseas and imported back 'home'.

In *Letters to Guy*, with the sense of the 'performance' of a gendered and racially marked British identity in mind, we can see how the colony – in this case Western Australia – can be presented as a backdrop to the progress of 'the white lady'. Barker arrived in the colony as, quite literally, the 'first' lady, the symbol of imperial rule and Queen Victoria's surrogate. Her progress around the colony was marked by floral tributes, with the construction of makeshift bowers in even the most remote locations. The tractability of the colony for this imperial performance was, in part, secured by Barker's mode of address in her book. Her letters are written to her thirteen-year-old son, Guy, who is in England; and she speaks in them as a mother, albeit an eminent.one. The colony is represented in the didactic, picturesque and occasionally comic terms appropriate for a younger readership, with the vice-regal dog, Monsieur Puppy, as a prominent character!

Barker contains the colony of Western Australia within a framework of domesticity and utility. Flora and fauna are foreign yet available:

> I often think it might be worth someone's while to teach all England, and indeed, all Europe, the advantage of 'black-boy', as kindling wood. It is just one of many things one sees in a new world like this, lying ready to man's hand, waiting for him to come and take it, and use it.[29]

The function of this kind of writing for a British audience becomes evident when, in the grounds of government house in Perth, Barker's youngest son, Louis, plays out a version of the Swiss Family Robinson settlement. If Robinson Crusoe is the archetypal narrative of the individualistic, masculine figure taming the wilderness, then Swiss Family Robinson is its communal, feminized equivalent. Here the solitary, isolated and egocentric man is replaced by the family; there is no contact with other races (as with Crusoe and Friday), and the Swiss Family Robinson enter an Eden-like setting with all creation at their service and disposal. The family respond to this abundance by making shelters, tree houses, domestic spaces right across the island. The domestic and feminized vision of settlement, so exemplified by Barker, finds its mythology here.

It is indicative that the Swiss Family Robinson mythology flourishes best where the illusion of social and cultural homogeneity prevails. As the letters from South Africa attest, 'Southern' colonies were by no means equally receptive to this narrative of colonization. Barker calls her reminiscence of Natal *A Year's Housekeeping in South Africa*, again signalling her perspective as a mother, wife and mistress of the house. Barker is not unique in seeking to represent South Africa in terms of the domestically pastoral, fabricating a sense of social stability around the nucleus of the farm; J. M. Coetzee identifies this as one of the major themes of South African 'white writing'.[30] However *Housekeeping* represents a specific variation of this discourse, whereby the Victorian cult of domesticity allowed women to make themselves and their houses privileged sites of political understanding and action.

South Africa is quite clearly a different kind of contact zone than Canterbury, New Zealand or Perth, Western Australia. From her very first letter, the land and its people are undisciplined. Barker's first sight of land is Robben Island, off Cape Town, 'a more forlorn and discouraging islet I don't think I have ever beheld'.[31] On the wharf are listless Malays and 'half-caste' boys, and men who are lounging about, displaying a lack of industry that Barker sees as characteristic of Boers and natives alike. She writes, 'Kafirs [*sic*] do not understand what Mr Carlyle calls the beauty and dignity of labour.'[32] Even the landscape refuses to yield to the educated sensibility: Table Mountain in Cape Town is a disappointment, for instead of having picturesque, craggy peaks 'it cuts the sky with a perfectly straight line'. For the South African landscape to even remotely resemble Britain, the indigenous peoples and the Afrikaners must be out of sight.

When Barker moves north to Natal, her house causes her to comment that 'architecture is at its lowest ebb in South Africa'.[33] The public buildings in Pietermaritzburg remind her of a dilapidated barn on a bankrupt farm, with the natural elements and wildlife seeming to enter at will. White settlement is 'precarious', as illustrated by these makeshift buildings, and in the manoeuvres of the Natal Mounted Volunteers, primed and ready for action. She wrote, 'Living as we do in such a chronically precarious position, a position in which five minutes official ill-temper . . . might set the whole kaffir population in a blaze of discontent . . .'.[34] The 'kaffirs' must learn to live in a decent and orderly fashion, with training schools established to develop thrift, industry, domestic arts among a labour force of domestic servants for white settlers. Barker sees the Africans as 'good material which is ready to our hands', needing

75

only domestication. Yet for all her attempts in this venture, her Zulu servants desire to return to 'the savage life, with its gorges of half-raw meat and native beer, and its freedom from clothes'.[35]

Natal's difference from the other colonies of the 'South' visited by Barker was also marked by its lack of resemblance to Britain, and the ease with which British traditions and codes were parodied and reduced by mimicry. Barker described 'Kafirland' [sic] as the old clothes-shop of the fighting world, where the cast-off clothes of European armies worn by the 'kaffirs' flouted the original, and strict, codes of military dress. The scarlet tunic once denoting the disciplined military officer was now donned with bare legs. Similarly, the names of English aristocrats were used for animals, so that as Barker travels into Durban the coach driver yells: 'Walk along, Lord Gifford: think as you've another Victoria Cross to get topo' this hill! Walk along, Lord Carnarvon: you ain't sitting in a Cab'nit Council here, you know.' She has the grace to be flattered when she then hears: 'Walk along, Lady Barker.'[36]

In Natal the contestation between radically different cultures – British, emergent colonial, and African – was manifest. Here, even Barker underwent a physical transformation, ruefully pointing out that references to her as 'the white lady' are only figures of speech, for she is almost as brown as a 'native'. It was a site where mimicry resisted the intention to produce the resemblance necessary for the production of a British-style domestic space. Instead, it generated grotesque parodies of Britishness. It was no coincidence that Olive Schreiner's anti-pastoral novel, *The Story of an African Farm*, with its stern turning away from European locations and its celebration of an austere African landscape, was published in 1883, soon after Barker's year in Natal. Although Barker's vision differed from that of Schreiner, she could not escape noting the presence of counter-knowledges and counter-histories in colonial South Africa.

As a dream of a racially homogenous, highly disciplined familial microcosm, the Swiss Family Robinson narrative so loved by Barker and her young son allowed the fiction of the contact zone as an empty space, receptive and tractable, to remain in place. It contained no 'Other' to mimic and displace the ritual performance of an imperial, middle-class domestic order. Of the three volumes of Barker's letters which describe the 'South', only that from Natal has remained out of print. The re-publication of *Letters to Guy* and *Station Life in New Zealand* continues the reproduction and recycling of docile bodies and dream houses in southern spaces. As Vron Ware points out, blackness and whiteness, and masculinity and femininity, are categories whose meanings are historically derived, always in relation to each other and rarely in a simple pattern of binary opposites.[37] Barker's 'white-souled state' is a fine example of the imperial interactions between gender, race, class. It is for post-colonial scholarship to uncover ideologies, subjectivities and knowledges as they emerge in such complex and compound aggregations in the post-colonial domain, with a 'fly's eye' view of not only those performances of power and authority – such as we find in Lady Barker's writings – but also the parodies and resistance which challenge the Lady's influence.

NOTES

1 Ian Reid, *Fiction and the Great Depression: Australia and New Zealand 1930–1950*, Melbourne, Edward Arnold, 1979; Russell McDougall and Gillian Whitlock (eds), *Australian/Canadian Literatures in English: Comparative Perspectives*, Sydney, Methuen, 1987; John Matthews, *Tradition in Exile*, Toronto, Toronto University Press, 1962; Terry Goldie, *Fear and Temptation: The Image of the Indigene in Canadian, Australian and New Zealand Literatures*, Kingston, McGill-Queen's University Press, 1989.

2 Edward Said, 'East isn't East: The impending end of the age of orientalism', *Times Literary Supplement*, 3 February 1995, pp. 3–6.

3 For example, Matthews' *Tradition in Exile* consistently made the case for comparative studies as the appropriate method for Commonwealth critical practice.

4 Anna Rutherford (ed.), *From Commonwealth to Post-Colonial*, Aarhus, Dangaroo Press, 1992, p. v.

5 Timothy Brennan, *Salman Rushdie and the Third World: Myths of the Nation*, London, Macmillan, 1989, p. 35.

6 Sara Mills, *Discourses of Difference: An Analysis of Women's Travel Writing and Colonialism*, London, Routledge, 1991, p. 85.

7 Alan Lawson, 'A Cultural Paradigm for the Second World', *Australian-Canadian Studies*, vol. 9, nos. 1–2, 1991, pp. 67–78; 'Un/Settling Colonies: The Ambivalent Place of Discursive Resistance' in Chris Worth et al. (eds), *Literature and Opposition*, Clayton, Victoria, Centre for Comparative Literature and Cultural Studies, Monash University, 1994, pp. 67–82.

8 Stephen Slemon, 'Unsettling the Empire: Resistance Theory for the Second World', *World Literature Written in English*, vol. 30, no. 2, 1991, pp. 30–41.

9 Christy Collis, 'Siting the Second World in South African Literary Culture', *New Literatures Review*, Summer, 1995, pp. 1–15.

10 Annamaria Carusi, 'Post, Post and Post, Or Where is South African Literature in All This?', *Ariel*, vol. 20, no. 4, 1990, p. 80.

11 J. M. Coetzee, *White Writing: On the Culture of Letters in South Africa*, New Haven, Yale University Press, 1988.

12 Mudrooroo Narogin, *Writing from the Fringe: A Study of Modern Aboriginal Literature*, South Yarra, Hyland House, 1990.

13 Robert R. Wilson, 'Seeing With a Fly's Eye: Comparative Perspectives in Commonwealth Literature', *Open Letter*, Eighth Series, no. 2, Winter 1992, p. 13.

14 Wilson, 'Seeing with a Fly's Eye', p. 23.

15 See David Carter, 'Tasteless Subjects', *Southern Review*, vol. 25, no. iii, Nov. 1992, pp. 292–303, and Rosemary Jolly, 'Contemporary Postcolonial Discourse and the New South Africa', *PMLA*, Spring, 1995, pp. 17–29 for a defence of institutional approaches in post-colonial criticism.

16 Dorothy Driver, ' "Woman" as sign in the South African colonial enterprise', *Journal of Literary Studies*, March 1988, pp. 3–20.

17 Anna Davin, 'Imperialism and Motherhood', *History Workshop Journal*, vol. 5, 1978, p. 49.

18 Jane Mackay and Pat Thane, 'The Englishwoman' in Robert Colls and Philip Dodds (eds), *Englishness: Politics and Culture 1880–1920*, London, Croom Helm, 1986, p. 204.

19 Quoted in Mackay and Thane, 'The Englishwoman', p. 204.

20 Patricia Grimshaw, Marilyn Lake, Ann McGrath, Marian Quartly, *Creating a Nation*, Melbourne, McPhee Gribble, 1994, pp. 191–3.

21 Grimshaw et al., *Creating a Nation*, pp. 191–3.

22 Lady Barker [Broome], *Station Life in New Zealand* (1870), introduced by Fiona Kidman, London, Virago, 1984, p. 105.

23 More recently the resurgence of interest in women's history has led to the republication of *Station Life in New Zealand* and *Remembered with Affection: Letters to Guy*, with new prefaces by Australian and New Zealand scholars who celebrate the 'accuracy' and 'appropriateness' of Barker's narrative of settlement! See, for instance, Alexandra Hasluck (ed.), *Remembered with Affection: A New Edition of Lady Broome's 'Letter to Guy' With Notes and a Short Life*, Melbourne, Oxford University Press, 1963.

24 Lady Barker [Broome], *Colonial Memories*, London, Smith, Elder, 1904.

25 Lady Barker [Broome], *A Year's Housekeeping in South Africa* (1880), London, Macmillan, 1894.

26 Isabella Beeton, *Book of Household Management*, quoted in Mary Poovey, *Uneven Developments*, Chicago, University of Chicago Press, 1988, p. 170.

27 Poovey, *Uneven Developments*, p. 166.

28 Mary Louise Pratt, *Imperial Eyes: Travel Writing and Transculturation*, London, Routledge, 1992, p. 6.

29 'Blackboy' is the grass-tree *Xanthorrhea hastilis*; Barker, *Letters to Guy*, pp. 132–3.

30 Coetzee, *White Writing*, p. 4.

31 Barker, *Housekeeping*, p. 2.

32 Barker, *Housekeeping*, p. 79.

33 Barker, *Housekeeping*, p. 57.

34 Barker, *Housekeeping*, p. 293.

35 Barker, *Colonial Memories*, p. 211.

36 Barker, *Housekeeping*, p. 85.
37 Vron Ware, *Beyond the Pale: White Women, Racism and History*, London, Verso, 1993, p. xvii.

BIBLIOGRAPHY

Barker [Broome], M. A., *A Year's Housekeeping in South Africa* (1880), London, Macmillan, 1894.

——, *Colonial Memories*, London, Smith, Elder, 1904.

——, *Remembered with Affection. A New Edition of Lady Broome's 'Letter to Guy' With Notes and a Short Life* (1885), A. Hasluck (ed.), Melbourne, Oxford University Press, 1963.

——, *Station Life in New Zealand* (1870), introduced by Fiona Kidman, London, Virago, 1984.

Brennan, T. , *Salman Rushdie and the Third World: Myths of the Nation*, London, Macmillan, 1989.

Carusi, A., 'Post, Post and Post, Or Where is South African Literature in All This?', *Ariel*, vol. 20, no. 4, 1990, p. 80.

Coetzee, J. M., *White Writing: On the Culture of Letters in South Africa*, New Haven, Yale University Press, 1988.

Collis, C., 'Siting the Second World in South African Literary Culture', *New Literatures Review*, Summer, 1995, pp. 1–15.

Davin, A., 'Imperialism and Motherhood', *History Workshop Journal*, vol. 5, 1978, pp. 9–65.

Driver, D., ' "Woman" as sign in the South African colonial enterprise', *Journal of Literary Studies*, March 1988, pp. 3–20.

Grimshaw, P., et al., *Creating a Nation*, Ringwood Vic, McPhee Gribble, 1994.

Jolly, R., 'Contemporary Post-colonial Discourse and the New South Africa', *PMLA*, Spring, 1995, pp. 17–29.

Lawson, A., 'A Cultural Paradigm for the Second World', *Australian-Canadian Studies*, vol. 9, nos. 1–2, 1991, pp. 67–78.

——, 'Un/Settling Colonies: The Ambivalent Place of Discursive Resistance', in C. Worth et al., (eds), *Literature and Opposition*, Clayton, Victoria, Centre for Comparative Literature and Cultural Studies, Monash University, 1994, pp. 67–82.

Mackay, J. and P. Thane, 'The Englishwoman', in R. Colls and P. Dodds (eds), *Englishness: Politics and Culture 1880-1920*, London, Croom Helm, 1986.

Mills, S., *Discourses of Difference: An Analysis of Women's Travel Writing and Colonialism*, London, Routledge, 1991.

Narogin, M., *Writing from the Fringe: A Study of Modern Aboriginal Literature*, South Yarra, Hyland House, 1990.

Poovey, M., *Uneven Developments*, Chicago, University of Chicago Press, 1988.

Pratt, M. L., *Imperial Eyes: Travel Writing and Transculturation*, London, Routledge, 1992.

Rutherford, A. (ed.), *From Commonwealth to Post-Colonial*, Aarhus, Dangaroo Press, 1992.

Said, E., 'East isn't East: The impending end of the age of orientalism', *Times Literary Supplement*, 3 Feb. 1995, pp. 3–6.

Slemon, S., 'Unsettling the Empire: Resistance Theory for the Second World', *World Literature Written in English*, vol. 30, no. 2, 1991, pp. 30–41.

Ware, V., *Beyond the Pale: White Women, Racism and History*, London, Verso, 1993.

Wilson, R. R. 'Seeing With a Fly's Eye: Comparative Perspectives in Commonwealth Literature', *Open Letter*, Eighth Series, no. 2, Winter 1992, p. 13.

Part II

CLAIMING LANDS, CREATING IDENTITIES, MAKING NATIONS

5

'SKIRTING THE EDGES OF CIVILIZATION'

Two Victorian women travellers and 'colonial spaces' in South Africa

Michelle Adler

During the nineteenth century many British women travelled to South Africa, writing letters, journals and travelogues about their experiences for a 'home' audience. These women were mostly middle-class – the wives or daughters of missionaries, soldiers, colonial officials – brought to South Africa in the wake of imperial expansion in the region. Their narratives focused on the difficulties of reproducing middle-class homes in an alien environment, where the amenities of 'civilized' society were often sorely lacking.[1] Discourses of domesticity characterized most female travel writing of the era and reflected the gender constraints of Victorian society, notably the way in which middle-class women's lives and writings were circumscribed and defined by the 'women's sphere' of home and hearth.[2] As women's opportunities widened, and empire was 'made safe' for British womanhood through conquest and settlement, it became increasingly possible for women to travel independently to South Africa, as scientists, philanthropists, nurses – or tourists with a 'sense of adventure'.[3] The plethora of women's travelogues during the last quarter of the century indicated the extent to which women had entered the male-dominated field of published travel writing, while their style and content reflected the changing roles and growing independence of British women beyond the confines of the domestic sphere.

In the late 1870s and early 1880s two fiercely independent women travelled to South Africa. Mrs Sarah Heckford (1839–1903), author of *A Lady Trader in the Transvaal* (1882), was a wealthy widow who left a comfortable life in Belgravia to 'leap the barriers of young-ladydom', as she put it, though they 'were armed with painfully sharp spikes': she followed a varied and unconventional path as trav-eller, farmer, and the first female *smous* (itinerant trader) in the northern Transvaal bushveld. Lady Florence Dixie (1855–1905) was the first female war correspondent, sent to South Africa by the *Morning Post* to cover the Transvaal Boer 'rebellion' of 1880. Travelling through Zululand in the aftermath of the Anglo-Zulu war, Dixie recorded her impressions in a politically controversial book, *In the Land of Misfortune* (1882).

Both women grew up in an era when gender divisions were rigidly circumscribed, and the ideal of British womanhood was the 'angel in the house'. But although Victorian gender ideology was powerfully constraining, it was also inherently unstable. Heckford and Dixie colluded with, modified and transgressed conventional mores to create independent lives for themselves: travel provided ideal opport-unities to do so. In sharp contrast to the domestic discourses found in most female travel writing, both Heckford and Dixie emulated the conventions of 'male' adventure narratives, a framework better suited to the narration of independent travel.

In exploring Heckford and Dixie's South African journeys, three key areas emerge: the 'spaces' that opened up for privileged women travelling in South Africa, allowing them to modify or challenge prevailing gender constructions; the geographical and social 'spaces' they described and codified in their travelogues; and the largely marginal 'writing spaces' available to women at a time when the public sphere of writing for publication was dominated by men. The theme of 'marginal spaces' weaves through the lives and writings of Heckford and Dixie: in the roles deemed appropriate for women at the time; in the 'outer edges' of frontier regions they chose to explore; and in the margins of history and literature to which their experiences and writings are usually assigned.

In England Heckford, like many leisured women, found that 'the easiest way to a life outside of the parlour lay not in overt rebellion, but in the virtuous path of charity work'.[4] Far from being helpless victims of male patriarchy, many privileged women exploited precisely those characteristics – gentleness, self-sacrifice, nurturing – that had been constructed to confine women to the parlour, as a means of escape into the world.[5] Philanthropy was Heckford's passport to an independent life; ill-health an excuse to travel. Dixie, by contrast, developed a reputation for nonconformity and rebelliousness. Membership of a wealthy aristocratic family offered some protection from society's disapproval of 'transgressive' or 'unwomanly' behaviour, a degree of independence not available to most women, and opportunities to travel to a series of exotic destinations.

Unlike most privileged women, who tended to confine their travels to settler enclaves, Heckford and Dixie chose to travel to the 'outer edges of civilization': the northern-Transvaal bushveld and Zululand. Frontier regions were not only dangerous and difficult to negotiate, but also provided scope for adventure, and freedom from the constraints of British colonial society: travelling towards imperial frontiers, women sometimes crossed the boundaries of 'femininity'. Typically, travel narratives revolve around the experience of alien geographical space. The landscapes through which Heckford and Dixie travelled were highly conflicted social and political terrains, in the grip of massive social transformation. Although they responded very differently to the 'contested spaces' in which they found themselves, their portrayals of Africa and African society centred on the theme of possession and dispossession of the landscape.

By 1878 South Africa was considered the 'coming country': armed with a hundred shares in the 'Transvaal Farming, Mining and Trading Association', Heckford planned to invest in land speculation in the Transvaal. The period covered in her book (1878–81) was an eventful one in South Africa's history. In 1875 the Secretary of State for the Colonies initiated his scheme to federate Natal and the Cape Colony with the Boer Republics and so form a single South African dominion. The principal exponent of this policy in South Africa was the High Commissioner, Sir Bartle Frere, who regarded independent African chiefdoms as anachronisms, and believed that the proposed dominion should be built on the basis of white self-government and the subjugation and 'civilization' of Africans. In 1879 'the Zulu kingdom and the Pedi polity, two vital obstacles to colonial control, were bludgeoned into submission by British-led armies.'[16] With the destruction of the two most powerful independent polities in the region, 'the balance of power in South Africa finally swung decisively in favour of a colonial society dominated by white settlers.'[17] These years also saw increased Boer resistance to British authority, the collapse of the myth of British military supremacy in engagements at Laing's Nek and Majuba, and eventual Boer control of the Transvaal in 1881.

Heckford disembarked at Natal in 1878. Most women would have travelled the 450 miles to the Transvaal in a wagon, but she set off on a pony, revolvers strapped to her waist and saddle. She accompanied a group of men, none of whom were 'gentlemen', or prepared to treat her with much deference. Heckford's refusal to conform to the stereotype of feminine compliance and helplessness once she found herself outside settler enclaves, is significant. The 'perfect lady' in Britain or in colonial towns, in the bush Heckford rode astride, slept under a wagon huddled with virtual strangers, wielded a bullwhip with dexterity, and was not above whipping servants and bullying her male companions. In the colonial context there were clearly opportunities for and advantages in stepping beyond the confines of ladylike behaviour. Although the lives of most middle-class colonial women were severely constrained,[8] as 'temporary sojourners' travellers were more easily able to challenge the boundaries of convention to 'create spaces' for themselves. In the words of veteran traveller Isabella Bird, 'travellers are privileged to do the most improper things with perfect propriety; that is one charm of travelling.'[9]

Emulating aspects of dominant 'male' values and behaviour provided a form of 'protective colouring' which allowed a woman travelling without family or husband to successfully maintain her independence, gain personal power and exert authority in a 'man's world'. Such self-empowerment also depended on supporting and exploiting existing belief systems regarding race and class. As an 'honorary man' Heckford could act independently, in ways that would have been unthinkable 'at home'. However, challenges to gender conventions were always contradictory and ambiguous, partly because of the need to appease the colonial community, but also because the majority of women believed in maintaining 'natural' gender divisions and 'feminine' identity. In colonial centres, even adventurous women travellers donned the mask of decorum.

Heckford regarded the dusty villages, lack of amenities, unfamiliar landscapes and people of South Africa with a critical British eye. Her first impression was of 'the drop-scene of an unknown opera',[10] but the landscape clearly fell short of the vision of an exotic country imagined at home:

> I must warn my readers, that although I shall have to tell them
> of rocks and valleys and wooded ravines, &c., they must not
> picture to themselves anything analogous to what they may
> have seen in Switzerland or Italy . . . The artist who would
> portray it need have but few colours in his paintbox.[11]

In 1879 Heckford reached Rustenburg, 60 miles west of Pretoria, crossing the Magaliesberg at Silkaatsnek, where the Boers had defeated Mzilikazi in 1838. The idea of the mountain range as barrier-frontier is ideally suited to 'narratives of difficult journeys into a remote world', which are characteristic of travel literature.[12] Beyond the barrier, experience will be entirely different: as Heckford put it, 'I was launched into my new life.'[13] One way in which Heckford could begin to imagine her new world was through writing, 'without which amusement I should have collapsed under the combined heat, dullness and anxiety of that time.'[14] She described Rustenburg as one of the last places 'inhabited by white people, and through whose streets numbers of Kaffirs . . . troop daily, dressed in skins, and adorned with barbaric ornaments.'[15] This world appeared exceedingly remote and alien, a frontier contact zone where 'savage' people intruded on the 'white' town.

On discovering that the farming scheme which had lured her to the Transvaal was a scam, Heckford was forced to find paid employment, first as a governess – a last resort for respectable women in straitened circumstances – and later, more unusually, as a farmer. The world she described was one enclosed within the universe of the farm, a microcosm of South African society, which she arranged into an ordered, apparently immutable social and racial hierarchy. Heckford's narrative portrays the English-speaking farming family of 1820 settler stock as the rightful owners of the landscape: poor Boer *bywoners* and African squatter tenants, from whom farmers extracted unpaid labour, are ephemeral intruders who leave few marks on the land. Africans are timeless ethnographic specimens, presented as comic or pitiful spectacles for the eyes of a British readership. The Boers scarcely fare better, being dirty, cunning, stupid and cruel – a perception reinforced by 'Boer scares' in the region. Beyond the universe of the farm is a scattering of English and Boer families, and beyond them, the ever-threatening 'tribes': 'in a pattern common to much colonial writing, the farm boundary is the line of exclusion beyond which lies the wilderness.'[16]

Heckford had little knowledge of the history of the area, or understanding of the conflicted social and political terrains she encountered: her narrative reflected dominant attitudes regarding class, race and national identity. She saw Africans as inherently savage and primitive, devoid of 'refinement and elevation of thought', undeserving of charity, and permanently excluded from the 'civilizing mission' to the poor she had championed in England. Occasionally

Heckford's life intersected with living strands of the region's recent past. Unable to grasp the intricacies of local politics and history, she sometimes generated her own framework for interpreting the world around her. In a rare moment of reflection Heckford acknowledged the existence of a different, submerged history of the region, upon which her own story and that of the surrounding farmers and settlers had been superimposed. Among the squatters was a son of Mzilikazi, living in wretched poverty:

> whether to a European or a Kaffir the sense of having to ask for favours when you once dispensed them, to obey where you once commanded – the feeling of dependence upon a stranger – must always be bitter. [Mzilikazi's son], looking down from my little aerie on the cultivated valley below, which had once been a wild bush, and his own hunting country, must in a miserable blind sort of way have felt something of what the exiled French Princes experienced when they looked across the channel to the distant shores of France.[17]

Farming in the remote, fever-ridden northern Transvaal was no easy task. Farmers cultivated a wide range of skills, including hunting, poaching, transport riding and trading. Suffering from bouts of malaria and struggling financially, Heckford was forced to devise survival strategies. As winter approached, Boer farmers in the area traditionally burnt depleted pastures and trekked deep into the bushveld with their large herds of cattle, camping far from any outpost of 'civilization' until springtime brought them back to the farms – a practice Heckford saw as further evidence of their inability to 'civilize' the landscape.

Heckford's most unconventional 'adventure' was her decision in 1880 to become a *smous* in the bushveld. The *smous* was a familiar figure in the rural Transvaal. But a female *smous* was unheard of; a 'lady' *smous* inconceivable. Heckford was alone, not very strong, lame, subject to severe attacks of malaria, and had no idea about trading. Nevertheless, she bought trade goods and horses, hired a *voorloper* and wagon driver, and with a team of 'salted' oxen,[18] set out for the Waterberg.

For Heckford the Waterberg – roughly north-east of Rustenburg – was a region at the very edge of the known world, an ideal context for reinventing one's social identity, or behaving in ways that else-where would be labelled transgressive. Early Boer settlers began trickling into the region in the 1850s, but fevers and flies made it one of the last areas of the Transvaal to be colonized. In the 1880s the region was still, from a European point of view, 'a remote and pestilential corner of Africa',[19] harbouring

> fractious chiefs, foolhardy hunters, desperate criminals on the run from the law, and unfortunate officials who from the 1860s had to contend with a region that was an administrative nightmare . . . It was in all a rather grim frontier.[20]

Trading at Boer camps, African households and mission stations, Heckford confronted the danger of wild animals and snakes, and the possibility of falling prey to typhoid, diphtheria, enteric and pneumonia, all of which claimed numerous lives in the 1870s. Sleeping in open veld in the bitter cold, she suffered chronic bronchitis, often 'not only tired in body, but I felt nearly mad'.[21] As Mary Gaunt, another traveller in Africa, explained, confronting danger could be empowering: 'there is something in the thought of danger that must be overcome . . . that quickens the blood and gives an added zest to life.'[22]

In these months before the outbreak of the Transvaal 'rebellion', Heckford and her Boer customers regarded one another with mutual suspicion. She expressed horror at Boer treatment of Africans, reporting that 'children had been dragged from their mothers' arms and taken away as slaves:'[23] The widespread use of indentured child labour, known as *inboekselings*, played an important role in the region at a time when the migrant labour system attracted Africans from the northern Transvaal to the diamond fields of Kimberley, resulting in labour shortages on white farms.[24] An emphasis on 'Boer cruelties' was typical of much travel writing about South Africa, and was intended to highlight the moral superiority of the British, and their concomitant superior claim to the region.

Heckford's career as a trader and farmer ended abruptly with the Boer rising, which brought financial disaster. Even the formidable Mrs Heckford could not survive the destruction of her farm, loss of trade, plummeting prices and diminished markets, and reluctantly she decided to return to England. She completed her travelogue during the voyage home.

In many ways Sarah Heckford's narrative is unremarkable. But, in the words of one critic, such 'lesser colonial documents from an obscure frontier' are of considerable interest as 'everyday testimony' from a region about which very little is known,[25] not least because they reveal the individual consciousness, its 'structures of feeling', and the lines of identity by which a woman's new place and world are imagined. Heckford's narrative reflects – through tensions, silences and contradictions – the ambiguities of her role as female traveller and writer in a 'man's world'. As Kay Schaffer argues, to write about colonial spaces at all, independent women had to take a 'masculine' position, since the most common narrative figure and role model was heroic, male and adventurous, setting out to conquer a land that was often represented as feminine and passive: 'to speak with authority she must wear a male disguise.'[26]

The colonial context allowed Heckford to subvert gender conventions and gain greater freedom and independence; the publication of her narrative was similarly a challenge to Victorian mores. The question of 'writing spaces' for women is an important one. Although many nineteenth-century women wrote for a living, the constraints on middle-class women entering the 'public sphere' meant that their main literary outlet was the 'private' diary, journal or letter. When entering the 'masculine' world of publication, women often chose low-status genres, such as travel writing, which followed the structure of the journal. The fact that women published at all must be seen as a challenge to hegemonic constructions of 'the feminine'. Although women often reproduced these constructions, they challenged, even as they seemed to support, the codes of gender and national identity.

By the 1880s the female traveller had become a familiar figure. However, women were still seen as peripheral to the imperial enterprise, and female travel writers continued to write 'in the margins' of colonial discourse. Their narratives were seldom regarded as 'important' or 'serious' contributions to Victorian society's knowledge about empire. That women writers were aware of this difference in status can be seen in the self-deprecating caveats with which they peppered their books. Crucially, women were unable to adopt an imperialist voice with the same ease as male writers: as Sara Mills points out,[27] female narratives reveal how women negotiated a series of constraints, ranging from the 'masculine' conventions of travel writing, to contemporary gender and colonial discourses. Certain discourses or subjects remained restricted or taboo. Moreover, the authors of most published female travelogues were privileged women, indicating the importance of wealth and leisure in shaping women's access to a public 'voice'.

In contrast to Heckford, Florence Dixie was a 'new woman'[28] who used the most public of writing spaces, the newspaper article, to express her views. Many Victorian women confronted the terrors of war and recorded their experiences,[29] but Dixie was the first female war 'special', with the task of reporting on the Transvaal Boer uprising for the *Morning Post*. Her appointment caused a sensation: female journalists were rare, but a woman war reporter was unheard of. Newspapers depicted a frivolous female trying to keep up with the troops, the general hilarity was enhanced by the fact that she came from a patrician family: 'even now, we understand, overtures are being made to a countess in her own right to proceed to the Transvaal.'[30] Dixie's appointment as war correspondent was an indication of the rapidly changing role of women during the last quarter of the nineteenth century: the ridicule it provoked shows that these changes were uneven and controversial.

For unconventional women freedom was more often than not associated with 'masculine' qualities and behaviour achievable only by modifying, where possible, conventions of femininity: 'the result was that an exceptional woman tended to identify with likeminded men rather than other women and to see herself as an "honorary man" – a unique exception to the constraints and rules which limited the lives of the other women.'[31] In South Africa Dixie was lauded for her 'manly' courage, while her 'masculine' abilities and dress evoked admiration.[32]

Indeed, as an 'honorary man' with the status of newspaper correspondent, Dixie could transgress social norms and enjoy a greater degree of independence and freedom than most women. By excelling in predominantly masculine activities and identifying strongly with powerful military men, Dixie gained access to the military establishment. At the same time she exploited her position as an attractive upper-class woman, thus ameliorating criticism of 'transgressive' behaviour.

Dixie's career as a war 'special' was short-lived. Before she could send her first report from the front the crisis in the Transvaal was over. The peace negotiations elicited all her flag-waving instincts: 'was it for such an inglorious ending that the lives of so many gallant officers and men have been thrown away? . . . making us ashamed of our country and the laughing stock of every Dutchman?'[33] Her dispatches vociferously demanded the continuation of the war, echoing the dissatisfaction of highly placed military men such as Sir Evelyn Wood. Never one to shy away from public controversy, Dixie denounced the Gladstone government for compromising timidity. Her dispatches to the *Morning Post* became increasingly impassioned and jingoistic, and were widely quoted in the South African press.

Most female travellers shared dominant ruling-class views regarding race and empire. But although Dixie openly endorsed the British imperial enterprise, her attitudes towards Africans are difficult to categorize: she developed great admiration, empathy and respect for the Zulu people, an attitude imbued with romanticism and to all appearances incompatible with her jingoistic fervour. However, her seemingly contradictory ideas about empire can to some extent be explained in terms of contemporary debates and attitudes.

Dixie's reputation as an adventurous 'eccentric' was enhanced by her curious role in contemporary debates surrounding the Zulu king, Cetshwayo, who in 1872 succeeded his father to the powerful, independent Zulu kingdom. The kingdom was seen as an obstacle to 'progress' in the region – an 'anachronism', according to Sir Bartle Frere – and in 1879 the British army and colonial forces invaded:

> the Zulu king was exiled and the Zulu military system term-
> inated, but the intensity of Zulu resistance persuaded the
> British to leave the Zulu in possession of most of their land,
> and they escaped annexation. The external forces of change,
> having failed in a direct assault, then started to erode Zulu
> independence.[34]

Dixie's fascination with Cetshwayo began in 1881 with a visit to the king, who had been captured in August 1879, at Oude Moulen, a farm near Cape Town. The visit was not unusual: Cetshwayo was something of a tourist attraction and a steady stream of notable figures paid homage to him. Dixie regarded the exile and imprison-ment of the king as reprehensible, and rapidly became an ardent proponent of his reinstatement:

> an instance of grosser injustice can nowhere be recorded than
> the detention of this brave but unhappy captive, who is
> suffering for the ambition and cupidity of others, and whose
> sole crime was his defence of his invaded country . . . In the
> dignity, patience, and fortitude under severe trial with which
> he bears his captivity, Cetshwayo has shown that he lacks not
> that which is found wanting in the breasts of his conquerors,
> i.e. generosity and nobility of soul, which it would be well for
> justice-loving (!) John Bull to imitate.[35]

According to Dixie, Cetshwayo begged her to visit Zululand and report to him on the extent of his popular support. Paradoxically, whereas she had vociferously demanded that the British should punish the Transvaal Boers and assert imperial authority, she now deplored the dismemberment of the Zulu kingdom and the destruction of its political and economic independence. Dixie was not the only one to become an ardent advocate of Cetshwayo's reinstatement. At the time of his capture the British public had accepted that he was a monstrous tyrant, whose barbarities had been vividly described by Sir Bartle Frere in official dispatches. By the time Cetshwayo was imprisoned in the Castle in Cape Town, his imposing, kingly appearance and presence was widely commented on. Many of those who met him personally were so impressed that they ensured that his petitions reached the British authorities and public. Many prominent people, notably Bishop Colenso of Natal, believed that Cetshwayo 'had suffered a great injustice and that Britain should make amends for this'.[36]

Undeterred by warnings that Zululand was still too volatile for a woman traveller, Dixie accompanied Sir Evelyn Wood on a tour of famous Zulu battlegrounds, including Isandhlwana, Ulundi and Rorke's Drift. She eulogized the 'gallant band of Englishmen' killed in battle, but also the 'warriors of Cetshwayo, who falling for King and country came to strike a blow at the invaders of their dearly beloved land'.[37] She was struck by Zulu loyalty to Cetshwayo, who 'had been stolen away from them'.[38] Dixie portrayed the Zulu in sentimental and utopian terms as 'noble savages', her own queenly progress through this 'romantic space' marked by salutations 'uttered by the stately sons of Zululand . . . there is a solemnity and dignity about it which is indescribable'.[39]

Dixie's admiration for the Zulu was not unusual. When in 1879 British troops invaded the kingdom, Zulu resistance was so fierce that they inflicted one of the greatest defeats in the history of Britain's colonial wars, and 'impressed the name Zulu indelibly on the popular imagination of Europe and America'.[40] The word 'Zulu' entered popular speech and writing, becoming widely identified with an idea of barbarous nobility.[41] Dixie's portrayal of the Zulu paradoxically combined popular martial imagery and the idea of the 'noble savage', with the gentler image required to 'defend' them from further assault upon their independence. Noble and heroic, the Zulu are nonetheless portrayed as a defeated people who no longer pose a threat to British colonial interests. Like several other women travellers, Dixie's construction of the myth of a 'primitive' society was intended to discourage further European intrusion.[42]

Dixie's ideologically complex narrative is characterized by a 'double discourse' of imperialist fervour on the one hand, and a desire to protect the 'noble Zulu' on the other. Avowedly endorsing the imperial enterprise and the propagandistic discourses of conquest, Dixie simultaneously presented a powerful critique of imperialism from its margins. Such internal contradictions in the text rupture the dominant discourse: a 'subversive' discourse is contained within the main narrative, resulting in the partial dismantling of the imperialist construction from within.

Dixie and Heckford, although in some ways markedly different from each other, both codified the geographical spaces of frontier regions in terms of divided landscapes – as contested terrains where struggles of possession and dispossession were acted out. But their portrayals of the 'Other' do contrast strikingly. Confronted in the western Transvaal with the dismemberment of African societies and the conquest of landscapes, Heckford, as farmer and itinerant trader, welcomed the transformation of 'savage wilderness' into productive white farmland: in her narrative the 'Other' is all but silenced. Dixie, on the other hand, who began as a war correspondent and then moved deeper into a sense of the colonized subject's narrative through her admiration for King Cetshwayo, regarded the Zulu kingdom as 'invaded space' that had to be protected from further assault. The subversive discourse in her writing disrupts the imperialist narrative flow, occasionally allowing the voice of the 'Other' to be heard. In this sense Dixie, unlike the (in some ways) more conventional Heckford, presents the reader with a counter-hegemonic voice within colonial discourse.

Although Heckford and Dixie were both unusual women, the ways in which they attempted to extend the boundaries of the 'female sphere' were representative of the strategies employed by a number of privileged women similarly negotiating roles for themselves outside the home. Each in their different way illustrate how the lives and writings of female travellers provide an arena for exploring how women attempted to create 'spaces' for greater freedom, self-expression and adventure. Journeys in faraway places allowed privileged women to subvert or challenge gender constructions in ways not always available to contemporaries at home. On the 'outer edges of civilization', where the rigid conventions of Victorian society begin to break down, women travellers could 'bend the rules' or sometimes openly challenge notions of the 'women's sphere', without appearing transgressive.

Heckford's independence as farmer and travelling trader rested on dissolving the barriers of gender where it was pragmatic to do so. As a *smous* in the bushveld she showed that it was possible to act outside traditional dictates of gender. Nonetheless she carefully preserved the image of conventional respectability, even when narrating far from conventional experiences. Such contradictions reveal the tensions implicit in women writers' engagement with empire and 'masculine' narrative conventions. In South Africa Heckford could, up to a point, assume the role of 'white man', taking on the accepted male colonial role of adventurer and entrepreneur; similarly Dixie, as a 'special' in the male world of journalism, identified with dominant masculine, ruling-class attitudes and behaviour, where this opened up opportunities for greater independence.

Although Dixie's behaviour and writing were more openly transgressive than that of Heckford – in that she entered the 'masculine' world of imperial politics – the double discourse of 'feminine' compliance and 'masculine' assertiveness that is in varying degrees present in both their narratives reveals the ways in which women were able simultaneously to collude with, resist or challenge dominant discourses and ideology.

Mills has argued that the most striking difference between male and female travel writing lies in the way they are judged and processed. The 'marginal space' occupied by female travel writing has recently been questioned, but in general, successive reconstructions of the social history of empire and African travel continue to confine women and their writings to the perimeters of history and literature. Travel narratives by Heckford, Dixie and other women who wrote about South Africa, although largely ignored and neglected, are important in several ways. Because the experiences and writings of travellers are gendered, they provide opportunities for exploring how relations of gender are perpetuated, exploited or transformed in a specific colonial context, and to what extent women accepted, colluded with, or resisted their marginal and subordinate status.

An analysis of female travel writing also challenges some of the generalizations of 'orientalism', in that it reveals the existence of counter-hegemonic voices within colonial discourse. Furthermore, it reveals a rich polyphony of voices, a variety of attitudes and experiences that not only bring into question the accuracy of dominant stereotypes of British women as 'God's Police' or intrepid eccentrics, but also expose a largely submerged perspective on empire and the ordering of colonial South Africa.

NOTES

1 See Gillian Whitlock's discussion of Lady Barker in this volume.
2 For example, Lady Barker, *A Year's Housekeeping in South Africa* (1879); Helen M. Prichard, *Friends and Foes in the Transkei: An Englishwoman's Experiences during the Cape Frontier War of 1877–8* (1880); and Harriet Roche, *On Trek in the Transvaal; or, Over Berg and Veldt in South Africa* (1878).
3 For example, Alice Balfour, *Twelve Hundred Miles in a Waggon* (1895); Louise V. Sheldon, *Yankee Girls in Zululand* (1890); and Mary Hall, *A Woman's Trek from Cape to Cairo* (1907).
4 Bonnie S. Anderson and Judith P. Zinsser, *A History of Their Own: Women in Europe from Prehistory to the Present*, vol. II, London, Penguin, 1988, p. 177.
5 See Frank Prochaska, *Women and Philanthropy in Nineteenth-Century England*, Oxford, Clarendon Press, 1980.
6 Peter Delius, *The Land Belongs to Us: The Pedi Polity, the Boers and the British in the Nineteenth Century Transvaal*, Los Angeles, University of California Press, 1984, p. 1.
7 Delius, *The Land Belongs to Us*, p. 246.
8 Indeed, Olive Schreiner found South Africa 'stifling', and yearned for the intellectual freedom of Britain.
9 Quoted in Pat Barr, *A Curious Life for a Lady: The Story of Isabella Bird Bishop*, London, Macmillan, 1970, p. 54.
10 Sarah Heckford, *A Lady Trader in the Transvaal*, London, Sampson Low, 1882, p. 1.
11 Heckford, *A Lady Traveller*, p. 6.
12 See Isabel Hofmeyr, 'Turning Region into Narrative: English Storytelling in the Waterberg', in P. Bonner et al. (eds), *Holding Their Ground*, Johannesburg, Witwatersrand University Press, 1989, pp. 269–70.
13 Heckford, *A Lady Traveller*, p. 67.
14 Heckford, *A Lady Traveller*, pp. 64–5.
15 Heckford, *A Lady Traveller*, p. 88.
16 Hofmeyr, 'Turning Region into Narrative', p. 271.
17 Heckford, *A Lady Traveller*, p. 175.
18 'Salted' oxen were immunized against 'sleeping sickness' and 'lung sickness', scourges of the far-northern Transvaal.
19 Roger Wagner, 'Zoutpansberg: the dynamics of a hunting frontier, 1848–67', in S. Marks and A. Atmore (eds), *Economy and Society in Pre-Industrial South Africa*, London, Longman, 1980, p. 336.
20 Hofmeyr, 'Turning Region into Narrative', p. 265.
21 Heckford, *A Lady Traveller*, p. 290.
22 Mary Gaunt, *Alone in West Africa*, London, T. Werner Laurie, 1912, p. 22.
23 Heckford, *A Lady Traveller*, p. 246.
24 See Delius, *The Land Belongs to Us*, p. 35.
25 See Hofmeyr, 'Turning Region into Narrative', pp. 261–2.
26 Kay Schaffer, *Women and the Bush: Forces of Desire in the Colonial Cultural Tradition*, Cambridge, Cambridge University Press, 1989, p. 103.

27 See Sara Mills, *Discourses of Difference: An Analysis of Women's Travel Writing and Colonialism*, London, Routledge, 1991.
28 Dixie's views on the 'woman question' are set out in her book *Gloriana: or, The Revolution of 1900* (1890).
29 See for example Harriet Ward, *The Cape and the Kaffirs: A Diary of Five Years' Residence in Kaffirland* (1851); Mrs Hutchinson, *In Tents in the Transvaal* (1879); and Lady Bellairs, *The Transvaal War 1880–81* (1885).
30 *Natal Witness*, 16 March 1881, p. 3.
31 Anderson and Zinsser, *History of Their Own*, p. 169.
32 See for example *Natal Witness*, 23 March 1881, p. 2.
33 Extract from Dixie's first dispatch from the front, quoted in B. Roberts, *Ladies in the Veld*, London, Murray, 1965, p. 94.
34 Jeff Guy, *The Destruction of the Zulu Kingdom: The Civil War in Zululand, 1879–1884*, Johannesburg, Ravan, 1982, p. xix.
35 Dixie, *In the Land of Misfortune*, London, R. Bentley, 1882, p. 11.
36 Guy, *Destruction of the Zulu Kingdom*, p. 124.
37 Dixie, *Land of Misfortune*, p. 329.
38 Dixie, *Land of Misfortune*, p. 340.
39 Dixie, *Land of Misfortune*, p. 341.
40 Guy, *Destruction of the Zulu Kingdom*, p. xix.
41 Music halls, which reflected the dominant imperial ethos of the day, satirized contemporary fascination with Zululand.
42 See for example Daisy Bates, *The Passing of the Aborigines*, London, John Murray, 1938.

BIBLIOGRAPHY

Anderson, S., and J. P. Zinsser (eds.), *A History of Their Own: Women in Europe from Prehistory to the Present*, vol. II, London, Penguin, 1988.
Barr, P., *A Curious House for a Lady*, London, Macmillan, 1970.
Delius, P., *The Land Belongs to Us: The Pedi Polity, the Boers and the British in the Nineteenth Century Transvaal*, Los Angeles, University of California Press, 1984.
Dixie, F., *In the Land of Misfortune*, London, R. Bentley, 1882.
Gaunt, M. *Alone in West Africa*, London, T. Werner Laurie, 1912.
Guy, J., *The Destruction of the Zulu Kingdom: The Civil War in Zululand, 1879–1884*, Johannesburg, Ravan, 1982.
Heckford, S., *A Lady Trader in the Transvaal*, London, Sampson Low, 1882.
Hofmeyr, I., 'Turning Region into Narrative: English Storytelling in the Waterberg', in P. Bonner et al. (eds), *Holding their Ground*, Johannesburg, Witwatersrand University Press, 1989.
Mills, S., *Discourses of Difference: An Analysis of Women's Travel Writing and Colonialism*, London, Routledge, 1991.
Prochaska, F., *Women and Philanthropy in Nineteenth-Century England*, Oxford, Clarendon Press, 1980.
Roberts, B., *Ladies in the Veld*, London, Murray, 1965.
Schaffer, K., *Women and the Bush: Forces of Desire in the Colonial Cultural Tradition*, Cambridge, Cambridge University Press, 1989.

Wagner, R., 'Zoutpansberg: the dynamics of a hunting frontier, 1848–67', in S. Marks and A. Atmore (eds), *Economy and Society in Pre-Industrial South Africa*, London, Longman, 1980.

6

'RESCUING' BARBARA THOMPSON AND OTHER WHITE WOMEN
Captivity narratives on Australian Frontiers

Kate Darian-Smith

Stories of white 'captivity' in Australia emerged from, and reflected, settler anxieties about racial and gendered interactions in Australia, and within the colonial world more broadly, during the nineteenth and twentieth centuries. Such narratives were always located on the edges of white settlement, in that peculiar colonial space of the frontier. While the parameters of Australian frontiers were constantly shifting as European control of the continent expanded, the frontier was always a culturally contested buffer zone or, in Mary Louise Pratt's terms a, 'contact zone' that separated European civilization from unknown, and as yet unconquered, lands and peoples. Pratt writes that taking a 'contact' perspective of the frontier treats the relations between the colonizers and colonized 'in terms of co-presence, interaction, interlocking understandings and practices, often within radically asymmetrical relations of power'.[1] On the Australian fringes of European settlement where the ownership of territory was disputed, the dynamics of black and white interactions were, as Pratt suggests, remarkably complex and diverse.[2]

Within colonial culture, however, the frontier was not only a geographical space, but a powerful imaginative site. The 'European vision' of Australia's unique landscape and natural 'marvels' was, above all, an imperial one.[3] Australian colonists made sense of their own experiences through collective memories, however fragmentary and inaccurate, of European colonization in other 'New Worlds'. In these memories, the frontier was constructed as a dangerous place where Europeans could be dislocated from their own society. Such

99

fears had been articulated since the first wave of European expansion in the late fifteenth century through tales of whites living with non-European peoples. By the eighteenth century this genre became associated mainly, although not exclusively, with the kidnapping of whites by native Americans in North America.[4] In the nineteenth century, as the market for sentimental fiction and historical romance increased, hundreds of accounts of white captivity were circulated in newspapers, journals and books throughout the English-speaking world, including the Australian colonies. The most popular variant of these increasingly formulaic expositions of white racial supremacy involved the 'capture', and sexual violation, of a white woman by non-Europeans.[5]

Racialized and sexualized captivity narratives were part of a colonial discourse that focused explicitly on the issues of interracial sexuality and biological hybridity. As Robert Young argues, 'Theories of race were also covert theories of desire'; they were 'about a fascination with people having sex – interminable, adulterating, aleatory, illicit, inter-racial sex'.[6] Historical and fictional incidents of white 'captives' living with black societies provided a ready-made set of circumstances in which Europeans could explore such taboos, and through this process interrogate the social and political categories of race and gender. The injection of whites into a non-white society, and the experiences of whites who were so 'unnaturally' placed, inverted imperial hierarchies of race and power. In order to reassert European dominance, non-white captors were constructed as the brutal, savage 'Other', and their cultures as 'primitive'.

When the white 'captive' was female, her real or imagined sexual defilement was emblematic of her racial subordination. The words 'white' and 'woman' were a powerful combination in the colonial imagination, fusing together multifarious cultural, racial and gendered ideologies, and constituting women as both symbols of European civilization and chattels of patriarchal capitalism. As cultural symbol and as property, the colonial white woman was constructed as the object of non-European sexual desire. Apprehensions about the racial and sexual threat to the status of white womanhood were echoed and amplified around the imperial world, rising to a pitch when localized friction between colonizers and colonized became intense.[7]

American captivity tales provided Australian colonists with one imaginative model through which to explore, and to act in response

100

to, perceived threats of interracial intimacy. The South Pacific provided an alternative geographical and literary locale for such speculations, prompting similar reactions. The nineteenth-century South Seas romance rejuvenated Robinson Crusoe-style narratives, which were fantastical but also historically and culturally referential.[8] These stories touched a chord within the Australian colonies, where isolation from Europe, and the unpredictability of maritime travel, led to a social preoccupation with the prospect of disaster at sea. Shipwreck was common in Australian and Pacific waters, and expeditions were frequently sent to locate survivors. If they included white women, the additional zeal of the rescue party often resulted in harsh punitive actions against 'native' peoples who held the women 'captive'.[9]

The material circumstances of the Australian frontier were, however, different from those in other colonial situations like North America or the South Pacific. Indeed, in the Australian colonies, indigenous peoples acted as the saviours, rather than the captors, of whites. Runaway convicts, bushrangers, castaways and explorers all depended on Aboriginal assistance to survive; Aboriginal resistance to colonization aimed to drive Europeans *away* rather than take them hostage. Written documentation reveals it was rare (in comparison, say, with North America) for Europeans in colonial Australia to be integrated into a traditional Aboriginal society for an extended length of time.[10] Nonetheless, the actualities of race relations on the Australian frontier did little to diminish the discursive and cultural power of the captivity narrative within settler society.

From the mid-nineteenth century, numerous Australian accounts of whites 'captured' by Aborigines were published. Some were unequivocally fictional, but many drew upon and embellished historical incidents, blending together fact and fiction. These texts were generically imperial in their treatment of race and sexuality; they produced, and were the product of, European colonial discourse; and their narrative structure and imagery were influenced by similar tales from other colonial theatres. But they were also distinctly Australian, and not only in a geographical sense. As the trangressive captivity plot was refashioned and recirculated in Australia, it gained momentum within the white Australian imagination, becoming indispensable to collective memories of colonial settlement. These narratives functioned to mythologize particular versions of the specificities of Aboriginal-settler conflict, and to disseminate certain Eurocentric assumptions about Aboriginal culture. And, when the captive was a woman, they enforced dominant ideologies concerning white female sexuality.

This chapter examines, across Australia's multiple and shifting frontier spaces, white responses to and representations of historical incidents where European women lived with Aborigines. These were, and remain, important in framing popular understandings of the history of Australian colonization. As Chris Healy points out, captivity narratives were 'one of the few modes in which women in Australia appear in histories', although the women concerned appeared not as historical actors but as 'a category of historical event'.[11] In the United States, where a sizeable historiography on captivity exists, Carroll Smith-Rosenberg has recently argued that through positioning white women as the 'innocent victims of barbarous savagery', captivity narratives authorized settler women as 'an alternative icon for America'.[12] Similarly, Kay Schaffer has termed stories about Eliza Fraser – probably the best-known female captive in Australia – as constituting a 'foundation fiction for the nation'.[13] As this chapter demonstrates, however, the influence of colonial captivity discourse in determining settler behaviour in cases where real white women 'captives' existed was not homogenous. White responses to these racially and sexually transgressive circumstances were shaped by the state of settler-Aboriginal relations, and the confidence of white society, that prevailed on specific contact zones at particular moments of time.

'RESCUING' BARBARA THOMPSON: THE MARITIME FRONTIER OF EUROPEAN EXPLORATION

October 16th, 1849: . . . the Blacks had brought a white woman down to the beach. I . . . began to run . . . [and] as we neared the party, saw a mixed group of Blacks and marines and sailors from the ship altogether . . . [with] a young woman very much browned by the sun. The men had given her two shirts; one white she wore in the same manner as a man, and the other, a blue one, hung tied around her waist so as to form an under petticoat. She sat on a bank with her head hanging down and had a tin plate with some meat and a knife and fork, which the men had given her, on her knees before her. One Black sat close to her with his arm passed behind her, two others were standing close to her. Her manner was very curious and she replied to our questions something in the manner of a person just waking up from a deep sleep . . . When she came on board tea was immediately made for her . . . she was asked if she would like to go back to the Blacks or go to Sydney. To this she simply answered, 'I am a Christian'.[14]

So Oswald W. Brierly, official artist on the survey vessel H.M.S. *Rattlesnake*, recorded in his private journal the 'rescue' of Barbara Crawford Thompson at Evans Bay, on the eastern tip of Australia's Cape York Peninsula. The *Rattlesnake*'s crew, who were busily bleaching the ship's laundry, initially failed to see Thompson's own whiteness. Her skin was darkly tanned, scarred from burns down one side of her face and body. They were only alerted to her race when she spoke some halting words of English. The sailors' stunned recognition was quickly followed by their transformation of a hitherto anonymous 'native' woman into the young white woman, Barbara Thompson. The now *white* nakedness of her body was washed and hastily covered. She was given a plate and cutlery to eat from the communal pot, and later, aboard the *Rattlesnake*, served meat and apple-pie. (Of the pie she appreciatively said, 'I never thought of tasting the likes of this again'.) For the first time in five years she sat at a table, and slept in a bed.

At the time of her reinstatement into European society, Scots-born Thompson's brief, but remarkable, life history spanned hemispheres and breached cultures. In 1844, aged sixteen, she eloped with William Thompson from Sydney to Moreton Bay. The Thompsons refitted a small cutter to salvage goods from a shipwreck in Torres Strait, but in a sudden summer squall their vessel was smashed on a coral reef. William Thompson and the remaining crew drowned while swimming ashore. Barbara Thompson clung to the cutter until she was collected by a turtling party of mainland Aborigines and Kaurareg from Muralag (Prince of Wales) Island. She was integrated into Kaurareg society until her adopted brother, Tomagugu, took her to her 'own people' at Evans Bay.

Thompson later recalled that the first question she was asked on the beach was 'whether I had been wrecked or taken by the blacks'. But the distinction between castaway or abducted captive was one of cause rather than effect. Both circumstances resulted in the same state of being: a white woman living among 'black savages'. Colonial discourse was permeated with polarized imagery about the power of one race over another: possession and dispossession, conquest and slavery, domination and submission; the exploiter and the exploited, the oppressor and the oppressed, the captor and the captive. The racialized and gendered assumptions of this discourse, and its ideological limitations, determined white interpretations of Thompson's experience. Thus, while Brierly, his colleagues and subsequent commentators all acknowledged that Thompson had been treated with great kindness by the Kaurareg, their choice of language belied this harmonious interracial existence. Thompson's peaceful re-entry into white society was expressed in terms of 'escape' and 'rescue'; the Kaurareg were reduced to 'captors', her life with them to a period of 'captivity', and the *Rattlesnake*'s crew assumed the heroic role of liberators. Brierly stressed Thompson's 'rescue' by emphasizing her moral and spiritual recovery in his *Journal*. He likened her inability to 'collect her ideas' to that of one surfacing from a 'deep sleep'. Her face bore 'a dreaming vacant expression', and in white company she was suddenly 'ashamed' of her nakedness.

Thompson's 'rescue' was most significantly marked in spatial terms. The beach at Evans Bay, where British sailors, marines and officers mingled with Aborigines and Islanders of both sexes trading artefacts and information, constituted a dynamic 'contact zone' between the European explorers and the indigenous culture. Thompson had returned from the 'wilderness' that lay beyond this frontier. But the beach was, at least in European eyes, no place for a white woman. In its indeterminate cultural space lay the possibility of bodily contact and sexual desire between races. Thompson's 'rescue' not only reconstituted her as a racialized and gendered subject, but as a sexualized one.

Thus, she was removed to the 'safety' of the *Rattlesnake*. Within its white space, there was no chance of intimate physical contact with her Kaurareg 'relatives'. Moreover, aboard the ship, Thompson was only permitted to communicate with other officers – including the Assistant Surgeon, T. H. Huxley – and was segregated from the curiosity, and the possible sexual advances, of the *Rattlesnake*'s crew. If the seamen harboured sexual fantasies about her, the officers, and Thompson's subsequent biographers, also speculated about her sexual activity on Muralag Island. Despite Thompson's admission that she had no 'black husband', the question of whether she did have intercourse with a 'savage' made her story particularly titillating. It was, for instance, the only detail English naturalist J. B. Jukes, on receiving first-hand news of the incident, selected to pass on to colleague J. Gould. Jukes wrote, in a tone of incredulity, that Thompson 'had been treated kindly by the black fellows all the time and that moreover none of them had —— [*sic*].'[15] Jukes' gentle-manly refusal to describe sexual relations between a black man and a white woman nevertheless identifies this as the pivotal meaning of Thompson's 'captivity'.

To be taken in by a society, and voluntarily instructed as a partic-ipant in its intricacies, has been described as the ultimate 'ethno-grapher's dream'.[16] This was not lost on Oswald Brierly. During the *Rattlesnake*'s long voyage back to Sydney, he interviewed Barbara Thompson (whom he came to call Mrs T.) for several hours each day. Brierly took notes in pencil, which he read aloud to the illiterate Thompson for approval before transcribing them more permanently in ink. Just as the narrative of Thompson's 'captivity' was trapped within the ideological framework of nineteenth-century colonial culture, her voice – her own account of her experience – was mediated through the middle-class, male, and scientific preoccupat-ions of Brierly. Thompson's narrative is thus subsumed within Brierly's endeavour to 'capture' the customs and cultures of the peoples of Torres Strait and Cape York before, as he anticipated, they would be obliterated or transformed by the system of British colonialism.

THE WHITE WOMAN OF GIPPSLAND: WAR ON THE FRONTIER

On a very different colonial frontier, in the Gippsland district of eastern Victoria, a war over ownership of territory was waged during the 1840s between the local Aborigines, the Kurnai, and white settlers. This was a contact zone dominated by violence, and where European control of the land was tenuous. In this context, the belief that the Kurnai held a white woman captive served to intensify and justify settler hostility, with perhaps as many as several hundred Kurnai being killed in retaliation.[17] In December 1840, in a letter to the *Sydney Herald*, Angus McMillan, the influential spokesman of a powerful group of Scottish settlers, had reported his discovery of European items in an abandoned Aboriginal camp at the Gippsland Lakes. These included adult and children's clothing, linen, blankets, tools, medicines, cooking utensils, a musket, newspapers from London, Glasgow and Aberdeen, a Bible, and life insurance policies. A dead child was found in a kangaroo skin bag, and according to

Dr Arbuckle, one of McMillan's companions, its parents had been white. Then, wrote McMillan:

> We observed the men with shipped spears driving before them the women, one of whom we noticed constantly looking behind her, at us, a circumstance which did not strike us much at the time, but on examining the marks and figures about the largest of the native huts we were immediately impressed with the belief that the unfortunate female is a European – a captive of these ruthless savages.[18]

McMillan's emotive imagery was highly conventional in its construction of black savagery and white civilization. The primitivism of the Aboriginal camp was contrasted with the material and spiritual trappings of a provident and literate family that was, by implication, Scottish.

There was no immediate response to McMillan's letter. In fact, during the next five years rumours about a white captive emerged in several districts in Victoria. But by 1845, as Aboriginal attacks on sheep and cattle became more systematic in Gippsland, sightings of a white captive were restricted to that region alone. With increasing regularity, lone shepherds and stockmen saw the White Woman. In all instances, she looked beseechingly at her observers as male Aborigines dragged her away.

The accumulation of these reports, were, as Robert Dixon points out, 'implicitly a call to action' for male settlers in Gippsland to mobilize against the Kurnai.[19] As the news drifted to the budding town of Melbourne, a communal panic, fanned by competition between the colonial press, arose about the captive's 'slavery worse than death'. Concern at her plight cut across class barriers, unifying the white settlers in a common cause (rescue of the female) against a shared enemy (the Kurnai). Meetings were called to decide a course of action. When the colonial administration declined to help, public subscriptions funded a search party led by Christian De Villiers and James Warman. By the end of 1846, a government expedition under the command of William Dana had also been despatched. Relations between the competing expeditions grew strained as they both headed towards the high country looking for the Kurnai 'chief' Bunjeleene, supposedly the White Woman's 'husband'. At the Gippsland Lakes, De Villiers and Warman discovered 'a great many skulls and human bones', and alleged that Dana's party, and local settlers, had been involved in massacres of the Kurnai.[20]

Both expeditions were disbanded, but hysteria about the White Woman failed to abate. One colonist wrote: 'I suppose if a person were to say in Melbourne that there was no white woman at all, he would be considered insane or put down as an unfeeling monster.'[21] In early 1847, public pressure became so intense that the government sent out a third expedition. Bunjeleene was eventually found, and his family were held as hostages while he was forced to lead the party to the Snowy Mountains. When winter set in, the search was abandoned. But as European control of Gippsland became more secure, and European women began to join their menfolk in Gippsland, public interest in the White Woman noticeably waned.[22] In November 1847 McMillan officially laid the White Woman to rest when he presided over a hasty inquest into the remains of 'an European woman and a half-caste child'.[23] Bunjeleene, who had been charged under British law with 'holding an European female as his Captive', soon died in prison.

Two points can be made about this colonial incident. The first concerns the White Woman's identity. Initially, there were attempts to 'prove' she was a 'real' European woman who had survived one of the numerous shipwrecks along the Victorian coast. But as it was impossible to give her a specific name, she was more often simply described. For William Lonsdale, Acting Superintendent of Port Phillip, the captive was 'in her mid twenties, with light brown hair, now cropped, and when shipwrecked was wearing a silk dress of quality, thin slippers and a boa'.[24] Scottish settlers were so convinced she was a compatriot, they distributed handkerchiefs and mirrors bearing messages in English and Gaelic: 'WHITE WOMAN! – There are fourteen armed men, partly White and partly Black, in search of you . . . Be particularly on the look out every dawn of morning.'[25] These constructions of the White Woman as young, physically attractive, middle-class and of desirable ethnic stock served to emphasize the racial, gendered and spatial displacement of her experience, and to elevate her to an object of sexual desire in the male settler imagination. She was thus the symbolic wife or daughter of every white settler, an idealized representative of European womanhood in a hostile land. It was therefore fitting that the only 'white woman' ever recaptured by the expeditions was a battered ship's figurehead of 'Britannia' – the icon of British nationhood.

Secondly, the tale of Gippsland's White Woman is one of colonial land-taking. While the expeditions were officially searching for the White Woman, they were also carefully appraising the economic potential of the 'wilderness'. The serialization of Warman's expedition journal in the *Port Phillip Herald* alerted intending settlers to the district's rich pastoral possibilities. Warman, although sympathetic to the Kurnai, portrayed them as a broken people, unable to resist the colonizers for much longer. The Melbourne newspapers, lamenting that the captive had not been found, stated that nonetheless 'the exploration of the country [had been] of the greatest public importance'.[26]

The 'burial' of the White Woman did not mean she was forgotten. Robert Russell, a Gippsland settler who contributed to the uproar over the White Woman in the colonial press, wrote the first of several fictional accounts based on the 'facts' of the incident in 1849; the most recent of these was published in 1994.[27] In contemporary Gippsland, the White Woman remains a significant feature of local folklore and pioneer reminiscences, and the story is historicized – albeit in a very different form – in the oral tradition of the region's Aboriginal community.[28]

The Gippsland incident was unique in colonial Australia, although fears that Aborigines would abduct white women were voiced by settlers on other frontiers where there was prolonged racial conflict. In 1881, Aborigines attacked a fishing station on Lizard Island in the Great Barrier Reef, forcing Mary Watson, her infant and a Chinese servant to flee in an iron *bêche-de-mer* pot to a nearby coral atoll, where they perished from thirst.[29] Watson's funeral was the largest ever held in north Queensland, and a memorial drinking fountain was erected in her honour. A poem dedicated to this pioneer 'heroine' in *The Bulletin* put into rhyming couplets what many settlers thought: that in death Watson had escaped 'nameless horrors' far worse – interracial captivity and rape.[30] Here, violent reprisals against the Aborigines were justified not only by Watson's death alone, but by the suggestion of what her fate might have been as a white 'captive'. Like the White Woman episode forty years earlier, the idea that a white woman was or could be captured by the Aborigines provided settlers with additional moral ammunition in their war for land.

'MRS WITCHETTY': INVERTING THE NARRATIVE ON THE TWENTIETH CENTURY FRONTIER

By the new century, and the federation of the new nation, Europeans had surveyed, tilled and stocked much of the Australian continent. Now, the modern frontier was characterized by the 'Great Australian Emptiness' of the sparsely populated lands lying 'out back' from the cities and towns strung along the seaboard. No longer threatening, the frontier remained an important imaginative site for white Australians, inciting nostalgia and a considerable curiosity. This fascination was met by a best-selling literary genre categorized as 'landscape writing, travel writing, descriptive writing, frontier writing, and several combinations of these labels'.[31] This genre popularized histories about the settler heroics of frontier life. By reiterating familiar, and ongoing, preoccupations with racial purity and miscegenation, such frontier writing authorized colonial captivity tales as historical record and ethnographic truth. Ion Idriess, for example, sensationalized Barbara Thompson's life in *Isles of Despair* (1947); while Charles Barrett strung several histories, including those of Thompson and Gippsland's White Woman, together in his *White Blackfellows: The Strange Adventures of Europeans Who Lived among Savages* (1948).

One of the most influential of these texts was Ernestine Hill's *The Great Australian Loneliness* (1938). Meaghan Morris has argued that Hill – 'an imperialist, a white supremacist and a patriot' – understood her frontier journalism to be about 'capturing life' at the very moment 'pioneer culture' was dying out.[32] In Nepabunna, a 'little village of wurlies' in the Flinders Ranges of South Australia, Hill stumbled across what she called the 'most amazing document in the annals of the Australian outback, the life history of Mrs. Jackie Forbes, otherwise Witchetty, the only authentic case to date of a white woman "living black" with the tribes.'[33] Hill, as an 'expert 'eye-witness, constructed Mrs Witchetty as a historical document; as living history, simultaneously embodying 'how things were' and 'how things are' on the contact zone of the interior.[34] And, as Morris points out, Hill's pen turned Mrs Witchetty into a 'living genre piece', a woman who liked to read 'hair-raising thrillers, blissfully unconscious that she is the most hair-raising thriller of the lot'.[35]

Hill's report of an interview with Mrs Witchetty played upon the cultural expectations of her readers. While conventional captivity narratives portrayed the inversion of imperial order, Hill turned the genre, and its sexual and racial order, upside down. Mrs Witchetty recalled that upon marrying her Aboriginal husband, 'I was worried lest the blacks should object to a white woman in their camp, but the [white] policeman promised if there was any trouble, *he would make them see reason* [my emphasis].'[36] White officialdom is thus utilized to enforce the entry of a white woman into Aboriginal society. The narrative inversion continues. Following the death of her husband, Mrs Witchetty chose to remain with their two 'initiated' sons in the camp. To 'live white' meant paying for rent and the children's education; in the camp there was 'no housework to do' and she existed happily on 'black's rations'. She concluded by telling Hill: 'If, as they say, a wife always takes her husband's nationality, I am an Australian, actually the *only real white Australian there is*' [my emphasis].[37] Mrs Witchetty's claim to 'real' Australian identity through interracial sexual union and miscegenation is presented by Hill as the most thrilling revelation of all. Assuming the voice of white rationality, Hill instructed her readers to waste no sympathy on Mrs Witchetty because of her refusal to acknowledge her own sexual and racial displacement. In this narrative context, Mrs Witchetty's voluntary 'captivity' is not portrayed as subversive, but simply as crazy.

In the Australia of the 1930s, with most of the surviving Aboriginal populations driven from their lands into missions, reserves and cities, Mrs Witchetty's choice to live as part of an Aboriginal society posed little threat to the self-confidence of white Australian nationalism. Government policies of Aboriginal assimilation at the time implied that, contrary to Mrs Witchetty's assertion, the 'only real black Australian' was one who could learn to 'live white'. Hill was not alone in believing in the inevitability of Aboriginal extinction: 'At the coming of civilization, the aboriginal tribes dwindle like chaff before the wind.'[38] Although she deplored the racial brutalities of the colonial frontier, Hill viewed these as existing in the past, as history. But that history included counter-narratives of racial submission, sexual violation and enforced captivity. From 1788, the abduction of Aboriginal men, women and children as guides and interpreters, labourers in the pastoral and fishing industries, domestic servants and sexual partners occurred throughout Australia.[39] Touring circuses, photographs and museums captured Aboriginal material culture and Aboriginal bodies as examples of 'savage man', thereby legitimating imperial expansion and racial dominance as civilization and progress.

At Roebourne, on the north-west coast, Hill discovered a white memorial to this civilization and progress. She was the sole guest at the Jubilee Hotel, where the walls of the public bar had been covered with murals painted by a 'blow-in' Englishman who 'had a flair for form and colour and action, and . . . knew his North-west history':

The masterpiece, discreetly displayed on the back of the billiard-room door, was a bearded pioneer travelling across the landscape and whirling his lassoo above the curly head of a lubra streaking before him, on her pathetically thin legs, for dear life.[40]

Hill made no direct comment on this extraordinary visual history, although she recorded how, that Saturday night, white stockmen and 'half-caste' women attended a dance at the hotel. The past depicted on the walls thus framed the contemporary racial inter-actions on the north-west frontier. But unlike the White Woman of Gippsland, or countless other white females in conventional captivity stories, the anonymous, terrorized Aboriginal woman on the Jubilee Hotel's mural was depicted not as a victim but as a rightful sexual spoil. While Mrs Witchetty represented an inversion of the trad-itional captivity story, the Jubilee mural represented a racial reversal of the imperial narrative: a black woman hunted down by a white pioneer. The enduring popularity of narratives of white female captivity in Australian culture no doubt served to deflect from such frontier realities – although the enslavement of Aboriginal women by whites was, within the ideological limitations of colonial discourse, not articulated as captivity but as conquest. The scene on the mural at the Jubilee Hotel serves as a reminder that on the contested spaces of the shifting frontier lay other hidden histories of interracial captivity and sexual desire through which the cultural dynamics of Australian identity were constituted.

NOTES

1 Mary Louise Pratt, *Imperial Eyes: Travel Writing and Transculturation*, London and New York, Routledge, 1992, p. 6.

2 For settler-Aboriginal interaction, see Henry Reynolds, *The Other Side of the Frontier: Aboriginal Resistance to the European Invasion of Australia*, Melbourne, Penguin, 1982.

3 See Stephen Greenblatt, *Marvellous Possessions: The Wonder of the New World*, Oxford, Oxford University Press, 1991, and Bernard Smith, *European Vision and the South Pacific*, Melbourne, Oxford University Press, 2nd edn., 1989.

4 See, for instance, Richard Slotkin, *Regeneration Through Violence: The Mythology of the American Frontier, 1600–1860*, Middleton, Conn., Wesleyan University Press, 1973, pp. 95–114; Annette Kolodny, *The Land Before Her: Fantasy and Experience of the American Frontiers, 1630–1860*, Chapel Hill, The University of North Carolina Press, 1984, p. 18.

5 See June Namias, *White Captives: Gender and Ethnicity on the American*

Frontier, Chapel Hill, The University of North Carolina Press, 1993.

6 Robert Young, *Colonial Desire: Hybridity in Theory, Culture and Race*, London, Routledge, 1994, pp. 9, 181.

7 Vron Ware, *Beyond the Pale: White Women, Racism and History*, London, Verso, 1992.

8 Ross Gibson, *South of the West: Post-colonialism and the Narrative Construction of Australia*, Bloomington, Indiana University Press, 1992, pp. 93–110; see also Joseph Bristow, *Empire Boys: Adventures in a Man's World*, London, Harper Collins, 1991, pp. 93–126.

9 See Jane Samson, 'The 1834 Cruise of HMS Alligator: The Bible and the Flag', *The Northern Mariner/Le Marin du Nord*, vol. 3, no. 4, Oct. 1993, pp. 37–47.

10 I refer here only to written documentation of cases where whites re-entered colonial society, including William Buckley and James Morrell.

11 Chris Healy, 'The Training of Memory: Moments of Historical Imagination in Australia', PhD thesis, Department of History, University of Melbourne, 1993, p. 192.

12 Carroll Smith-Rosenberg, 'Captured Subjects/Savage Others: Violently Engendering the New American', *Gender and History*, vol. 5, no. 2, Summer 1993, p. 179.

13 Kay Schaffer, 'Captivity Narratives and the Idea of "Nation" ', in Kate Darian-Smith, Roslyn Poignant and Kay Schaffer, *Captured Lives: Australian Captivity Narratives*, London, Sir Robert Menzies Centre for Australian Studies, University of London, 1992, pp. 1-13; also her *In the Wake of First Contact: the Eliza Fraser Stories*, Melbourne, Cambridge University Press, 1995.

14 Oswald Brierly, 'Journal of the H.M.S. Rattlesnake, Second Visit to Cape York, October–December 1849' in David R. Moore (ed.), *Islanders and Aborigines at Cape York: An Ethnographic Reconstruction Based on the 1848-1850 'Rattlesnake' Journals of O. W. Brierly and Information He Obtained from Barbara Thompson*, Canberra, Australian Institute of Aboriginal Studies Press, 1979, pp. 76–80. All subsequent references to Brierly's 'Journal' are from this publication.

15 J. B. Jukes, letter to J. Gould, Wolverhampton, 24 Feb. 1850, Gould Papers, British Museum (Natural History), Box 7, File: J. B. Jukes.

16 Mary Louise Pratt, 'Fieldwork in Common Places', in James Clifford and George E. Marcus (eds), *Writing Culture: The Poetics and Politics of Ethnography*, Berkeley, University of California Press, 1986, pp. 27–33.

17 Don Watson, *Caledonia Australis: Scottish Highlanders on the Frontier of Australia*, Sydney, Collins, 1984, p. 178.

18 *Sydney Herald*, 28 Dec. 1840; quoted in Watson, *Caledonia Australis*, p. 162.

19 Robert Dixon, *Writing the Colonial Frontier: Race, Gender and Nation in Anglo-Australian Popular Fiction, 1875–1914*, Cambridge, Cambridge University Press, 1995, p. 48.

20 For a fully referenced account of the expeditions and settler responses, see Kate Darian-Smith, 'The White Woman of Gippsland: A Frontier Myth', in Darian-Smith et al., *Captured Lives*, pp. 14–34.

21 *Port Phillip Patriot and Morning Advertiser*, 6 Feb. 1847.

22 see Watson, *Caledonia Australis*, pp. 178–9.
23 *Port Phillip Herald*, 5 Nov. 1847.
24 Letter, W. Lonsdale, to Colonial Secretary, 13 Oct. 1846; tabled, NSW Legislative Council, *Votes and Proceedings*, 21 Oct. 1846, p. 11.
25 The Gaelic version was addressed to 'ANNA!'. A photograph of the handkerchief is held at the Centre for Gippsland Studies, Monash University, Gippsland.
26 *Port Phillip Herald*, 21 Jan. 1847.
27 Early texts include Robert Russell, *The Heart*, Melbourne, *c.* 1849; Henry Gyles Turner, 'The Captive of Gipps Land', *The Illustrated Journal of Australia*, Vol II, Jan.–June 1857; Angus MacLean, *Lindigo – The White Woman: the Highland Girl's Captivity Among the Australian Blacks*, Melbourne, H. T. Dwight, 1866; and more recently, Liam Davison, *The White Woman*, St Lucia, University of Queensland Press, 1994.
28 Phillip Pepper with Tess De Araugo, *The Kurnai of Gippsland*, Melbourne, Hyland House, 1985, p. 76.
29 Jillian Robertson, *Lizard Island: A Reconstruction of the Life of Mrs Watson*, Melbourne, Hutchinson, 1981; *Brisbane Courier*, 23 Jan. 1882, pp. 2, 3.
30 'A. F.', 'Dead With Thirst', *The Bulletin*, 4 Feb. 1882, p. 2; see also *Brisbane Courier*, 25 Jan. 1882, p. 3.
31 Margriet Bonnin, 'A Study of Australian Descriptive and Travel Writing, 1929–1945', PhD thesis, Department of English, University of Queensland, 1980; see also Meaghan Morris, 'Panorama: The Live, The Dead and The Living', in Paul Foss (ed.), *Island in the Stream: Myths of Place in Australian Culture*, Sydney, Pluto Press, 1988, pp. 166–79.
32 Morris, 'Panorama', pp. 172–3. Morris quotes Roland Barthes: ' "Capturing life" really means "seeing dead" '.
33 Ernestine Hill, *The Great Australian Loneliness*, Melbourne, Robertson & Mullens, 1st edn 1937, 1940, p. 271. Witchetty grubs are nutritious larvae eaten by some Aboriginal groups; Hill uses the name here in a racist and derogatory sense.
34 In claiming Mrs Witchetty was the 'only authentic case', Hill may be referring to contemporary rumours, incited by the hoax of the ethnographic film *Blonde Captive*, about a white woman living with the Aborigines in Australia's remote north.
35 Morris, 'Panorama', p. 176; Hill, *Loneliness*, p. 274.
36 Hill, *Loneliness*, p. 273.
37 Hill, *Loneliness*, p. 275.
38 Hill, *Loneliness*, p. 35.
39 See Henry Reynolds, *With the White People*, Melbourne, Penguin, 1990.
40 Hill, *Loneliness*, p. 34.

BIBLIOGRAPHY

Darian-Smith, K., Poignant, R., and Schaffer, K., *Captured Lives: Australian Captivity Narratives*, London, Sir Robert Menzies Centre for Australian Studies, University of London, 1992.
Dixon, R., *Writing the Colonial Frontier: Race, Gender and Nation in Anglo-*

Australian Popular Fiction, 1875–1914, Cambridge, Cambridge University Press, 1995.

Gibson, R., *South of the West: Post-colonialism and the Narrative Construction of Australia*, Bloomington, Indiana University Press, 1992.

Hill, E., *The Great Australian Loneliness*, Melbourne, Robertson & Mullens, 1st edn. 1937, 1940.

Moore, D. R., *Islanders and Aborigines at Cape York: An Ethnographic Reconstruction Based on the 1848–1850 'Rattlesnake' Journals of O.W. Brierly and Information He Obtained from Barbara Thompson*, Canberra, Australian Institute of Aboriginal Studies Press, 1979.

Morris, M., 'Panorama: The Live, The Dead and The Living', in P. Foss (ed.), *Island in the Stream: Myths of Place in Australian Culture*, Sydney, Pluto Press, 1988, pp. 160–187.

Namias, J., *White Captives: Gender and Ethnicity on the American Frontier*, Chapel Hill, The University of North Carolina Press, 1993.

Pratt, M. L., *Imperial Eyes: Travel Writing and Transculturation*, London and New York, Routledge, 1992.

Schaffer, K., *In the Wake of First Contact: The Eliza Fraser Stories*, Melbourne, Cambridge University Press, 1995.

Smith-Rosenberg, C., 'Captured Subjects/Savage Others: Violently Engendering the New American', *Gender and History*, vol. 5, no. 2, Summer 1993, pp. 169–95.

Ware, V., *Beyond the Pale: White Women, Racism and History*, London, Verso, 1992.

Watson, D., *Caledonia Australis: Scottish Highlanders on the Frontier of Australia*, Sydney, Collins, 1984.

Young, R., *Colonial Desire: Hybridity in Theory, Culture and Race*, London, Routledge, 1994.

7

NAMES AND THE LAND
Poetry of belonging and unbelonging,
a comparative approach

Liz Gunner

Recent studies on orality have stressed the porous nature of the boundaries between orality and literacy while stating emphatically that they remain different territories. Both Hofmeyr and Tonkin – working respectively on oral historical narrative from the Transvaal region of South Africa, and from Liberia in West Africa, direct our attention to the complex textuality of oral forms and oral genres.[1] They are 'not' – as the novelist Chinua Achebe once remarked about stories – 'innocent'. Oral genres, as much as written, come with their own hinterland of specific cultural and historical imperatives and their own subjectivities. Far from existing fenced off and out of time – a little like the world of the Reserve in Huxley's *Brave New World* – they impinge, often awkwardly, on written genres and the discourses constructed from them. Sometimes they seem so awkward that their powerful, difficult presence is largely ignored or at best underrated.[2] Certainly in the case of names and the land in both the South African and Aboriginal poetry I will be discussing there are ways of regarding the body and the land, ways of belonging, which are difficult to ascertain without the crossing and recrossing of cognitive boundaries, a revision of what constitutes 'text' and 'post-colonial text', and a search for a new aesthetic.

Yet the pitfalls in discussing oral poetry are numerous. 'Who recorded the texts – outsiders? Whites?' 'Are the texts not so period- and culture-bound that they must, rightly, remain in "Huxley's Reserve"?' 'Who were the informants – elders? Or schoolboys?' 'Surely it is essentialist to compare poetry from such different societies with their own very specific experiences of being colonized?' And again in the case of this particular paper: 'After all − the sweep of history in operation is so wide: the frontier wars between the Cape Colony and the Xhosa in the early eighteenth century; the fractured Basotho creating a nation and facing the Boers in the mountainous centre of South Africa in the mid-nineteenth century and later; the exploits of the militaristic Zulu leader Shaka in the 1820s, recalled in praise poetry one hundred years later when the Zulu kingdom remains only as a mirage and when Zulu men form part of the labour force on the mines of the Reef and the monotonously green sugar estates of Natal; the Aranda of Central Australia, their poetry recorded in the 1930s, having since the mid-nineteenth century faced settler incursions that totally disrupted their "land based rel-igious institutions", and dispossessed them.[3] Not to mention the contemporary poetry that comes into play as well!' 'It all seems so messy and imprecise.'

Nevertheless, with the above caveats in mind, I will continue with my comparative exploration. I will explore whether there are conceptions of textuality and of poetry and value which engage with the aesthetics of 'settler' poetry and language in a way which is both subversive and innovative.

In the case of the Aboriginal Aranda poetry, I am working from the translations made by T. G. H. Strehlow at Alice Springs in 1933 during the months of May and June, when he was present at the Ilbalintja cycle of commemorative ceremonies of the Northern Aranda. The ceremonies were at Alice Springs because the Ilbalintja soak was dry, but more importantly, because it was in the land of a white cattle owner.[4] The texts have been carefully contextualized. Strehlow, reared on the Hermannsburg Luthern Mission at Alice Springs and a speaker of Western Aranda since childhood, stresses the importance of being familiar with the language of those whose poetry and ceremonies one is attempting to document. He emphasizes, too, the importance of knowing the status of one's informants. Although an outsider, he is acutely aware of the dispossession of those whose words and performance he is witness to. There is a sense of a poetry which − in 'traditional society' − functioned in a religious and historical sense as well as aesthetically. There may be a touch of the conservationist romantic in the following account of the last night of the Ilbalintja cycle, but the anger − and the empathy − are palpable as well:

It was a clear star-bright night, with the crescent moon already low in the sky. The men were deeply moved as they remembered the time when Karora had been ruling at Ilbalintja in the pride of his strength. For the time being they were no longer the dispossessed, despised, miserable underdogs of the usurping white race. They were again proud, free men, glorifying and re-living the deeds of those Northern Aranda ancestors of whom they were the latter-day reincarnations. Not only was the earth on which they were standing their very own soil: the sky and its luminaries too belonged to them, linked to their tribal lands by the ties of myth and tradition. The sun, ancestor of Ilbalintja had already gone to his rest, after covering his face with a veil of hairstring; but the moon and stars were still in the sky, and they too had once been men and women who had roamed about in Central Australia.[5]

In documenting the 'sung verse' of the Aranda, Strehlow returns a number of times to the power inherent in a name, to the point that when the song of each totemic ancestor is sung it must be the correct couplets: 'they must be able to call them by those names which the ancestors had bestowed upon themselves at the beginning of time.'[6] And again, Strehlow emphasizes that a totemic ancestor's song consisted of his own name, and he would then

> 'name' . . . the place where he had originated, the trees or rocks growing near his home, animals nearby, strangers visiting etc. . . . In this way a series of couplets loosely associated by time, space and story, was brought into being; and this series constituted the song that each ancestor left behind for the benefit of those human beings who were to be re- incarnated from himself and from his own supernatural children.[7]

Names in this Aranda poetic tradition, to which I shall return later, clearly signify a complicated belonging to, and intimate identification with the land, through stones, animals, flowers, plants, trees. The South African Nguni (Xhosa and Zulu) and Sotho praise poetry on which I draw is also a poetic tradition of naming. An individual acquired praise names during his or her life and also composed them. These names, or praise poems (known as *izibongo* in Zulu, *iibongo* in Xhosa and *dithoko* in Sotho) were both laudatory and critical and acted as brief (auto) biographies of the person, which commemorated and represented them after their death. Praise poetry – the poetic collection of names by which an individual was known – were, in the case of chiefs and leaders, often a part of political authority, and in the case of leaders their poetry often formed a crucial conduit between them and their subjects. Commentary, that was often far from flattering, was put into the praise names so that public opinion could be aired through the recitations of the praise poet (known as *imbongi* (Zulu and Xhosa) and *seroki* (Sotho)). In the case of Nguni and Sotho praise poetry, the poetic tradition is still an active one in South Africa and Lesotho.[8]

These poetic traditions from two regions, two 'southern spaces', while existing within very different symbolic systems and time frames, seem nevertheless to be linked through their metaphysical embodying of the land and their presencing of the land in the identity of the individual. What they have to say needs to be read in consonance with contemporary writings about land and identity. Certainly in the South African case, such oral textuality has had a strong influence on some written traditions, as I will show. The Aranda poetry which speaks of a complex transaction of body, space and being can be seen to have links with the Nguni and Sotho poetry's personifying of place, and natural and heavenly objects. In each instance the complicated voice of the so-called colonized subject can be heard constructing a discourse in relation to the land. In the South African poetry, which moves (in the examples that follow) through the oral form into the written and then to a sung genre, the discourse relates to both possession and conquest, then resistance and nationalist longing and finally possession through speech.

OF BELONGING AND CONQUEST

What emerges from Nguni and Sotho oral poetry of the early nineteenth century is the sense of belonging which is established through a multitude of references to place and to the names of homesteads and individuals, forebears, friends and foes. It is not, however – particularly in the case of Zulu and Sotho poetry – a settled poetry but rather one turning on restless movement, skirmishes, conquests. The sense of settled place which is present in the poetry provides a verbal corroboration of some eighteenth- and early nineteenth-century travellers' accounts of the densely settled nature of the land in what is now the Transkei and in the old Zulu kingdom. Yet such poetry, particularly the genre of praise poetry, is not of a kind that unproblematically represents settled harmony or static tradition. The two opposed impulses of movement and stasis often operate within the same texts. Thus an early nineteenth-century leader is hailed (in a contemporary remembering of his praise poem) as 'You Builder of your Lineage by way of the Spear'.[9] And in one version of the praise poem of the Zulu king, Shaka, from the same period, movement, conquest and place are linked into a triad of belonging:

> He went up one ridge and down another
> He returned by way of Boyiya son of Madakwa
> He passed through the bones of the children of Tayi . . .
> The hawk which I saw sweeping down from Mangcengeza;
> When he came to Phungashe he disappeared . . .
> He is like the cluster of stones at Nkandla
> Which sheltered elephants when it had rained.[10]

Thus place becomes familiarized as points of conquest and of living. To take another example of an Mkhize chief, a contemporary of Shaka's father:

> Stabber who is on the inside of the hut at Diza . . .
> Our rock of Sijibeni
> That makes a man slip even as he seems to be holding onto it
> Giver without stint unlike the one from Ngonyameni.[11]

In such 'naming' of an individual, place becomes familiarized both as points of conquest and of habitation. People are lodged within the landscape. Even when it is a terrain of conquest it is peopled, it is familiarized, it is not alien. The statements of conquest and belonging can even be seen as reinforcing each other. Even the sky, so often featured in paintings and poetry by settler English and Afrikaans speakers as a great emptiness over another emptiness of land, becomes personalized[12] and, up to a point, benign, although in the Basotho example here the benevolence is itself ambivalent and set within a reference to aggression:

> Overarching Sky, Lekena,
> That arches over the nations,
> Lately he entered the place of Majorobela and scorched it;
> Lately he entered Maseru and set it alight.[13]

J. M. Coetzee has spoken of the schema of seeing which operates in turning terrain into landscape and which modifies the vision of white painting and letters.[14] What operates as a schema in the Zulu and

119

Sotho poetry from which I have been quoting is what could be called a schema of naming; what is in fact in operation is an *aesthetics of naming* as the land and the elements are absorbed into the names of people and become the signifiers of poetry that is both biography and autobiography. These names in turn become reabsorbed into the poetic (auto)biographies and statements of identity of successive generations. It is this aesthetics, or better still what we could call the metaphysics of naming, which is central to a sense of 'text' in both South African praise poetry and the Aboriginal sung poetry mentioned above.

Even very fine details of flora and fauna as well as place in the sense of locality, of particular places, mountains, ridges, plains can be absorbed into the personal through praise poetry which names and identifies a person. Thus Hintsa, an early nineteenth-century Xhosa chief who was tricked and murdered by the British, is called:

The Sweet tall grass of Khala
Whose movements are a blessing
Who stares without blinking
Whose eyebrows reveal his anger.[15]

Elsewhere in praise poetry the identification between the individual and nature is modified and the fine specifics of place are tied to a narrative moment within the praise poem as a whole:

It was spring and the wild olive trees were blooming,
The willows too and the blooms were on the twigs;
Among the grasses the most beautiful was the diritshwane,
Among the birds were such as the masked weaver bird.

In the aesthetics of naming in this poetry, the land frequently becomes the person, and becomes part of the body's text; the social and the historical self is perceived through the land.

The narratives of conquest and of belonging which this poetry holds cannot be unwound easily the one from the other. It also contains a sense of the shifting emphases of a local discourse in which the idiom of landscape is important – the impression of 'layers of sediment in a long memory'[16] which involves histories of settlement, migration, conquest sometimes existing within the same praise poem, the same 'name'. The presence in Zulu poetic idiom of the phrase 'crossing the fords' and the association of this with courage may be such a 'trace' of memory of the long journey south and the crossing of rivers now known as the Limpopo and the Zambezi. It works as a trope of travel gesturing to past journeys and to both belonging and conquest.

OF POETRY AS RECLAMATION

While one can trace trajectories of oral poetry continuing in the mainstream of South African culture today alongside the written text – for instance the presence of praise poets at the May 1994 inauguration of President Nelson Mandela – it is still important to look at the ways in which the dynamics of oral poetry were engaged with by those who turned to the use of the written tradition.

In the work of two poets who drew on the genre of praise poetry, the relationship between land and naming is central although the sense of land and the naming of the individual is no longer as strongly present as in the oral poetry. But the links are clear: it is the poetry of the peopled land, the territory so intimately brought into the biographies of individuals, clans and peoples through praise poetry which is – at least in part – the material and inspiration on which these poets draw. H. I. E. Dhlomo and B. W. Vilakazi both had Zulu as their mother tongue. The former wrote in English and the latter in Zulu; both were active as writers in the 1930s and into the 1940s. Dhlomo and Vilakazi were aware that they were heirs to a powerful artistic tradition which by the 1930s was, in terms of the dominant culture, denigrated and marginalized. It was useful to those in power only in so far as it validated the burgeoning ideology of racial difference and could be used to define a separate (and ghettoized) 'Zulu culture' with no national voice and no access to national memory. Yet alongside such hegemony very different uses were being made of the cultural forms to hand. Each writer was concerned with loss – of land, nation, history – and each (in somewhat different ways) was intent on a process of reclamation through culture. Dhlomo's long meditational and at moments pastoral poem, 'The Valley of a Thousand Hills', written in 1941, sets out the poverty of the present and the multi-layered nature of its dispossession expressed within the physical boundaries of the once beautiful but now barren and over-populated Valley of a Thousand Hills. He frames this loss within a reference to the power and nobility of the past which is at times a particularly Zulu past and at other moments expands into a wider, inclusive black nationalist gesture which calls on the names of a galaxy of leaders from over the whole of Southern Africa. What points to the continuity with the oral poetry is his

attempts to reclaim through summoning up place upon place in a
kind of litany, an incantation which could be seen as a pastiche –
almost – of the oral style. It is however much more than style that
Dhlomo is after. It is the remapping of the present, the conceptual
reclaiming of land (and a *national* land and space) with which he is
concerned.[17] He begins the poem with a litany of place names of
rivers and locales:

> Mfolozi Black and Mahlabathini!
> Inkandhla, Nongoma and Ulundi!
> Mfolozi White and Umkhambathini!
> Mgungundhlovu and Sibubulundi!

> O brave and magic names of Zululand . . .[18]

Alongside this remapping in which naming – of people and of place
– is central, as is the capturing of their association with the Zulu
kingdom of the last century, Dhlomo writes of loss and dislocation,
of being 'an outcast in my own land'. The poem becomes a counter-
point of possession and dispossession and has rightly been seen as
one of the first significant South African nationalist poems, even
though, as Ari Sitas has pointed out, it failed at its time of publication to find the response it deserved because it was cut off from a
Zulu-speaking audience through language, idiom, and because it
was in the medium of print.[19] The dislocation within Dhlomo's work
is two-fold, not only is he an outcast in his land, he is also an outcast
from the oral poetic tradition with which he is trying so hard to re-
engage. Next to the oral texts his grand gesture of reclamation can
be seen as – at least in part – a failed attempt at uniting two separate
artistic terrains, writing and orality.

B. W. Vilakazi's poetry, written in Zulu, also engages with the
disparity between what is perceived as the impoverished and dispossessed present and the richness of a lost heroic past. In the 1934
collection, *Inkondlo kaZulu* (Anthem of the Zulu),[20] the contrast
between past and present is at times conceived in terms of space: the
present is constricting and confined, the past wide, inhabited with
the free movement of figures such as the Zulu king Shaka who
ranges over named rivers like the Umvoti, the hillocks of Zenzeleni,
and along ridges with sheer cliffs below them. The map of the past
presses heavily on a different present. Vilakazi, who was himself a
fine critic of oral poetry, is able to make use of the naming of places
in a far less stilted way than Dhlomo, perhaps partly because he is

writing in Zulu. Both, however, see mapping through poetry as central. Place names are crucial in this exercise of reclamation and the re-named land becomes once more something to which an outcast can return and belong. In general, the *Inkondlo* collection gives a sense of multitudes of plenty, of throngs of people, of belongings, of moments in the collective past, and a 'thick' sense of place. All this collectively constitutes a form of repossession. Vilakazi also, in a very self-conscious, writerly way, gives an impression of the 'traces' of history contained in the oral praise poems, the sense of a palimpset of times, voices, places. History speaks through the rewriting of the land and its names.

Yet so intense is the effort at reclamation that the bleakness of the present is only hinted at, as a kind of absent presence. The weight of the creative effort is directed at creating a fullness and richness of being which seeps from the past into the present, reshaping it. Place, therefore, and the possession of it through active remembering, forms an important part of the project of reclamation in which he too, like Dhlomo, was engaged. Although Vilakazi was not, as Dhlomo was, a self-consciously South African nationalist writer neither was he a narrow, ethnic chauvinist. He was intent, as Pushkin had been with Russian, to explore new forms such as the confessional and meditational modes. At the same time he mined and reshaped the oral forms, pushing the language into new semantic and expressive areas.

While Vilakazi was conscious of the exiled state of the present, he escaped the double exile of Dhlomo and was able to achieve a far greater resonance of continuity with the oral form in terms of both its aesthetics and its metaphysics. He was able at least to give a sense of crossing cognitive boundaries, rather than writing what could look dangerously like pastiche. Constantly, his poetry gives a sense of names being more than referential. Instead they are closer to a summoning up of an individual, calling them back into being – as do the oral praise poems – and so collapsing linear time and allowing the past to sit within the ambit of the present. Vilakazi is able to do that in a collective sense as well, referring to the ancestors rather than to the names of a particular person. In one of his most telling poems he speaks explicitly of the presentness of the ancestors and combines this with making a powerful political point. It is the poem called 'Because' which is addressed to the (white) dispossessor – 'You':

Because I am always smiling . . .
You think I am like something inanimate
Something that feels no pain . . .
You think that I accept my lot
And have no cause for tears
But what drips from my heart
Falls from the beautiful hands
Of the ancestors who watch over everything. [21]

Vilakazi carries the naming power of praise poetry into new dimensions in the written form, knits past and present in a way that is both new and old and refashions the reader's sense of what constitutes – in both the metaphysical and contingently possible sense – land and being.

OF SONG, SELF AND DISPOSSESSION

A contemporary form of oral poetry also takes the land, and works with it in a way which relates not so much to the 'present-past' of Vilakazi's poetry but to a particular contemporary South African experience – that of the migrant worker. I am referring to the Sotho form known as *difela*. In this body of sung poetry, performed in the shebeens (the bars) in Lesotho and South Africa's border towns, the trope of travel predominates. Place features as a point of departure, of arrival and of return. In a way that is dramatically different from the older praise poetry, and from that of Dhlomo and Vilakazi with their self-conscious projects of reclamation, the singers move, in their verse, across land to which they do not belong and which they do not own. These are the songs of the dispossessed who travel over the land rather than existing within it. The triad of belonging, made up of movement, conquest, and meshed place and being which marked the earlier oral poetry is no longer operative. Yet the songs, as David Coplan has pointed out,[22] are used by performers – who are both men and women – to create an integrated and positive self-concept in the face of displacement, fragmentation and dehumanization. The singers exist *out* of place, yet place, in terms of a fixed point, particularly of return, is central to their songs. In the brief extract quoted below, the restless movement of the older praise poetry is present, but the thick sense of place and the thronging of people (which marks both that and Dhlomo and Vilakazi's written forms) is erased and replaced by a single fixed point representing departure and return. The female singer calls out (in Sotho):

> Give me a ticket gentlemen
> A ticket and my stick
> When I leave home I wander about
> I am going home, home to Lesotho
> When I leave I move fast. [23]

The impulse to define oneself through song and to link this in the modern context to travel and place is evident in the migrants' *difela* songs. Although very different from the older praise poems (and specifically from the more elite Sotho praise poems, *dithoko*) *difela* are also clearly linked to them in their knitting together of the discourse of self and of place. In their life as performance genres the two exist – particularly in Lesotho – side by side, the one seen as a valuable national property, the second new form of the dispossessed, still largely unrecognised by the establishment as an expression of national or transnational identity.

NAMING, LAND AND IDENTITY IN ARANDA POETRY – CROSS RESONANCES?

Naming in the context of Aranda oral poetry, and specifically the relation of naming to land and to belonging, has, I have already suggested, resonances with South African praise poetry (which is also a poetry of naming). In the Ilbalintja song cycle (referred to earlier) the sacred songs of the ceremonial cycle restate the link between clan – in this case the bandicoot clan – and the land. The cycle, which was performed in forty-two parts between 4 May and 29 June 1933, enacted, glorified and relived the deeds of the Northern Aranda ancestors of whom those present were, according to Aranda belief, the latterday reincarnation. Strehlow focuses on male songs and male participation but acknowledges that there are women's songs: he refers to 'the undoubted existence of a body of women's lore kept jealously secret from the men'.[24] The impression given, though, is that in this particular song cycle it was men who participated in the dramatic re-enactment of the clan myths, and who sang the songs relating to particular ancestors and to place. Thus as the headgear which represented the Ilbalintja soak itself was being prepared, the songs for the soak were sung:

White creek sand!
Impenetrable hollow!
White limestone band!
Impenetrable hollow!
Rich yellow soil!
Impenetrable hollow!
Red and orange soil!
Impenetrable hollow![25]

Karora, the ancestor of the bandicoot clan, has his own verses which he is believed to have composed, which describe himself and the place near where he originated; also the trees and rocks growing near his home, the animals nearby; the strangers who visited him; his wanderings and quest for food, and what happened when the time came for him to pass into his deep sleep.[26]

Another ancestor connected with the bandicoot clan myth is Tjenterama. Strehlow describes how his informant, Gura, had as his secret name, his 'great name', Tjenterama. The ancestor, who features towards the end of the bandicoot myth, is speared by Karora's sons in a hunting encounter. After the final catastrophe has overwhelmed them in the form of a great flood of honeysuckle nectar which sweeps over the plains and forces them back to drown in the Ilbalintja soak, Tjenterama becomes their ceremonial chief. In the performance of the song cycle, Tjenterama's special verses, his names, would be sung as the actor representing him was decorated. The verses of Tjenterama were also, though, the private property of (Strehlow's informant) Gura, and they are as follows:

He is frisking about at the back of his nest
In the thick arabera grass.
'Are you a bandicoot?
Are you one indeed?'
'I Tjenterama have now grown lame
Yes lame and the worawora flowers are clinging to me.
Nodding sleepily he keeps on listening
Fast asleep he is resting without a stir'.[27]

The naming that is in operation here may not work in precisely the same way as in praise poetry, yet there are similarities. There is – even in the brief examples given here – a sense of the operation of a particular combination of poetry and value; as in the praise poetry, the categories of land, body and being are cut across and restated.

126

Time is collapsed, identities merged. At one moment in the cycle, as the actors are being decorated, two couplets of song are heard time and again. The first is:

> The whirlwind is encircling his waist;
> Stripes fall down his back from his shoulders
> and the whirlwind is encircling his waist.

and the second:

> Are you a bandicoot?
> Are you a bandicoot indeed?[28]

Both these verses and their performance in the context of the enactment of the Ilbalintja clan song cycle demonstrate the breaking down of the categories of land, body and being. The Nguni and Sotho praise poetry quoted earlier also operates in this way in its naming of people in terms of land, flora and fauna. Thus rocks, ridges, valleys, tall grass, the sky, the moon, become part of the individual's being and sense of self; here, too, there is a linking of categories. In both cases, the ancestors are present through their names.

In a situation such as this, where the poetic tradition of each region has an aesthetic and a metaphysic of naming which marks it off from the incoming settler tradition – diverse as the latter may be in some aspects – questions of continuity are bound to be both fraught and interesting. I have outlined some directions in which the South African making of poetry has moved, but what of continuities in Aboriginal poetry, of which the Aranda poetry forms a part? What kind of trajectories and connections are being worked through as specific cultural forms are produced in response to the pressures of Australian history and the particularly Australian experience of colonialism and colonizing?

Adam Shoemaker has pointed out that a preoccupation with the themes of injustice and an emphasis on the concept of a venerable, autonomous Aboriginal history is present in almost all Black Australian literature, regardless of the genre of expression. He mentions that the verse of Oodgeroo Noonucal and Jack Davis hold themes and concerns and a world view that are undoubtedly 'black Australian, but their poetic technique is not'.[29] Here Noonucal and Davis would seem to be unlike Dhlomo and Vilakazi who try to recreate in some way the oral form (and what embodies it). Shoemaker is also wary of the white poet Les Murray's attempts at syncretic convergence of cultures in a poem such as 'Thinking about

Aboriginal land rights I visit the land I will never inherit'. He sees as most connected, and simultaneously most innovative, the poetry of a writer such as Aileen Corpus who uses poetry which has an inbuilt, phonic imperative quite unlike anything White Australian poets have produced. He refers to her poem, 'blkfern jungle' for instance.[30]

Shoemaker also mentions Tjapangati and Lionel Fogarty as poets attempting to work in this oral imperative. Neither seem to incorporate what I have called an aesthetics and metaphysics of naming – the poetry of Mudroroo Narogin may come closer to that[31] – yet both, with Narogin, seem to point in important ways to the creation of a cross-border Australian aesthetic which claims orality, consigning it not to an unreachable past but to a more inclusive present. This kind of move to inclusivity may go some way to redefining 'literature' and the 'text' in the Australian context, as it should in the South African setting of 'literature' as well. If we are really to understand the ways in which land and identity have operated as sites of contestation and creativity in both these Southern spaces, the cross-border categories of the poetry discussed above must be recognized. They press on the present unsatisfactory boundaries of the post-colonial text just as the ancestors are seen to press on the present in both Nguni and Sotho praise poetry and Aranda song-cycle.

NOTES

1 My thanks to William Beinart, Kate Darian-Smith and Paul Gready for their comments on drafts. Isabel Hofmeyr, 'We Spend Our Years as a Tale that is Told': Oral Historical Narrative in a South African Chiefdom, Johannesburg, Witwatersrand University Press, 1993; Elizabeth Tonkin, Narrating our Pasts: The Social Construction of Oral History, Cambridge, Cambridge University Press, 1992.

2 As in B. Ashcroft, G. Griffiths and H. Tiffen The Empire Writes Back: Theory and Practice in Post-colonial Literatures, London and New York, Routledge, 1989.

3 A phrase used by C. D. Rowley in The Destruction of Aboriginal Society, Sydney, Penguin Australia, (1st edn, 1972), 1986, p. 206. Rowley is quoting T. G. H. Strehlow but does not give a precise source reference.

4 See T. G. H. Strehlow, Songs of Central Australia, Sydney, Angus & Robertson, 1971.

5 Strehlow, Songs, p. 371.

6 Strehlow, Songs, pp. 120–4.

7 Strehlow, Songs, p. 126.

8 See Jeff Opland, Xhosa Oral Poetry: Aspects of a Black South African Tradition, Cambridge, Cambridge University Press, 1983; Leroy Vail and Landeg

White, *Power and the Praise Poem: Southern African Voices in History*, London, James Currey, 1991; Jeff Opland and Peter Mtuze (eds), *Izwi Labantu* [The Word of the People], Oxford, Oxford University Press, 1994; Liz Gunner and Mafika Gwala (trans. and eds) *Musho! Zulu Popular Praises*, Michigan, Michigan State University Press, 1991, Johannesburg, Witwatersrand University Press, 1994.

9   Ngqengele Buthelezi in Gunner and Gwala, *Praises*, p. 113.

10 Shaka's praise poem by Gwebisa, from E. W. Grant, 'The izibongo of the Zulu Chiefs', *Bantu Studies*, 3, 1927–29, pp. 201–44, quoted in Opland (ed.), *Words that Circle Words: a Choice of South African Oral Poetry*, Johannesburg, Ad Donker, 1992, p. 186.

11 Quoted in Opland, *Words*, pp. 189–90.

12 This idea is discussed extensively in J. M. Coetzee, *White Writing: The Culture of Letters in South Africa*, Massachusetts, Yale University Press, 1989.

13 From the manuscript referred to as Moletsane M3 quoted in D. P. Kunene, *Heroic Poetry of the Basotho*, Oxford, Clarendon Press, 1974.

14 Coetzee, *White Writing*.

15 Opland, *Words*.

16 A phrase used by Cohen and Odhiambo in their discussion of Luo landscape and local discourse in *Siaya: The Historical Anthropology of an African Landscape*, 1989, quoted by Megan Vaughan in 'Colonial Discourse Theory and African History or has Postmodernism passed us by?', African History Seminar paper, School of Oriental and African Studies, 10 February 1993.

17 For a fuller discussion of Dhlomo's nationalist aspirations in this poem see Ari Sitas, 'Traditions of Poetry in Natal' in L. Gunner (ed.), *Politics and Performance: Theatre, Poetry and Song in Southern Africa*, Johannesburg, Witwatersrand University Press, 1994, pp. 139–61.

18 H. I. E. Dhlomo, *Collected Works of H. I. E. Dhlomo*, T. Couzens and N. Visser (eds) Johannesburg, Ravan Press, 1987, p. 293.

19 Sitas, 'Traditions of Poetry', pp. 140–2.

20 B. W. Vilakazi, *Inkondlo kaZulu*, Johannesburg, Witwatersrand University Pres, 1934. My translations.

21 Vilakazi, *Inkondlo*, p. 37.

22 David Coplan, 'Eloquent Knowledge: Lesotho Migrants' Songs and the Anthropology of Experience', *American Ethnologist*, 14, March 1987, p. 429.

23 Coplan, 'Eloquent Knowledge', p. 428.

24 Strehlow, *Songs*, p. 649.

25 Strehlow, *Songs*, p. 353.

26 Strehlow, *Songs*, p. 121.

27 Strehlow, *Songs*, p. 356.

28 Strehlow, *Songs*, p. 356.

29 A. Shoemaker, *Black Words, White Page: Aboriginal Literature 1929–1988*, St. Lucia, University of Queensland Press, 1989, p. 128.

30 Shoemaker, *Black Words*, p. 192.

31 See Colin Johnson (Mudrooroo Narogin), *Dalwurra: The Black Bittern, a Poem Cycle*, Veronica Brady and Susan Miller (eds), Perth, Centre for

Studies in West Australian Literature, University of Western Australia, 1988.

BIBLIOGRAPHY

Arbousset, T., *Relation d'un voyage d'exploration au nord-est de la colonie de cap de Bonne Esperance*, Paris, Arthus Bertrand, 1842; trans. as *Narrative of an Exploratory Tour to the North-East of the Cape of Good Hope*, Cape Town, Robertson & Solomon, 1846, repr. Cape Town, Struik, 1968.

Attwell, D., *The Transculturation of English: The Exemplary Case of the Rev. Tiyo Soga, African Nationalist*, Pietermaritzburg, University of Natal Occasional Papers in English Studies no. 1, 1995.

Cope, Trevor (ed.) *Izibongo: Zulu Praise Poems*, Oxford, Clarendon Press, 1968.

Coplan, D., *In the Time of Cannibals: The World Music of South Africa's Basotho Migrants*, Chicago and London, University of Chicago Press, 1995.

Dhlomo, H. I. E., *Collected Works of H. I. E. Dhlomo*, T. Couzens and N. Visser (eds) Johannesburg, Ravan Press, 1987.

Hofmeyr, I., *'We Spend our Years as a Tale that is Told': Oral Historical Narrative in a South African Chiefdom*, Johannesburg, Witwatersrand University Press; Portsmouth, New Haven, Heinemann, 1993.

Johnson, Colin (Mudrooroo Narogin), *Dalwurra: The Black Bittern, a Poem Cycle*, Perth, Centre for Studies in Australian Literature, University of Western Australia, 1988.

Kaschula, R., 'Imbongi in Profile', *English in Africa*, 20 Jan. 1993. pp. 65–76.

Opland, J., *Xhosa Oral Poetry: Aspects of a Black South African Tradition*, Johannesburg, Ravan Press; London, Cambridge University Press, 1983.

—— (ed.) *Words that Circle Words: A Choice of South African Oral Poetry*, Johannesburg, Ad Donker, 1992.

Rowley, C. D., *The Destruction of Aboriginal Society*, Sydney, Angus & Robertson, (1st edn, 1972), 1986.

Strehlow, T. G. H., *Songs of Central Australia*, Sydney, Angus & Robertson, 1971.

Vilakazi, B. W., *Inkondlo kaZulu*, Johannesburg, Witwatersrand University Press, 1934.

8

IMAGINATION, MADNESS AND NATION IN AUSTRALIAN BUSH MYTHOLOGY

Sue Rowley

Recent theories of nationalism and national culture and identity have emphasised the active role of the imagination in the formation of nations. Benedict Anderson's most influential and persuasive argument for theorizing nations as 'imagined communities' exemplifies a recurrent theme in writing on nation formation.[1] Anderson cites Ernest Gellner's frequently quoted observation that nationalism '*invents* nations where they do not exist'.[2] The centrality of the imagination is echoed in the titles of recent publications on the formation of Australia as a nation: *Inventing Australia, Creating a Nation, Illusions of Identity*, and *National Fictions* are examples of well-known texts across a range of disciplines.[3] Significantly, though the titles emphasize imagination or creativity in 'inventing' nations, these pivotal concepts are treated cursorily as though the act and capacity for imagination, invention, illusion and creativity were self-evident.

But the meaning of 'imagination' is not self-evident, and nor is there necessarily tacit agreement about how the concept is to be employed. Theories of nationalism and national culture appear unresolved on the issue of imagination, implicitly resting on a modernist construct of creativity to suggest that nations are invented, fabricated or manufactured. 'There is no "real" Australia waiting to be uncovered,' writes Richard White. 'A national identity is an invention. There is no point asking whether one version of this essential Australia is truer than another because they are all intellectual constructs, neat, tidy, comprehensible – and necessarily false.'[4] The wariness and ambivalence that frequently characterizes critical analyses of nationalism derives from the perceived likelihood that these inventions might be mistaken for reality, with very real consequences.

The critical focus of contemporary theories of nationalism is, therefore, on the cultural process of invention. At this point, writers are likely to circumvent the vexed issues of authorship, originality and imagination which have been subject to sustained post-modernist critique. Nations are understood, not as the original inventions of those who penned the stories and painted the pictures which articulate the cultural imagination, but as the products of culture. Graeme Turner, for example, writes of 'the forms and meanings constructed through Australian storytellers'. 'As the culture produces its texts,' he states, 'it prefers certain meanings, thematic structures and formal strategies.'[5] In Anderson's writing, agency is vested in the print media: the 'overwhelming and bewildering concatenation of events', he writes in reference to the French Revolution, were 'shaped by millions of printed words into a "concept" on the printed page, and, in due course, into a model'.[6]

Ironically, late nineteenth century writers and artists whose work articulated an emerging national consciousness in Australia also saw themselves as a conduit for cultural experience and were disturbed by the notion of imagination when it intruded in the process of nation formation. Rather than emphasising the act of invention, they sought to deny the fictionality of representations in order that the 'imagined community' they were engaged in constructing could be construed as real.

Theories of imagination, according to Paul Ricoeur, may be arranged along two intersecting axes: 'on the side of the object, the axis of presence and absence; on the side of the subject, the axis of fascinated or critical consciousness'.[7] At one pole of the first axis, Ricoeur places reproductive (or representational) imagination in which 'the image relates to a perception of which it is merely a trace, in the sense of a weakened impression'. At the other extreme of the same axis he places productive (or creative) imagination in which 'the image is essentially construed in function of absence, of what is other than present'. Contemporary post-modern cultural theorists are likely to perceive imagination as a representational process, but their insistence on the fabrication of nations permits a degree of slippage in the location of imagination along this axis, without going so far as to impute authorship to specific writers, intellectuals or artists to whom a more passive role is generally ascribed.

The ambivalence of writers and artists of the late nineteenth century to imagination arose from their perception of the creative capacity to generate imaginary worlds – imagination could intrude a disruptive, transgressive element into the representation of the emerging nation. Jochen Schulte-Sasse notes that radical social and material changes occasioned by modernization 'profoundly changed the conception of the imagination and, presumably, the imagination itself'.[8] From the eighteenth century, he observes, two reactions were common. The first was a fear of the disruptive potential of the imagination, leading to the demand that it be 'tamed' by reason. The second reaction was a concern that imagination, alternatively seen as a mode of critical resistance to modernity and a counterforce to rationality, might be unable to withstand the process of modernization. The resolution of this ambiguity lay in the separation of art from everyday life and the exclusion of the imagination from discourses that most directly legitimated the existing social order. Contained within the field of art, the 'productive' imagination could be given free reign. But 'untamed fancy' should be held in tight check. It goes without saying that nation formation was a central area of human activity into which this 'productive' imagination must not intrude, especially in the Australian literature and paintings of the 1890s which embraced the need to imaginatively project Australia's nationhood as an achievable goal for that decade. Consequently the act of imagination through which the nation was constituted was necessarily suppressed. Thus, imaginative literary and visual works of art were charged with forging an imagined national community in a process that implicitly denied the fictionality of either the representations or the nation.

In spite of differences in the ideological projects of creators and critics of nationalism, an unresolved distrust and tension between imagination and nation is a recurring theme in writing about national cultures. This tension derives from the perceived human capacity to confuse image with its real-world referent. This is Ricoeur's second axis, which intersects with the first 'according to whether the subject of imagination is capable or not of assuming a critical consciousness of the difference between the real and the imaginary'. At one end of this axis, he places non-critical consciousness in which the image is confused with, or mistaken for, the real. At the other end, where 'the critical distance is fully conscious of itself, imagination is the very instrument of the critique of reality'.[9] From Ricoeur's analysis, these variations in the ways in which the concept of imagination has been theorized appear considerable and perhaps irreconcilable. 'What after all,' Ricoeur asks, 'could be in common between the state of confusion which characterises that consciousness which unknown to itself takes for real that which for another consciousness is not real, and the act of distinction which, highly self-conscious, enables consciousness to posit something at a distance from the real and thus produce the alterity at the very heart of existence?'[10]

Many late nineteenth-century writers and artists understood their images of 'Australia' to be representations drawn from late colonial life rather than fabrications. In characterizing Australian nationhood on the basis of colonial experience, they contested and revised a legacy of European invention that pre-dated European occupancy of the continent by centuries. The European imaginative and intellectual investment in the idea of a southern continent is expressed in the notion of the 'Antipodes'. Dating from colonization, the European antipodean fantasy, based on curiosity, desire, dread and anticipation, was counterbalanced by a colonial and emerging national Australian (albeit non-Aboriginal) representation of experience in a 'new country'. As images of *terra australis incognito* were re-formed on the basis of experience, colonial perceptions, expectations and aspirations shifted, frequently (as Ross Gibson has argued[11]) in order to accommodate disappointment and disillusionment.

These re-formed images of the new country grew out of the actual experience of journeys to and within Australia and inevitably the fact of journeying has played a pivotal part in the imaginative process of representation. 'The Australian story' is one of travellers, most of them men: of transportees, explorers, immigrants, pioneers, drovers, shearers, gold-seekers, bushrangers and swagmen. However, the centrality of the journey theme as a metaphoric and structural device in national imagery and narrative is not purely a function of historical mobility. Journeying infuses the representation of explorers, pioneers and bushmen with the potency of the quest, the pilgrimage and the passage of life itself. The journey is integrally bound to narratives of transformation of the masculine subject. The conventional gender-specificity of the journey theme has been invested in Australian myths of nation – not only in content but at the deeper level of narrative structure and organization of meaning. To use Hayden White's formulation, the journey functions as a poetic prefiguration of both the plot structure of the narrative and the explanation of its meaning and significance.[12]

It is significant, therefore, that the journey motif is also employed as a structural device and metaphor in critical studies of nationalism and national identity. For example, in his use of the notion of the pilgrimage, Anderson's study of nationalism is prefigured by this most deep-rooted poetic device. Along the 'upward-spiralling road', he says, the functionary 'encounters as eager fellow-pilgrims his functionary colleagues, from places and families he has scarcely heard of'. In spite of the diversity of their backgrounds, their common destination, which is also the ceiling to their careers, creates 'a consciousness of connectedness'. In his use of the journey motif, however, Anderson naturalizes elements which he might otherwise have questioned. Assuming women's national conscious-ness to have been formed in the same manner as men's, he accounts for its formation with reference to experiences which were specific to men, or arguably had different consequences for women's sense of identity. In choosing the pilgrimage as a structuring device, Anderson implicitly frames his study of national consciousness in terms that are both gender-specific and gender-blind.

SPATIAL PERCEPTION IN JOURNEYS OF NATION

Where the journey functions as the central imaginative device for nation formation, the representation of national space is likely to be determined by this device. Australian bush mythology is shaped by the journeying of bushmen: by their departures, adventures and homecomings. The space of the bush and home is represented from the perspective of the journeying bushman. Implicitly, other charact-ers – themselves understood partially by 'a visitor' whose difference from them is a precondition of the narration – would perceive the space they inhabit differently.

Henry Lawson writes of the bush in terms of 'its everlasting, maddening sameness of the stunted trees':

> Bush all round – bush with no horizon, for the country is flat. No ranges in the distance. The bush consists of stunted, rotten native apple trees. No undergrowth. Nothing to relieve the eye save the darker green of a few sheoaks which are sighing above the narrow, almost waterless creek.[13]

But his account of the Drover's Wife's Sunday afternoon walk with her children along the bush-track permits a complex discussion of perception as determined by experience of bush life. For the Drover's Wife, the pleasure in and commitment to this ritual walk are acknowledged. However, its meaning for her, and for her children, is undercut by the suggestion that strangers would not understand it because, for them, '[t]here is nothing to see, however, and not a soul to meet'.

In both 'The Drover's Wife' and the later story, ' "Water Them Geraniums" ', the reader is persuaded to experience the bush as a stranger might, as one who 'might travel for miles without seeming to have moved':

> You might walk for twenty miles along this track without being able to fix a point in your mind, unless you are a bushman.[14]

The monotony 'makes a man long to break away and travel as far as trains can go, and sail as far as ships can sail – and further'. The Drover's Wife and the stranger, it is implied, would perceive and respond to both the bush and the activities of its inhabitants in different ways. In ' "Water Them Geraniums" ', Lawson introduces a third point of view – that of a Bushman who 'soon picks out differences among the trees, half unconsciously as it were, and so finds his way about'.[15] Unlike the stranger who is unable to discern differences, the bushman traverses the bush by blazing a track or *fixing a point* in his mind. The Drover's Wife is neither bushman nor stranger. She belongs here in the bush, and 'is used to the loneliness of it' and 'would feel strange away from it'. In fact, she represents a *fixed point* in the bush, as far as the bushman/narrator is concerned.

As readers, we see the bush almost invariably through the eyes of an outsider, at times a stranger, at times a bushman. Sometimes the bush is seen from the track to form a backdrop which appears static, shallow and undifferentiated. At other times, the bush may seem impenetrable or empty. Aspects of the bush world may be obscured from view, or patterns of meaning may be implied that would not be shared by the inhabitants of this space. Understood in this way, a lack of discernible differences and sense of depth of the bush may be a consequence of the point of observation and we may be unaware that the bush is seen from vantage points which permit only fragmented and incomplete vision.

Spatial descriptions reflect the perceptions, experience and forebodings of the male narrator. They articulate his dread of living in the bush. In this sense, it is the narrator who emerges as the protagonist and bush stories are episodes in his journey. For the narrator, the bush and its inhabitants are closely interconnected. As characters who are immobilized in relation to plot – whom Jurij Lotman describes as 'functions of plot-space'[16] – bushwomen and sedentary bushmen appear mad, queer or eccentric. To the extent that the narrators identify with these characters, they realize that they too could become 'bush-like'. The narrator may not recognize the effect of his prolonged stay in the bush until later. 'It's only afterwards, and looking back, that you see how queer you got,' says Joe Wilson.[17] Thus, incessant, endless journeying is motivated not only by the imperatives of nation formation, but also by the need to avoid immersion in the life of the bush. The narrator recognizes that if he were to dwell there, he too would be assimilated into the bush, and therefore become deranged relative to the standards of normality and sanity which he represents as 'natural'.

A similar distinction between those who travel and those who do not is structured into Benedict Anderson's theoretical framework for the formation of national consciousness, but the implications of this definitive difference are not considered. Amongst those who do not embark on career 'pilgrimages', Anderson argues, national consciousness is formed through reading print media. The distribution and the content of vernacular colonial print media elicits an identification with other readers and this identification forms the basis of an imagined community. The question arises: what is the relationship between those who have embarked on a pilgrimage and those who in effect 'read themselves into national consciousness'? The formation of a national consciousness is based not only on identification amongst 'fellow-pilgrims' from diverse backgrounds, but also on differentiation from those who are not 'travelling'.

The spatial metaphor of the journey in narratives of nation formation distinguishes between points of departure and return, and the locations of the 'action', through which Anderson's spiralling road passes. Similarly, Australian bush mythology represents national landscapes through a specific and limited experience of the land. Since it is inherent in the logic of the journey motif that the transformative experiences of the mobile protagonist determines the treatment of both the terrain of the journey and its inhabitants, it follows that the representation of national place and character is dependent on the perception of the traveller, which is predicated on mobility, transience and difference.

BUSH-INDUCED MADNESS

The representation of certain kinds of experience as formative of the emerging nation rested on the plausible identification of reader and author with a narrator whose journeying anchored the narrative to the real world inhabited by authors and readers. Significantly, these journeys permitted the imaginative negotiation not only of the distance between the city and the bush, but also metaphorically between the present and the past. The eccentricity or madness of bush characters is understood by the narrator in terms of his perception of the bush as a 'maddening place'. The question of perception remains problematic as the narrator defines both the place and characters who inhabit it in terms of his own experience of mobility and nomadicism. Nevertheless, the theory of bush-induced madness advanced in Lawson's writing is significant for the light it throws on the notion of imagination that underpins the imaginative formation of nationhood.

In bush mythology, the breaking of the mind can serve to mute unendurable grief and pain forged in the bush. Lawson's bushmen and women attempt to reconstruct their world as a more manageable but more constricted mental space in which the experience of actual loss is balanced by imagined restitution. The bush, to which the initial loss is attributed, permits this contracting of mental space. Literally, isolation makes outside disruption unlikely and sheer physical labour exhausts body and mind. More significantly, the bush itself is depicted as a constricted space of stultifying sameness which dulls the mind to other possible worlds.

Some of Lawson's characters are able to form other worlds in the imagination and to convince themselves sufficiently of their reality to almost inhabit them.[18] For others, such as Mrs Spicer in ' "Water Them Geraniums" ', the more austere but arguably saner approach is the numbing of the mind against the intrusive events of the wider world, in order to anaesthetize the heart against its unendurable pain. Though Mrs Spicer does not seek to create and dwell within imaginary worlds, she has cut herself adrift of the world beyond the confines of the present time and her immediate surrounds. She rests precariously on the edge of sanity. Of the rest of the world we are told that she had 'lost all her curiosity':

> But sometimes when she got outside her everyday life on this selection she spoke in a sort of − in a sort of lost groping-in-the-dark kind of voice.[19]

This loss of contact with events outside her selection is signified by the 'groping voice' she adopts when she tries to put into words her perceptions, memories and links with the world beyond. Her managing of grief and hardship has depended on her ability to contract the mental space within which she imagines and remembers her life, and to anaesthetize her mind against enduring pain.

Mrs Spicer's precarious mental stability is thrown off balance when she revives her connections with this world beyond her immediate struggle, through recollection of her past, or interaction with the bush community. Though she describes herself as 'past carin' ', her present friendship with Mary and Joe Wilson are ill-afforded reminders of loss. The value she places on hospitality, the pleasure of the company of the Wilsons, the benefits the children derive from their acquaintance, the material help Joe provides, and her protective concern for Mary draw Mrs Spicer into the world they represent. But, she says, 'the visits doesn't do me any good. I git the dismals afterwards.' Ill and dying, Mrs Spicer's last instructions to Annie are to milk the cows, to feed the pigs and calves, not go to Mary Wilson for help, and to water the geraniums. Much has been said about the injunction to 'water them geraniums', but why should Annie not go for Mary Wilson? Mrs Spicer dies because she cannot grow 'past carin' ' as long as she must still respond to the events of the world over which she has no control, a world that Mary Wilson represents.

The poignancy of Lawson's studies of madness lies in the inability of the characters in fact to sever links with the social world and inhabit the asylums they have created.[20] Lawson emphasizes the role of imagination in generating madness: 'going ratty' describes the queerness of thought and deed that is the consequence of loneliness 'provided you have any imagination at all'. Mrs Spicer maintains an equilibrium by denying mental activities − by neither remembering nor imagining another life. Within the circumscribed world of the farm, she is alert, sensitive to absurdity, eloquent, and innovative in times of great hardship. It is because she is neither stupid nor lacking in imagination that the defences she has erected against the despair of her life are so vulnerable. Joe Wilson's first comment about Mrs Spicer is that

I supposed the reason why she hadn't gone mad through hardship and loneliness was that she hadn't either the brains or the memory to go farther than she could see through the trunks of the apple trees.[21]

'Going ratty' depends on the imaginative capacity of the mind. If the mind will not break, then the only possible way out of the unbearable pain of living is to grow 'past carin' '.

As far as narratives of nation formation are concerned, it could be argued that these mad characters play only a marginal role in the national cast of characters and that their stories are located similarly on the margins of the national mythology. However the possibility that such immobilized characters, whether male or female, may become 'adapted' to the bush in such a manner that others perceive them to be mad, suggests an anxiety is attached to journeying that colours the apparently buoyant journeys of nation formation. Adaptation to the bush also is perceived as absorption by the bush. While the journey represents a quest to claim and domesticate the land as the national territory, inhabiting the untamed land threatens madness and death. The mobility of bushmen is a product not only of quest but of anxiety.

The possibility of the narrator succumbing to madness is implicitly dependent on two factors: the first is the prolonged dwelling in the bush, and the second is the mental faculty through which the response to this experience is formed. Implicitly the narrator does not lack either the brains or the memory that are preconditions for madness, since these are employed in the act of narration itself. Two observations follow from this recognition of the vulnerability of the narrator to bush madness. The first is that his implied mobility, and his incessant travelling, underwrites the reliability of his observation and narration. The narrator is necessarily familiar with, but not immersed in, bush life. The realist attitude of 'objectivity' and 'reliability' in the account of bush life is a function of the transience of the narrator's encounter with the bush.

The second implication of the susceptibility of the narrator to bush-induced madness relates to an attitude to imagination on the part of not only the narrator, but also, implicitly, the writer. This attitude is one of wariness. The imagination, without which no tale can be told, has the capacity to derange the narrative, and to undermine its veracity. The literary responses to this problem are not unlike the fictive responses of bush inhabitants to their experience of the bush. A primary response is to clearly delineate the products of 'imagination' from the representation of the 'real' world, to encircle the imagination within boundaries which indicate that this imaginary 'space' is not that of the real world. Richard Kearney alludes to this strategy when he comments that the nineteenth-century imagination 'felt more and more compelled to recoil into a magical world of its own making'.[22] Such a world appears as the product of the imagination, but it is not represented as holding up a mirror to the real world. Just as bush characters cannot inhabit delusive worlds without losing their footing in the real world, readers are warned against imaginatively 'inhabiting' these fantasies. The reader, like the narrator, should imaginatively travel through fictional worlds.

The literary and visual exploration of madness and fantasy emerges out of an exploration of the mind's construction of an image of that which does not exist. By contrast, the representations of the emerging nation are assumed to depict aspects of history and culture which impart a distinctive national character and provide a basis for national identity and coherence. The images are assumed to reproduce that which does exist, or has existed, in the 'real' world.

Henry Lawson, Joseph Furphy, Steele Rudd and Frederick McCubbin – writers and a painter who consciously articulated a concept of 'Australia' and sought to contribute to its cultural formation – all display a direct interest in the 'productive' imagination, typically in its negative association with madness, hallucination and childishness, and generally on the margins of what might be called the nationalist centres of their work. In their treatment of fantasy, madness, enchantment and imagination, Lawson and McCubbin, in particular, appear to have understood the imagination as having a capacity to generate imaginary worlds which could be delightful or frightening. But they saw danger in the inability to distinguish these worlds from the 'real' world which they themselves inhabited. In the formal and stylistic sense, these artists appear resistant to the use of imagination as an instrument of their own practice, since such a use of imagination may appear to undermine the 'truth claims' made in the work. The association of madness and imagination suggests a degree of distrust of imagination which has implications for both their writing and the imagined national community.

NATION, MODERNITY AND IMAGINATION

The necessity of this imaginative restraint – the 'veto' of the imagination, in Luiz Costa Lima's terms – was urged in the aesthetic debates of the 1890s published in the *Bulletin*. As Douglas Jarvis has argued, the *Bulletin*'s 'rejection of aestheticism, classicism and romantic idealisation as literary or artistic creeds is based largely on moral and ideological grounds'.[23] The aesthetic vogue of the 1880s, which found expression in popular fashion and taste as well as literary and artistic forms, was denounced as reflecting aristocratic and imperialist values, to the neglect of contemporary social conditions. Literary realism, Jarvis argues, was favoured on moral utilitarian and nationalist grounds, and seen as reflecting radical, egalitarian and nationalistic ideas. Lawson's writing was valued for its apparent 'artlessness', his detailed, objective style was seen to report 'truthfully' that which he observed, and his capacity for observation was derived from the depth of his experience of the bush. Nevertheless, Lawson made use of an obtrusive authorial presence to give the impression of 'a mature man remembering, retelling a past incident or a yarn heard in the past'.[24]

The interplay of past, present and future was effected by the use of the narrator as a character who remembers the past. In this way, the bush story takes place in the 'past' of the narrator, who implicitly is speaking in the 'present' of the reader, thus establishing a national past which appears to be continuous with the present. The imagined formation of the nation is inscribed as a remembered past. The constricted space of imagination facilitates partial recall of a past in which painful and de-stabilizing experiences are repressed. Both memory and imagination are subject to wariness and constraint as they serve the imaginative formation of the nation. Just as bush mythology is able to provide a 'usable' past, based on the selection of some historical elements and the erasure of others, so the role of the narrator as a perceiving, remembering subject of his stories ensures that the perception of the imagined past is determined by the present constraints on imagination.

NOTES

1 Benedict Anderson, *Imagined Communities: Reflections on the Origin and Spread of Nationalism*, London, Verso, 1986.
2 Ernest Gellner, *Thought and Change*, London, Weidenfeld & Nicholson, 1964, p. 196, cited in Anderson, *Imagined Communities*, p. 15 (Anderson's emphasis).
3 Richard White, *Inventing Australia: Images and Identity 1688–1980*, Sydney, Allen & Unwin, 1981; Patricia Grimshaw et al. (eds), *Creating a Nation 1788–1990*, Melbourne, McPhee Gribble, 1994; Anne-Marie Willis, *Illusions of Identity: The Art of Nation*, Sydney, Hale & Iremonger, 1993; Graeme Turner, *National Fictions: Literature, Film and the Construction of Australian Narrative*, Sydney, Allen & Unwin, 1986.
4 White, *Inventing Australia*, p. viii.
5 Turner, *National Fictions*, p. 1.

6 Anderson, *Imagined Communities*, pp. 77–8.
7 Paul Ricoeur, 'L'Imagination dans le discours et dans l'action', cited in Richard Kearney, *The Wake of Imagination: Ideas of Creativity in Western Culture*, London, Hutchinson, 1988, p. 400.
8 Jochen Schulte-Sasse, 'Afterword: Can the imagination be mimetic under conditions of modernity?', in Luiz Costa Lima, *Control of the Imaginary – Reason and Imagination in Modern Times* (trans. Ronald W. Sousa), *Theory and History of Literature*, vol. 50, Minneapolis, University of Minnesota Press, 1988, p. 203.
9 Ricoeur, 'L'Imagination', p. 400.
10 Ricoeur, 'L'Imagination', p. 400.
11 Ross Gibson, *The Diminishing Paradise: Changing Literary Perceptions of Australia*, Sydney, Sirius, 1984.
12 Hayden White, *Tropics of Discourse – Essays in Cultural Criticism*, Baltimore and London, The John Hopkins University Press, 1987, p. 128.
13 Henry Lawson, 'The Drover's Wife', *A Camp-Fire Yarn*, Sydney, Lansdowne, 1988, p. 238.
14 Lawson, 'Drover's Wife', p. 238.
15 Henry Lawson, ' "Water Them Geraniums" ', in Lawson, *Camp-Fire Yarn*, p. 720.
16 Jurij Lotman, 'The Origin of Plot in the Light of Typology', *Poetics Today*, vol. 1, no. 1–2, 1979, p. 168.
17 Lawson, ' "Water Them Geraniums" ', p. 724.
18 For instance, Ratty Howlett in Lawson's 'No Place for a Woman' and Maggie Head in Lawson's 'The Babies in the Bush'.
19 Lawson, ' "Water Them Geraniums" ', p. 727.
20 The exception – 'The Bush Undertaker' – is not a sad or pathetic story. Here the congruence of the bush and the imaginative world is most readily perceived. The old man has adapted his mental space to that of the bush, undisturbed by the intrusion of a discerning narrator, and nature's cyclical pattern of life and death subsumes the linear plot of civilized life.
21 Lawson, ' "Water Them Geraniums" ', p. 722.
22 Kearney, *The Wake of Imagination*, p. 186.
23 Douglas Jarvis 'The Development of an Egalitarian Poetics in the *Bulletin*, 1880-1890', *Australian Literary Studies*, vol. 10, no. 1, May 1981, p. 27.
24 Jarvis, 'Egalitarian Poetics', p. 60.

BIBLIOGRAPHY

Anderson, B., *Imagined Communities: Reflections on the Origin and Spread of Nationalism*, London, Verso, 1986.
Costa Lima, L., *Control of the Imaginary – Reason and Imagination in Modern Times* (trans. R. W. Sousa), *Theory and History of Literature*, vol. 50, Minneapolis, University of Minnesota Press, 1988.
Gibson, R., *The Diminishing Paradise: Changing Literary Perceptions of Australia*, Sydney, Sirius, 1984.

Grimshaw, P., et al. (eds), *Creating a Nation 1788–1990*, Melbourne, McPhee Gribble, 1994.

Kearney, R., *The Wake of Imagination: Ideas of Creativity in Western Culture*, London, Hutchinson, 1988.

Lawson, H., *A Camp-Fire Yarn*, Sydney, Lansdowne, 1988.

Turner, G., *National Fictions: Literature, Film and the Construction of Australian Narrative*, Sydney, Allen & Unwin, 1986.

White, H., *Tropics of Discourse – Essays in Cultural Criticism*, Baltimore and London, The John Hopkins University Press, 1987.

White, R., *Inventing Australia: Images and Identity 1688–1980*, Sydney, Allen & Unwin, 1981.

Willis, A-M., *Illusions of Identity: The Art of Nation*, Sydney, Hale & Iremonger, 1993.

9

INSCRIBING IDENTITY ON THE LANDSCAPE
National symbols in South Africa

Nhlanhla Maake

INTRODUCTION

One of the oldest national anthems in the world, 'God Save the Queen', which was adopted in 1825, was sung in all parts of the British Empire as the national anthem. As the winds of change began to blow in Africa, new flags were hoisted, and new anthems were adopted and sung in the place of the song of Empire. Place names also changed from the colonial to post-colonial ones. These new names and flags were to be understood as symbols which expressed new aspirations, and the overthrowing of the *ancien régime*.

National anthems, flags, and place names are the most important genres, if not monuments, which bear outward testimony of what a society holds dear in a given country. This is where the signifier is transformed into myth, where it 'points out and it notifies, it makes us understand something and it imposes it on us' as Barthes would put it.[1]

Flags and national anthems are an inscription of the self on the landscape. If one were to look at these myths in Saussurean semiotics of *langue* and *parole*, taking the land as a *tabula rasa* upon which any *parole* can be inscribed, the significance which is attached to the signifier moves beyond mere paradigmatic relations of combination and selection, and becomes a myth, which is not static but dynamic. It is through the study of these two genres that we can come to an understanding of the nature of myth, trace the psychology of conflict, not actual or historical, but as 'mythized' by the *parole* of national symbols. It is not the past which we conceive in the study of national symbols, but a distortion of it, which bears all the qualities of myth as opposed to history. As Barthes would put it, '*myth hides nothing*: its function is to distort, not to make disappear. There is no latency of the concept in relation to the form: there is no need of an unconscious in order to explain myth.'[2] This feature of myth is more true of the South African myth-making than that of any other independent African state. My intention here is to study the myths out of which national flags and anthems have been created in South Africa, and how these myths have been transformed through historical change. In addition to the above, I will consider the significance of place-names as powerful national symbols.

THE SOUTH AFRICAN FLAG

In one definition of a national flag it is suggested that 'the colours and designs of national flags are not usually arbitrarily selected but rather stem from history, culture, religion of the particular country.'[3] This is a handy definition, but problematic, in the sense that it attaches a certain natural relationship between the signifier and the signified. Indeed, the South African flag, *Die Vierkleur* (the Quadricolour), not officially recognized until 1994, bears testimony to the history and culture of the country. It consists of three main colours – orange, white and blue, with three small flags in the centre, two of which represent the two northern Boer Republics, and one the British colonies, all of which merged to form the Union of South Africa in 1910. Though the official flag had to wait until 1928 for official adoption by the Union Nationality and Flag Act of 1927, it had been in existence since 1652, when Jan van Riebeeck hoisted the Netherlands flag, which was then probably orange, white and blue. Thus, the flag was a symbolic erasure of the indigenous inhabitants of the sub-continent from the landscape of both history and myth.

A few decades after the formation of the Union, the South African landscape was carved into enclaves of dry land called Bantustans, which were later to be granted false independence. Their independence could not be complete without outward symbols, thus they improvized their own flags and national anthems. This was the ultimate act of attempting to create myth through symbols, and to reinforce a false historical identity. Barthes' words could not be more true of the situation – 'myth essentially aims at causing immediate impression – it does not matter if one is later allowed to see through the myth, its action is assumed to be stronger than the rational explanations which may later belie it.'[4]

South African history is an inscription of a series of myths on the landscape of memory. Between the South Africa Act of Union (1909) and the introduction of the Land Act came the birth of the South African Native National Congress at Bloemfontein in 1912. In order to create its own myths the liberation movement adopted a three-coloured flag, consisting of green, gold and black. The green was said to represent 'the land', gold 'the wealth of the country', while black represented 'the people'. The majority of the dispossessed found in it a symbol with which they could commemorate their dispossession, and assert their rightful possession of the land. From then on South Africa had to contend with two flags. So it was to be with the anthem. These were to become outward symbols of the battle of the minds; symbols of identity and representation engaged in a battle of mutual annihilation. Later, offshoots of the liberation movement in the 1950s and 1970s added a collage of yet more colours to the landscape by adopting their own flags. The banning of the ANC and the Pan-Africanist Congress (PAC) in the 1960s, and the Black Consciousness group and the Azanian People's Organization (AZAPO) in the 1970s, was synonymous with the obliteration of their symbols from the landscape of mass political rallying.

In the 1980s, as the people became more defiant, the Tricolour became more conspicuous, going hand in hand with the re-emergence of 'Nkosi Sikelel' i-Afrika' especially after the rise of the United Democratic Front (UDF) in 1983, until it reappeared in full sail after the release of Robben Island prisoners in 1989 and the ultimate release of Nelson Mandela and the unbanning of political organizations in February 1990. Since the ANC was no longer an illegal organization, the flag was *de facto* unbanned. The organization, including others, was allowed to rewrite itself on the landscape of political contest.

After the 1990 Troika the colours of the Tricolour bloomed like a spring of liberation, and translated themselves into garments – hats, shirts, lumber-jackets, coats, skirts, trousers, socks, shoes and bags. Perhaps even the most intimate undergarments worn underneath were splashed with green, gold, and black. It was soon hard to imagine that in the not-so-distant past wearing anything which resembled the Tricolour could invite a charge under the Suppression of Terrorism Act. It was a scene reminiscent of Mao Zedong's dictum: 'Let a hundred flowers bloom and let a thousand schools of thought contend.' The colours of the Quadricolour were overwhelmed, and it was seen only at the Nationalist Party's (NP) and the Conservative Party's (CP) meetings. A similar fate befell the Afrikaner National anthem. This was not the end but the beginning of the rivalry of symbols, which was to culminate in the transparency of myth and the adoption of a hybrid anthem in 1995. But before we leap to the conclusion of the saga, let us look at the national anthems, for their stories, like all myths and symbols, are similar.

THE AFRIKANER NATIONAL ANTHEM

A national anthem is defined as a 'hymn or song expressing patriotic sentiment and either governmentally authorized as an official national hymn or holding that position in popular feeling . . . sentiments of the text vary, from prayers for the monarch to allusions of nationally important battles or uprisings.'[5] South Africa's two contending national anthems fitted this description, but perhaps the Afrikaner one more than 'Nkosi Sikelel' i-Afrika', because it was officially recognized by the government, and it exclusively alluded to the history which concerned the Afrikaners.

The words of 'Die Stem van Suid-Afrika' were composed by the Afrikaans poet and writer, C. J. Langenhoven (1873–1932) on the last two days of May 1918. There were originally three verses, and the fourth, which completed the present version, was added later. Round about 1921 the South African Broadcasting Corporation (SABC) closed their daily broadcasts with both the then official 'God Save the King' and 'Die Stem'. The Afrikaners were not content with the adoption of Afrikaans as the second official language in 1924. They wanted to have their own national anthem. In keeping with his concept of creating all-embracing symbols of nationhood, General J. B. M. Hertzog (Prime Minister 1924–39) authorized 'Die Stem' to be played at the opening of Parliament in 1938. It was from then on generally accepted as an official anthem.

The English version of 'Die Stem' was adopted in 1952. There was and there still is no translation in any of the African languages, which are spoken by a far greater majority of the population than the Afrikaans and English speakers put together. This is another sad reminder of the negation of common identity and ownership of the land, and the writing of a history, like the *Vierkleur*, which seeks to obliterate the earlier inhabitants of the sub-continent. In 1961, when South Africa became a Republic, the *Vierkleur* was regarded as the sole national flag, and the Union Jack was lowered forever and relegated to oblivion. 'Die Stem' not only celebrates an exclusively Afrikaner culture, language and history, but also makes a claim to all the land and space. The first stanza (in translation) opens as follows:

> Ringing out from *our* blue heavens, from *our* deep seas breaking round,
> Over everlasting mountains where the echoing crags resound;
> From *our* plains where creaking wagons cut their trails into the earth;
> Calls the spirit of *our* country, of the land that gave *us* birth.
> At thy call *we* shall not falter, firm and steadfast *we* shall stand,
> At thy will to live or perish, oh South Africa dear land.
>
> [my emphasis]

This stanza commemorates one of the most important historical moments in the history of the Afrikaner folk, their migration or 'trek' by ox-wagon from the Cape in protest against the British government, which started in the third decade of the last century. At the same time the anthem celebrates the beauty of the landscape – the blue sky and the mountains. The lyrics are poetry *par excellence*, presenting us with vivid visual images which the Afrikaans language renders far more poetically than the English version.

'Die Stem' is the only national anthem on the sub-continent (perhaps on the whole continent) which opens with four possessive pronouns within the first four lines of the first stanza, followed by three cataphoric references of the first person plural in the immediately following lines, 'we' and 'us'. Compared with the African national anthem, and even anthems of other nations in southern Africa, it is the most powerful in terms of evocative imagery, but its lack of the magnanimity which characterizes the other anthems can only be matched by its vigour. In the second stanza, the cataphoric reference of the first person plural is the recurrent feature, repeated ten times, as if to emblazon the Afrikaner identity indelibly on the landscape. Images of what constitutes the essence of the *volk* are evoked in physiological images of 'marrow', 'bones', 'blood', 'heart' and 'spirit', and the unbending recalcitrance of the Afrikaners is celebrated through alliteration in the third line, '*will . . . werk . . . wandel*' ('will . . . work . . . striving'), which is lost in the translation. Patriotism is expressed through lexical reiteration in 'loving' and 'enduring love'. The unoccupied land is apostrophized and addressed directly in the second person. The historical past is also celebrated, and the future asserted through linking with the past: 'in the promise of our future and the glory of the past'. Poetry is, indeed, the staff of which myth is made. The third stanza carries over the claims of the first and the second, extending the metaphors of space and identity:

> In the golden warmth of the summer, in the chill of the winter's air,
> In the surging light of springtime, in the autumn of despair;
> When the wedding bells are chiming, or when those we love depart,
> Thou dost know us for thy children and dost take us to thy heart:
> Loudly peals the answering voice: We are thine, and we shall stand,
> Be it life or death, to answer to thy call, beloved land.

The *glorificamus te* of the landscape of the first stanza is taken up in this stanza, and the land is once again apostrophized, and patriotism expressed through unquestioning commitment of obedience to it. A domestic atmosphere is expressed through the metaphors of 'wedding bells'. The metaphor of life and death – 'from cradle to the grave' – of the first stanza is carried over into this one: 'Be it life or death' (a line which was to become the most controversial in the adoption of a new national anthem in 1995), which reinforces the Afrikaners' readiness to die for what they regard as their land – to fight to their last drop of blood, as they tend to express it, a myth which was created through the writing of their history. The final stanza is an appeal to divine intervention; God is certainly no newcomer in the Afrikaner sense of patriotism, for throughout their history, since the Blood River (Ncome) battle with the Zulus in 1838, they have made covenants with him. He is called upon to give strength to the Afrikaner folk, and the prayer is that the land, the legacy of their forefathers, should pass to the next generations intact.

Like the Afrikaner anthem, the naming of places, cities, mountains, rivers and other natural phenomena celebrate the culture and history of the Afrikaner, to the exclusion of other peoples. Most cities in South Africa have a Voortrekker Street; cities like Pietermaritzburg and Pretoria are named after Voortrekker leaders; and almost every major landscape feature has an Afrikaans name. In addition to the presence of the Union Jack in the centre of the Afrikaner flag, the English also have the privilege of having their history and culture inscribed on the landcape, with names which commemorate their imperial past. Durban, for instance, is named after Sir Benjamin D'Urban (1777–1849), Governor of the Cape from 1834–38; Grahamstown after Colonel John Graham, 'whose troopers had cleared the Zuurveld of Xhosas in 1815'; and King William's Town after King William IV of Great Britain.[6]

In order to obliterate further the history of the dispossessed, townships were deliberately given names which did not bear any historical connotations, but instead stand as a monumental irony and mockery of the Africans who were condemned by the Group Areas Act (1950) and other laws of discrimination to live in them. They provide evidence, once again, of the way myth can distort through silence. Examples are: Gugulethu, which in Xhosa means 'our pride'; Langa, the Xhosa name for 'sun'; Lekaneng, meaning 'sufficient', 'place of suffciency'; and Katlehong, translated as 'place of success', or 'place of happiness'.[7]

No major town or city has an African name, except in the Bantustans. There are also other township names whose irony is an abominable mockery of humanity, such as the artificially constructed settlement outside Bloemfontein, which is called 'Botshabelo' – 'place of refuge'. The now famous 'Boipatong' also means 'a place of refuge'. In the introduction to his sourcebook of South African place names, Raper writes about the connotative meanings of place names:

associations attach themselves to the name via the feature to which the name refers . . . The connotative or associative is subjective, dependent on one's knowledge of the place. Thus the name *Durban* may call to mind an experience in a particular hotel, the beach and all its attractions . . . a honeymooon, or whatever.[8]

What more can we ask for, if that is all there is to connection between the signifier and the signified? This is clearly the case of a meta-myth, a distorted reading of what has already falsified history.

THE AFRICAN NATIONAL ANTHEM

The African national anthem, 'Nkosi Sikelel' i-Afrika' was composed by Reverend Enoch Sontonga in Xhosa in 1897. It was initially sung on different social occasions, until it was adopted by the ANC, and then became the unofficial anthem sung by Africans at political gatherings. It was later sung in Nguni, and attached to it was a second part, which was sung in Sesotho:

Morena boloka setjhaba sa heso,
O fedise dintwa le matshwenyeho,
O se boloke . . . Morena.
[Lord we ask you to protect our nation,
To keep us free from conflict and tribulations,
Protect us ... Lord.]

This part is anonymous, but the first two lines seem to have been adopted from the second stanza of the national anthem of Lesotho, composed by a French Missionary, Reverend François Coillard (1834–1904) and adopted as the national anthem in May 1967, which reads: 'Lord, we ask you to protect Lesotho / Keep us free from conflict and tribulations.'[9] 'Nkosi Sikelel' i-Afrika' was composed as a hymn, with eight stanzas. One of the earliest publications in which it appeared was a book of songs entitled, *Imihobe Nemibongo Yokufundwa Ezikolweni*, in 1927, with an English sub-title, *Xosa* [sic] *Poetry for Schools*, by the renowned Xhosa poet, S. E. K. Mqhayi. Mqhayi is said to have completed Sontonga's composition. At present only the first stanza is used as the national anthem. In explaining its evolution from Sontonga's composition to a national anthem, D. D. T. Jabavu says:

'Nkosi Sikelel' i-Afrika' was composed in 1897 and first publicly sung in 1899 at the ordination of the Rev. M. Mboweni, a Shangaan Methodist Minister . . . The piece was commonly sung in Native Day Schools and further popularized by the Ohlange Zulu Choir of the Secondary School founded by the Rev. J. L. Dube . . . When the African National Congress flourished its leaders adopted this piece as a closing Anthem for their meetings and this soon became a custom in the other provinces in connection with all types of Bantu organization.[10]

It was thus that the hymn and prayer became the song of the people, and a representation of their identity, and aspirations for a free South Africa. What is interesting in the evolution of this national anthem from a hymn to a secular song is the similarity of the transformation of the Tricolour into fashion, where the sanctity of a myth is violated when it becomes popular or vulgar, losing its concept as a sacred myth.

It is a magnanimous song, embracing the whole of the continent of Africa, without discriminating. The other seven stanzas, which have been done away with, open with naming all people in the nation: kings, men, women and girls and ministers. The prayer goes on to ask for a blessing in all things: agriculture and stock, efforts towards union and self-upliftment, and the whole of Africa. Despite government efforts to ban 'Nkosi Sikelel' i-Afrika' and confine it to the homelands, it proved indelible. There are many evocative descriptions of its power and impact in literature. Mbulelo Mzamane, in his documentary novel about the events of 1976, *Children of Soweto*, writes how students at a political gathering sang the anthem alternately in Xhosa and Sesotho, bringing tears to the eyes of many of the people present,[11] and Don Mattera, in his award winning autobiography, *Gone with the Twilight*, describes an ANC meeting in 1955 in Sophiatown: 'First the delicate shrill of the women's voices that appeared to be rolling from the slopes and grassy hillocks of our land, to burst into thin, melodic sound, then to be raised to the ceiling of the hall by the sonorous baritones of the men'.[12]

'Nkosi Sikelel' i-Afrika' was never recognized by the government. At best it was either sung or played on air for a visiting Afrikaner official. In the SABC Radio Bulletin of 10 September a choir of Africans has the following caption: 'Southern Sotho and Zulu members of Radio Bantu's announcing staff in Johannesburg rendering their national anthems under the direction of Alexius Buthelezi on the occasion of the visit of the Commissioner-General for Southern Sotho . . . Mr S. F. Papenfus.'[13] After the release of Nelson Mandela and the un-banning of political organizations, the two anthems were to express the polarized streams of ideology and aspirations, and the two flags to compete in public places. The space for the battle of the flags and anthems was consecrated in the sporting field, the second religion of South Africa.

GROUND OF CONTEST

In July 1991 the International Olympics Committee announced that South Africa would be allowed back into their games, and to participate in the 1992 Olympic games in Barcelona. This was done not without the blessing of the ANC, whose head of sport, Steve Tshwete, wept unashamedly in public when the South African all-white cricket team went to play in India, in November 1991, under the old banner. One of the conditions for the admission of the South

Africans back into the Olympics was their commitment to the ANC that the official national anthem would not be sung at the Olympic games. There was also some debate about the adoption of the 'Springbok' as an emblem for the South African team, which has now ended with the reinstatement of the symbol. The animal had been used as a symbol of the South African élite sporting body of that name, whose colours were, by some ironic coincidence, gold and green. The most logical choice for an anthem should have been 'Nkosi Sikelel' i-Afrika', but instead, a neutral anthem was to be sung, and the protea flower was chosen as the symbol for South African sportsmen who went to the Olympics.

In the latter half of 1992 the ANC were embarrassed by the Afrikaners' act of defiance at the mecca of rugby, Ellis Park, when the spectators sung their national anthem and waved the old flag. But it was on the very same ground that South Africa was to win the 1995 rugby tournament, waving a banner of National Unity, consisting of the three colours of the Tricolour, green, black and gold, and three of the *Vierkleur*, blue, red and white. The lie of the old myth had been uncovered, and a new inscription, a new myth, was beginning to unfold.

NOTES

1 S. Sontag, 'Myth Today' in Sontag (ed.) *Barthes: Selected Writings*, Glasgow, William Collins Sons & Co., 1989, p.102.

2 Sontag, 'Myth Today', p.107.

3 *Encyclopaedia Britannica*, Chicago, Chicago University Press, vol. 4, p. 812.

4 Sontag, 'Myth Today', p.117.

5 *Britannica Macropaedia*, Encyclopaedia Britannica Inc., Chicago, Chicago University Press, 1989, vol. 8, p. 530.

6 E. Raper, *Dictionary of Southern African Place Names*, Johannesburg, Lowry Publishers, 1987, pp. 27–133, 187–260, 447.

7 Raper, *Place Names*, pp. 233–274.

8 Raper, *Place Names*, p. 21.

9 W. L. Reed and M. J. Bristow, *National Anthems of the World* (8th edn.), London, Cassell, 1993, p. 295.

10 D. D. T. Jabavu, 'The Origins of "Nkosi Sikelel' i Afrika",' 1934, (unpublished paper).

11 M. Mzamane, *Children of Soweto*, Johannesburg, Ravan Press, 1982, p. 217.

12 D. Mattera, *Gone With the Twilight*, London, Zed Books, 1987, pp. 84–5.

13 A. Luthuli, *Let My People Go*, London, Fontana Books, 1962, p. 29.

BIBLIOGRAPHY

Davenport, T. H. R., *Southern Africa: A Modern History*, London, Macmillan, 1977.

Jabavu, D. D. T., 'The origins of "Nkosi Sikelele' i Afrika" ', 1934 (unpublished paper).

Luthuli, A., *Let My People Go*, London, Fontana Books, 1962.

Mattera, D., *Gone With the Twilight*, London, Zed Books, 1987.

Mqhayi, S. E. K., *Imihobe Nemibongo Yokufundwa Ezikolweni*, London, The Sheldon Press, 1927.

Mzamane, M., *Children of Soweto*, Johannesburg, Ravan Press, 1982.

Raper, E., *Dictionary of Southern African Place Names*, Johannesburg, Lowry Publishers, 1987.

Reed W. L. and Bristow, M. J., *National Anthems of the World* (8th edn), London, Cassell, 1993.

Sherman, J., 'Liberation songs and popular culture', *Staffrider*, (8) 3 & 4, 1989.

Sontag, S., 'Myth today' in Sontag (ed.) *Barthes: Selected Writings*, London, Fontana Press, 1989.

Thompson, L., *A History of South Africa*, Yale University Press, New Haven, 1990.

10

'GREAT SPACES WASHED WITH SUN'[1]

The Matopos and Uluru compared

Terence Ranger

INTRODUCTION

Since 1985 I have been working on the modern history of the Matopos mountains south of Bulawayo in Zimbabwe.[2] In December 1992 and January 1993 I was Alexander Visiting Professor at the University of Western Australia in Perth and I was able to read a good deal of recent work on Aboriginal history.[3] One of the first things I read, of course, was Robert Layton's study of Ayers Rock/Uluru.[4] Like the Matopos, Uluru is at one and the same time an extraordinary rock formation, an icon of national identity, a major tourist attraction, and the site of struggle between black and white over possession, representation and control. I was eager to discover how closely comparable the modern history of these two southern spaces might turn out to be.

I was at first struck by the great number of comparisons that could be made. In many ways it seemed as if one really could talk about essentialized southern spaces, characterized by an age-old symbiosis of land and people, and threatened by northern appropriation, with all its consequences of intervention, exploitation and expulsion. But then I began to appreciate equally great differences between the two cases, and these seemed to me to be differences not only of history but of historiography. In what follows I want first to state the similarities; then to state the differences; then to interrogate the historio-graphy of Uluru from a southern Africanist perspective; and finally to interrogate my own original account of the Matopos from the vantage point of a comparative study.

THE MATOPOS AND ULURU COMPARED

There are indeed many similarities between the history of these two extraordinary rock formations over the last hundred years. Prior to the last two decades of the nineteenth century, both were landscapes constituted by indigenous myth and ritual and traversed by pilgrims. The story of the two boys who built Uluru from the mud they were playing in after the rain is paralleled by the myth of Mudzanapabwe, who created water and the Matopos simultaneously, by stamping with his foot on a rock and bringing the rain-clouds down to earth. The messengers who come to the rain shrines in the Matopos as representatives of communities all over south-western Zimbabwe and beyond are paralleled by the Aboriginal groups described by Layton, 'living over a wide area and owning many dreamings', who 'come together in ceremonies' at Uluru in which 'speakers of many dialects are united'. (In the Matopos, too, speakers of many dialects and indeed languages are received at the shrines – 'God is Language', say the priests). The words of an Aboriginal elder quoted by Layton – 'That's a rock, but that's got to have something else, because that's got all those old men's memories inside' – resonate with my own instruction by the shrine adepts in the Matopos in how to read the constantly changing messages of the stones, which have led me to entitle my account of the modern history of the Matopos *Voices From the Rocks*. In both cases the rocks incarnate history, culture and environmental knowledge.

Their subsequent history has also been similar. In both cases white settlers and administrators arrived some hundred years ago. In both cases there was violent appropriation – in the Matopos the military campaigns of the 1896 war; around Uluru violence between Aborigines and settler herders of cattle and sheep. The hills came to be surrounded in both cases by a settler ranching economy which gave rise both in Southern Rhodesia and in central Australia to black cowboy cultures. The rocks were appropriated by renaming – Uluru becoming Ayers Rock, and the Matopos becoming the Rhodes-Matopos Park. In both cases, the white state, ignoring immemorial indigenous knowledge of the environment, imposed its own 'scientific' criteria of conservation and proclaimed national parks. In both cases indigenous hunters and gatherers (and in the Matopos case, farmers) found themselves frustrated by park regulations and

158

exclusions. Tourists came pouring in. There was indiscriminate photography at Uluru and a complete appropriation of the landscape of the Matopos by white photographs and water-colours. Yet alongside this, both in central Australia and in the Matopos, schools of indigenous Christian water-colourists arose, to baffle commentators who could not tell whether their work represented mere mimicry of white visions of landscape or some sort of a reappropriation.

And then there arose very similar cultural resistances, coming to their head both at Uluru and in the Matopos in the 1970s. Contrary to most expectations, indigenous religion had not been in fatal decline. In the Matopos the shrines revived in influence during the mass nationalist period of the 1960s. In the 1970s black guerrillas operating in the rugged terrain of the hills were sustained by the spiritual support of the rain-shrines and promised to return the land to the people. At Uluru Aborigines waged a less violent struggle to keep tourists away from sacred places and in 1979 laid claim to Ayers Rock and the surrounding land on the basis of their ritual ownership. Their assertion that 'the Whiteman has known of these places for only a little time and he cannot own them and they are not his country' parallels the cultural nationalist repudiations of white claims in the Matopos. And then in the 1980s African rule was achieved in Zimbabwe and, in Australia, the Aborigines of Uluru were given shared rights of management in the National Park.

At Uluru today Aboriginal rangers may prohibit tourists from taking photographs or painting representations of the holy places. The British painter Sarah Raphael has recently described her visit to what she stills calls Ayers Rock. She sat down to paint the Olgas, 'a group of strange, round, orange domes about 30 kms away'. For the first time in her encounter with the Australian landscape everything went right – and then a female Aboriginal ranger appeared and told her that she was not allowed to paint 'a sacred rock'. She was allowed to finish the painting on condition that she never showed it to anybody.[5] In the Matopos today the inhabitants are still unable to control photographers or painters, but at least they have been able to re-assert control over their shrines. Sitwanyana Ncube, one of the claimants to the guardianship of the senior Matopos shrine, Njelele, forbade me to enter the shrine because I wore or carried hard, shiny objects – a wrist-watch, a camera, a tape-recorder. I offered to abandon them all, but to no avail. 'White *minds* are hard and shiny', he said. Sitwanyana would have been fully in agreement with the elder quoted by Layton: 'We must protect our sacred places from visitors. These are for Aboriginals alone and essential to us if our culture is to survive.'

THE MATOPOS AND ULURU CONTRASTED

So many comparisons. And yet, as my hard and shiny mind thought through Layton's book, I became increasingly struck by the contrasts.

A fundamental one seemed to lie in the relationship of these sacred places to history. In the Matopos the rain-shrines, as well as controlling the environment, also propagate a linear version of a long historical past.[6] This narrates a sequence of the rise and fall of successive regimes in south-western Zimbabwe, reaching back to the seventeenth century. It constitutes an elaborate statement of how rulers legitimate themselves by 'making peace' with the land – and how they lose legitimation through arrogance and greed. The shrine historiography inspired nationalist resistance to the arrogant Rhodesia Front regime, and also inspired reflection on the incomplete legitimacy (as seen from Matabeleland) of the Mugabe government after 1980. The shrine priests turn every drought into a crisis of legitimacy. By contrast, the past at Uluru seems to be part of a 'consciously ahistoric' Dream Time, in which all change is assimilated to the order established at the Creation.[7]

And this contrast, of course, relates to many others. The mark of 'San' hunter-gatherers has been left on the Matopos in the form of the many rock-paintings which survive, but black cattle-keepers and farmers have dominated the hills for some two thousand years. At Uluru, on the other hand, hunting-gathering is defined as the essential Aboriginal way of life. The pilgrims who come to the Matopos rain shrines represent not egalitarian descent groups 'made up of two or three families . . . whose estates lie on the same dreaming track', as Layton writes, but messengers from chiefs and headmen. In the Matopos, control of the environment is exercised by the shrines through the chiefs. In contrast to the argument of seamless continuity and timeless occupation advanced by the Aboriginal Central Land Council in its 1979 claim to Ayers Rock, residents of the Matopos well remember several African appropriations of the hills before the colonial seizure. At the wider level they remember conquests and the creation of new states: at the local level they remember struggles between families to control fertile valleys – and even shrines. The very name Matopos was imposed by the Ndebele conquerors in the nineteenth century, before which time the hills were known as Matonjeni (as they still are among the Shona to the east of them). Many of the great rocks in the Matopos have borne first Banyubi/Kalanga names, then Ndebele ones, and finally have been re-christened by the whites. The Matopos have thus had a much more active, or at least more actively remembered, black history than has Uluru. They have also had a much more active white history, since Rhodes by choosing the Matopos as his burial place, consciously proclaimed a new symbolic era and made his hill-top grave into the 'Rhodesian Valhalla', while Uluru was not a popular tourist destination for white Australians until the 1960s.

These differences extend to the nationalist movements in the two places. In the Matopos, nationalism was at first led by African Christian progressives, who had been ploughing in the hills, and only later infused with the moral cultural nationalism of the shrines. The hills were liberated by ZIPRA and ZANLA guerrillas, from the armies of Joshua Nkomo and Robert Mugabe respectively, who combined their resort to the shrines with radical Marxism. By contrast to the traditionalist essentialism of the Aboriginal movement to reclaim Uluru, the Zimbabwean nationalist movement was Janus-faced, fusing 'tradition' and modernism in an unstable combination.

Consequently what has happened since 1980 has been very different in these two southern spaces. In Zimbabwe the whole country, and not just particular holy places, has fallen under the authority of a black government. But the Matopos National Park has remained under the National Parks Department of the central government, which regards itself as representative of the people. Unlike Uluru, the national park itself is *not* managed in partnership with locals; the modernist doctrines of international conservation are embraced by the Zimbabwean state, which in the interests of the 'whole community' does not allow locals to collect plants, or hunt, or visit holy places within the park. The imperatives of international tourism have ensured that the park still presents much the same symbolic face that it did under settler rule. People still visit Rhodes's grave and the other colonial monuments; still camp out and have barbecues; still photograph indiscriminately; and are still ignorant of the African history and cosomology of the hills. Sitwanyana Ncube was only able to exclude me from Njelele cave because it lies outside the southern boundaries of the national park.[8]

President Mugabe sometimes invokes the world movement of

indigenous peoples, including the Aborigines, when stating the case for further acquisition of land from white commercial farmers. But the incongruity of this comparison was revealed by a San correspondent to the Zimbabwe *Herald* who wrote tongue-in-cheek to say that he was glad to hear that his people were soon to get their hunting grounds back from Ndebele and Shona usurpers! The acute sense of white Rhodesians in 1980 that they had 'lost' the Matopos was not balanced by a sense among local people that they had 'regained' them.[9]

ABORIGINAL HISTORIOGRAPHY CONFRONTED

These contrasts seemed to outweigh the apparent similarities between Uluru and the Matopos. It seemed, after all, that it was not northern appropriation which first introduced the Matopos into linear history and state exploitation and contested land-use and differential imagination of the landscape, even though the Rhodesian settler state outdid all previous regimes in its symbolic and practical seizure of the land and the expulsion of its people.

Yet, as I read the recent work on Aboriginal history, I wondered whether these contrasts did not reside partly in the historiography as well as in the history of the two areas. After all in southern African studies, not only the historiography of black cattle-keepers and farmers but also the historiography of hunter-gatherer peoples is much more dynamic than the idea of changeless continuity which characterizes most writing on pre-colonial Aboriginal history. To give only two examples, both Edward Wilmsen and Robert Gordon have vigorously attacked the essentialism of definitions of 'the Bushman' or the 'San', and also the current idea of them as the 'First People'.[10] They have demonstrated how many different groups have been subsumed under a single heading and argued that serf status rather than race or ethnicity has been the historically distinguishing feature of the composite 'San' people. As Wilmsen has argued: 'The discourse reifies its subjects not only beyond race but paradoxically, given its intentions, beyond humanity. The image of the "First People" leads in the wrong direction, feeding a spurious traditional/ modernity divide.'[11]

Gordon spells out some of the practical consequences of esssentialism for living 'Bushmen'. He shows that wherever reserves or national parks have been created in Namibia or South Africa, permission for 'Bushmen' to stay on the land is always subject to the requirement that they maintain a 'traditional' life-style. Thus 'Bushmen' were expelled from Etosha National Park for 'non-traditional' conduct – the raising of oxen! In Tsumkwe likewise, 'nature conservancy was strongly opposed to stock farming, as this would destroy the "pristine" image of the game park.' 'Bushmen' would be allowed to live in the park, provided they lived 'traditionally' (as defined not by themselves but by the local white nature conservator). Even the demand for improved housing was seen as a fatal breach with tradition. Gordon quotes Johannes Kloppers on 'Bushman' demands in South Africa's Kalahari Gemsbok National Park, where they wanted to keep dogs, to hunt freely, to improve housing. Kloppers found all this 'utterly untraditional' and urged that 'in the course of the years they have racially disqualified themselves from protection in a national park.' It is hardly surprising that Gordon does not find much reassurance in the proposals by independent Namibia's Department of Nature Conservation for a 'Bushman' game reserve, in which 'Bushmen' will be allowed to remain, provided that they hunt and gather 'traditionally'.[12]

Gordon's remarks have resonances both for the Matopos and for Uluru. In the Matopos earlier conservationist ideas that preserving the hills in their 'pristine' condition meant keeping the 'picturesque kraals, costume, cattle, crops and customs' of "traditional" Africans', gave way to later demands that Africans 'spoilt' by urban life and Christianity should be evicted wholesale from the national park.[13] At Uluru the management partnership of Aborigines and park authorities might be thought to offer protection against penalties for breaches of tradition. Nevertheless, all the advantages of Aboriginal essentialism when urging claims to sacred sites are balanced by the danger of excluding Aborigines from the 'humanity' of change and adaptation, and of setting up a spurious traditional/modernity divide.[14]

It seemed to me, when reading recent Aboriginal historiography, that there are ways forward to making an understanding of the Aboriginal past – and of Australian landscape – more dynamic.

I found a way in to a more contested and dynamic view of Aboriginal relationships to the land in Peggy Brock's collection of studies of female 'rites' and 'sites'.[15] Brock and her contributors demonstrate that the whole process of 'dream time' myth and of 'song line' movement, as it is described by scholars who focus on male ritual, is cross-cut by the alternative possibilities of gender. As

Catherine Ellis and Linda Barwick point out: 'A woman's desire to live near her parents in order to share in matrilineally transmitted rights to ceremonies and resources was often in conflict with the desire of her husband to live in and have children born in his own country.'[16] As they also point out, women can 'dream' new ceremonies, can be taught by an ancestor, in a dream, new myths, songs, dances, and so on.[17] These processes of multiple and conflicting claims to territory and of the invention or re-invention of myth and ritual were plainly a source of dynamism in pre-contact times.

Helen Payne writes in the Brock collection of another process of innovative appropriation whereby, on Aboriginal groups entering a new territory, 'familiar looking landscape features' are attached to already existing and known myth cycles, and thus give a misleading impression of timeless co-existence between people and land.[18] This idea is developed by a cultural geographer, Phillip Clarke, in an essay on 'Adelaide as Aboriginal landscape'. Clarke explicitly attacks the notion of 'tribal relations with a more or less constant area of terrestial landscape' producing a 'true' tradition expressed in myth. He argues that there were always 'wide-ranging geographic views' and 'perceived connections with distant landscapes'; Aboriginal groups had either passed through many ecological zones in the past, or still exploited their various resources in the present; they had profoundly shaped their various environments by fire-stick farming, thus creating open grassland and purposive tracks. Hence there were no simple or constant human/land relationships which could be expressed in static bodies of ancient myth.

Moreover, there were in addition other 'landscapes' – an imagined 'land of the dead', a perceived spatial organization of the heavens. All this generated a variety of myth idioms which could be applied to the new experiences of migratory groups as they entered new lands, or as they enlarged the geographical scale of their experience. Both migration and enlargement of conceptual scale took place in pre-contact times, Clarke argues, but both became a common experience after contact. He shows how myth idioms adapted, and in particular how the apparently immemorial myth of the creative Tjibruke spirit, creator of the springs and hills of the Adelaide hinterland, was an invention or reinvention of tradition dating from the 1930s.[19]

Gender studies and cultural geography, then, can add dynamism to an older anthropology's all-too-static and 'given' account of Aboriginal territory.[20] But anthropologists themselves have begun to develop new analyses. The leading contemporary anthropologist of the Aranda, that much anthropologized people, is John Morton. Morton remarks that patrilineally descended clans are now deemed, in the modern jargon, to be 'primary owners' of parcels of land, but that there are many other equally important ways of being associ-ated with land units – matrilineal descent through female members of a country clan gives rights to 'manage' the country of another; one can inherit rights in the country of one's paternal grandfather or one's maternal grandmother; and there are non-descent criteria of association as well. People are linked with their place of conception, where their mother felt the first quickening of the foetus. Hence fathers, brothers, sons would all have quite different 'dreamings' and be linked with different 'song lines' even while sharing a territory.

We are back with the notion of alternative: and we are soon back with the notion of creativity. Morton insists that the role of the dreaming ancestors – not so much *making* the country as making it *significant* – differs little from current hunting, fishing, gathering, cooking generations. The ancestors are not gods but human fore-bears; their descendants can dream and sing and project names on to the landscape. Hence 'mythical creation is not simply a thing of the dim and distant past'; the living possess the creative techniques of the ancestors, and in ritual performance they 'install themselves as ancestral beings' with the power to use these techniques. New land-scapes can be created – and have often had to be created. As Morton writes:

> The boundaries of local group areas, together with the patri-lineal groups who own these areas, may change quite dramat-ically as a result of political shifts in history. Small estate groups, averaging less than 100 living persons, must have been constantly prey to the vagaries of demography . . . In this contest claims to a country are established and relinquished . . . Different persons come to hold dreamings and sacred sites by very different means.

Senior men speak of their territories 'as if they could never leave them – indeed, as if they had never left them'. But in fact 'foraging bands were in constant flux' and 'residence was probably very flexible'.

Here Morton brings the territorial and landscape history of western and central Australia much closer to the history of other continents. 'There is every reason to suppose', he writes, 'that the map of western Aranda territory has over the years been just as volatile as the map of Europe' – or, one might add, as the map of the Matopos.[21]

THE HISTORIOGRAPHY OF THE MATOPOS CONFRONTED

In these ways, I thought, the history of Uluru might be made more like that of the Matopos. But I realized that the perspectives of Brock's contributors, of Clarke and of Morton, not only interrogated previous work on Uluru but also previous work on the Matopos themselves, including my own.

It has been just as true for Zimbabwe as for Australian Aboriginal studies, that work on ritual and religion has focussed on male belief and practice. In Zimbabwe, just as in Australia, attention to 'female rites and sites', or to female environmental knowledge, would have a radical cross-cutting effect on our understanding. Thus I knew, but had not earlier paid adequate attention to, the fact that ecological religious practice in the Matopos was gendered. Reading the Brock anthology has made me seek to bring out in *Voices From the Rocks* the gendered history of Matopos religion and the gender balance in the myths and practices of the Mwali cult. It seems that before the emergence of the Mwali shrines – and thereafter simultaneously with their operations – rain-making in the caves of the Matopos was the task specifically of young girls and old women; it is possible that the word 'Mwali' itself has particularly female connotations, being used elsewhere in Africa to relate to women's ritual roles or to female initiation; within the now patriarchally dominated Mwali cult itself, God is praised as both male and female, and individual shrines are seen as representing variously Mwali's male and female manifestations. (Thus in the Matopos Communal Area, where there exists today the greatest cluster of shrines, one of these, Dula, is thought of as male and as particularly concerned with war, while another, Dzilo, is thought of as female and particularly concerned with rain and fertility. Dula is controlled by a patrilineally descended line of priests; Dzilo should be controlled by a matrilineally descended line of priestesses, though both black and white patriarchal assumptions have constantly obscured this.)

The work of Clarke and Morton has made me think hard about the earlier stages of human history in the Matopos. It may be true that the recent indigenous history of the hills seems much more dynamic than that of Uluru. But this is certainly not true of studies of the Zimbabwean hunter-gatherer period. One of the few white Rhodesian contributions to human knowledge was the study of the Stone Age by means of surveys of rock paintings and excavations of rock shelters mainly carried out in the Matopos. Today the paintings remain a major tourist attraction. But they have been presented as the work of a long-vanished people who had no connection with the current African farmers of the Matopos communal areas. Moreover, while African farming and stock-keeping is thought of by conserv-ationists as mortally dangerous to the Matopos environment – despite having been practised there for some two thousand years – hunter-gatherers are depicted as having been in perfect symbiosis with the land.

Peter Garlake's excellent short history of 'early Zimbabwe' writes of the San inhabitants of the hills that

> their lives had a regular pattern. The country was rich in animals and wild fruits and vegetables. On these they lived, taking food and killing game as they needed it, moving with the herds and seasons across a territory recognized by all as theirs by right. In rich areas, like the Matopo Hills, many people could live and never have to move far. However, they did not have to put anything back into the land. They did not have to plan for future needs, keep food for the lean months or wait for the harvest. No one could sell his food or hoard it. No one could become wealthy. There was no threat from people hungry for land.[22]

It is an idyllic – perhaps too idyllic – picture. One would like it to be bombarded by the complexities and insights introduced by Clarke and Morton. One would like a study of the ways in which hunter-gatherers in the Matopos changed their environment – by fire-stick farming or other means. One would like some speculation about their movement from territory to territory; their gendered and other variant claims to land and myth. Peter Garlake himself has recently begun to explore the ways in which the cave paintings were designed to operate upon rather than merely to reflect the land and the landscape. I look forward to archaeological and other studies of the transition to farming in the Matopos – hitherto an entirely neglected subject. I anticipate that such studies will show a much greater inter-action between hunter-gatherer and farming populations than has hitherto been supposed. In the religious and ritual field particularly,

I expect that San rain ceremonies – and perhaps even myths – are still reflected in the rites of the Mwali shrines.

In short, even the most historically static studies of Aborigines have the advantage of being about a contemporary as well as an 'ancient' people, while the more dynamic work of Clarke and Morton and others raises a whole series of questions that have not yet been asked in Zimbabwean work on hunter-gatherers. But I don't think that the interest of their questions is restricted to the San period in the history of the Matopos. Black farmers and cattle keepers have their own ways of asserting ancestral identity with the land; they, too, speak of their territories as though they could never leave them. While historians of these societies are well aware of the actual processes of migration, conquest, displacement and competition, we still need to deconstruct myths of land and environment. I am aware that even now my presentation of the environmental knowledge of the Mwali cult is too essentialist and static by contrast to the rapidly changing versions of white dominance–exploitation–conservation–preservation of the land.

CONCLUSION

I have found, in short, that comparisons and contrast between the historiographies of the Matopos and Uluru – or between southern African and Aboriginal historiography more generally – can be very fruitful. They modify the simplest form of the contrast between human/land relationships in southern spaces, on the one hand, and northern appropriation and intervention on the other. But they leave a contrast in place while making it dynamic on both sides. This perception seems to me to be very important for the present and future. Control of sacred space which depends upon park regulations – as at Uluru – may be more complete but at the same time less real than control which arises, as at Njelele, from the continuing dynamics between chiefs and cults and people.

In Zimbabwe today there is a living micro-politics in the Matopos as well as the macro-politics which sustains the National Park. Rhodes's grave has long lost the power which Kipling's elegy attributed to it:

The immense and brooding Spirit still
Shall quicken and control.

Living he was the land, and dead
His soul shall be her soul.

There shall he patient make his seat
(As when the Death he dared!)
And there wait a people's feet
In the paths that he prepared.[23]

Tourists still beat the path to the grave, but the people of these 'great spaces washed with sun' move along tracks prepared by Njelele and the other shrines, which still 'quicken and control'.

NOTES

1 'Great Spaces Washed with Sun' is a line from Rudyard Kipling's elegy to Cecil Rhodes, 'The Burial', which was read at his interment in the Matopos on 10 April 1902. The burial — and the elegy — were crucial assertions of white symbolic appropriation of the Matopos. I return to this elegy at the end of my chapter. For a published edition of the poem, see *Rudyard Kipling's Verse: Inclusive Edition 1885–1926*, Garden City, New York, 1927.

2 Two of my writings on the Matopos are particularly relevant to this chapter. These are my monograph, *Voices From the Rocks: A Modern History of the Matopos*, London, James Currey, 1996, and an article forthcoming in the University of Cape Town journal, *Social Dynamics*, 'Making Zimbabwean Landscapes: Painters, Projectors and Priests'.

3 I subsequently wrote a paper, 'Aboriginal and Khoisan Studies Compared' which I delivered at seminars in Oxford and London during 1993. I draw on material from that paper in this chapter. I must gratefully acknowledge the practical and intellectual hospitality of Norman Etherington and Peggy Brock, which both stimulated and made possible my explorations of Aboriginal historiography.

4 Robert Layton, *Uluru: An Aboriginal History of Ayers Rock*, Canberra, Aboriginal Studies Press, 1989.

5 Sarah Raphael, 'Down to Earth', *Guardian Weekend*, 20 May 1995. I found Raphael's article fascinating because she described the same difficulties in representing the central Australian landscape that were encountered by early colonial water colourists in the case of the Matopos, and which I have described in 'Making Zimbabwean Landscapes'.

6 I describe the theocentric historiography of the shrines and the modern political consequences of it in 'The Politics of Prophecy in Matabeleland', Sattherthwaite Colloquium on African Religion and Ritual, April 1989. The theme is further developed in *Voices From the Rocks*.

7 Thus the anthropologist John Morton, speculating about radical change in Aboriginal land-ownership and occupation, remarks that 'because

much of the depth of Aboriginal history is subsumed in myth, [the] people themselves are not conscious of this.' See John Morton, 'Country, People, Art: the Western Aranda, 1870–1990', in Jane Hardy, J. V. S. Megaw and M. R. Megaw, eds, *The Heritage of Namatjira: The Watercolourists of Central Australia*, Victoria, Heinemann, 1992, p. 37.

8 Soon after the 1980 Zimbabwean elections, a ZAPU Member of Parliament called on the new black government to allow the expelled residents of the National Park to graze their cattle and to farm there. The new Minister, Joseph Msika, replied that 'it would discredit Zimbabwe internationally were we to embark upon a programme of reducing our parks and wildlife estate.' See Terence Ranger, 'Whose Heritage? The case of the Matobo National Park', *Journal of Southern African Studies*, 15, 2 1989, p. 248.

9 Whites fleeing Zimbabwe after the 1980 elections often took paintings of the Matopos with them to remind themselves of their lost heritage.

10 Edward Wilmsen, *Land Filled with Flies: A Political Economy of the Kalahari*, Chicago, Chicago University Press, 1989; Robert Gordon, *The Bushmen Myth*, Boulder, Westview, 1992.

11 Edward Wilmsen, 'Primal Anxiety and the Production of the Ethnography of True Primitiveness', Conference on Symbols of Change, Berlin, January 1993.

12 Gordon, *The Bushmen Myth*, pp. 166, 183, 254–5.

13 I trace this change in *Voices From the Rocks*. The expressions quoted come from Eric Nobbs, the first advocate of the idea of a national park in the Matopos. See Nobbs to Acting Treasurer, 31 October 1919, file A 3/28/46, National Archives, Harare.

14 Kevin Keefe, himself a member of the Aboriginal Cultural Awareness Camps of the 1980s, with their emphasis on 'Aboriginality-as-persistence', and their 'belief in the persistence of an inherently unique identity . . . a nation of an essential, enduring and unilinear Aboriginal culture, transmitted through the blood', has recently warned of the static and conservative political implications of such a belief. In Australia, he says, it is all too easy to co-opt such Aboriginal spokesmen into 'multi-culturalism'. Keefe has himself come to portray Aboriginal culture as 'the ongoing product of human agency' and to emphasize 'resistance and diversity.' See Kevin Keefe, 'Aboriginality: Resistance and Persistence', *Australian Aboriginal Studies*, 1, 1988.

15 Peggy Brock, ed., *Women, Rites and Sites: Aboriginal Women's Cultural Knowledge*, Sydney, Allen & Unwin, 1989.

16 Brock, *Women*, p. 27.

17 Brock, *Women*, p. 30.

18 Brock, *Women*, p. 51.

19 Philip Clarke, 'Adelaide as Aboriginal Landscape', *Aboriginal History*, no. 15, 1991.

20 A text sold in the University of Western Australia's bookshop as core reading in anthropology tells us that 'tribal membership was based on birth in the same tribal territory'; that there were 'over 500 distinct tribes, each with their own distinct territory, history, dialect and culture'; the territory '*was* life' to its inhabitants; the deeds of the

ancestors, marked on the environment, constantly generated life; 'there was no reason to desire or try to possess the country of another group: it would have seemed meaningless to them since their creation stories only related to their own country.' See Richard Broome, *Aboriginal Australians: Black Response to White Dominance, 1788–1980*, Sydney, Allen & Unwin, 1982, pp.10–14. This is certainly very different from the pre-conquest history of the Matopos, where there were constant attempts to 'possess the country of another group'.

21 John Morton, 'Country, People, Art: The Western Aranda, 1870–1990', pp. 29, 35, 37, 41.

22 Peter Garlake, *Early Zimbabwe: From the Matopos to Nyanga*, Gweru, Mambo, 1983, pp. 3–4.

23 Kipling, 'The Burial', see note 1.

BIBLIOGRAPHY

Brock, P., ed., *Women, Rites and Sites: Aboriginal Women's Cultural Knowledge*, Sydney, Allen & Unwin, 1989.

Broome, R., *Aboriginal Australians: Black Response to White Dominance, 1788–1980*, Sydney, Allen & Unwin, 1982.

Philip Clarke, 'Adelaide as Aboriginal landscape', *Aboriginal History*, no. 15, 1991.

Garlake, P., *Early Zimbabwe: From the Matopos to Nyanga*, Gweru, Mambo Press, 1983.

Gordon, R., *The Bushmen Myth*, Boulder, Westview, 1992.

Hardy, J., J. V. S.Megaw and M. R. Megaw, (eds), *The Heritage of Namatjira: The Watercolourists of Central Australia*, Victoria, Heinemann, 1992.

Layton, Robert, *Uluru: An Aboriginal History of Ayers Rock*, Canberra, Aboriginal Studies Press, 1989.

Ranger, T. O., 'Whose Heritage? The Case of the Matobo National Park', *Journal of Southern African Studies*, 15, 2 Jan. 1989.

—— *Voices From the Rocks: A Modern History of the Matopos*, London, James Currey, 1996.

—— 'Making Zimbabwean Landscapes: Painters, Projectors and Priests', *Social Dynamics* 1995.

Wilmsen, E., *Land Filled with Flies: A Political Economy of the Kalahari*, Chicago, University of Chicago Press, 1989.

11

'A LAND SO INVITING AND STILL WITHOUT INHABITANTS'

Erasing Koori culture from (post-) colonial landscapes[1]

Tony Birch

> You get somebody coming in, a foreigner at that, trying to tell
> us to rename our mountains.
>
> Bob Stone, Stawell Town Councillor.[2]

In 1989 the Grampians National Park in the western district of
Victoria became a landscape that would test the memory and historic
identity of the European 'settler' society which dominates the region
numerically and culturally. The then Labor Victorian Minister for
Tourism, Steve Crabb, announced that certain natural features in the
Park would 'revert to their Aboriginal names', with the name of the
mountain range which dominates the park being restored to
Gariwerd. This met with widespread criticism. Europeans in the
district feared the indigenous name restoration project threatened
their own history of 'pioneer settlement'. In addition, the recognition
of a Koori past in the area incorporated the reality of a *living* Koori
community in the western district. In turn this raised the spectre of
the squattocracy's worst nightmare, the possibility of a land rights
claim. Such a fear is evident in hundreds of written complaints
against the restoration project, in which the local Koori communities
were derogatorily described as either a 'cultureless remnant', or as
terra nullius, absent from both the physical and historical landscape.

Although the initiative came solely from the Victorian Tourism
Commission, without consultation with the local Koori community,
the Minister felt that he was in a position to decide which names
would be 'restored':

I expect that the Grampians will be known as Guriward [*sic*], the Black Range as Burrunj, the Glenelg River as Bugara, Halls Gap as Budja Budja, Victoria Gap as Jananginjawi and so on.[3]

The local white community responded with a level of racist hysteria which flared like the picking of a scabby sore. An 'ex-Labor voter' warned of an electoral backlash: 'remember Mr Crabb the tax payer pays your salaries not the lazy, dirty, counter-productive black sector of Australia'.[4] The Mayor of Stawell, Peter Odd, claimed a 'radical group' had forced the proposal on the government:

It seems to me more like a little group that can get what it wants like all the minority groups. The government just bows down to them and the government is ruled by the loudest noise all the time.[5]

Yet no 'noise' on the issue had come from the local Koori community. The five indigenous groups of the western district are represented by Brambuk Incorporated, which at the time was constructing the Brambuk Living Cultural Centre in the Grampians National Park. A spokesperson, Geoff Clark, criticized the government's continuing refusal to consult local Kooris on policies affecting Australian history and culture. Although he supported the 'refreshing and positive gesture' of the name restoration, Clark compared Crabb's approach with that of an earlier visiting Scot: 'he [the minister] and Major Mitchell are guilty of ignoring the Aborigines' past and present association and ownership of the Grampians area . . . over thousands of years.'[6]

The name restoration met opposition from a variety of groups. The Stawell Shire Council wrote to all local governments in Victoria, and gained wide support from both rural and urban shires. The Victorian Place Names Committee received petitions of protest with 60,000 signatures.[7] The Council of Clans regarded the proposal as a threat to 'Scottish heritage and pioneers'.[8] The Balmoral Golf Club voiced concern over the effect the name restoration would have on its greens: 'Our club is close to the Glenelg River and uses the water for irrigating the course'. A Horsham shire councillor, Don Johns, expressed similar concerns about Horsham's water supply.[9]

The Koori rock-art of the park, central to Koori spirituality, was also ridiculed by local Europeans. Pat Reid of Stawell claimed that visitors to her farm had 'little or no interest in our Aboriginal pre-history', and whatever there was 'dissipates completely upon inspecting Bunjil's cave' (the most significant Aboriginal art site in Victoria).[10] E. R. of Mount Waverley informed Crabb that in twenty years of visiting the Grampians she had seen 'not one Aboriginal person' and only 'a few miserable rock paintings'.[11] C. S. of Stawell wrote to 'point out some facts associated with Aboriginal myths of Dreamtime'. He denied a Koori presence ('no Aboriginals ever entered the Grampians due to evil spirits') and repeated a dominant pioneer folk myth that the rock-art was painted by 'a French artist who had a great appreciation of Aboriginal art of central Australia'.[12]

The name restoration had been initially proposed in February 1985 by archaeologist Ben Gunn in a report for the Tourism Commission on 'Recommended changes to Aboriginal site names in the Grampians'.[13] The region contains 80 per cent of Victoria's iden-tified Koori rock-art sites, and Gunn suggested that these be given more appropriate names in line with the 'planned promotion of certain sites as public attractions'. He noted that the existing 'euro-centric descriptive names' (such as 'Cave of Ghosts') could produce 'inappropriate expectations in visitors . . . disappointment or worse, ridicule'. Gunn suggested that Koori names be given to the sites, in consultation with 'the local Aboriginal communities'. A following survey alerted the Tourism Commission to the possibility of exploiting the region's Koori culture: 'Guided tours of Koori sites have the potential to be very successful. The opportunity is there to bring together the product and the potential customers.'[14]

Crabb wanted to promote the region as 'Victoria's Kakadu', referring to the famous World Heritage site in northern Australia. But this false advertising by the Tourist Commission ignored the regionally specific indigenous culture and history of the Gariwerd area, causing visitors to be 'disappointed' with the local rock-art.[15] An officer of the Victorian Archaeological Survey stated that 'people were disappointed in the art itself. They were expecting something like Northern Territory art.' Tourists not only expected to view the 'ancient', but also to see its readily identifiable signifiers, the art of 'outback' and 'real' Aborigines. However, an exploitative tourist industry does little to encourage an appreciation of the rock-art, and respect for past and present indigenous culture, in the western district of Victoria. Denis Rose, a Koori cultural officer from Brambuk, feels that this will only occur when the 'significance of the sites as places of occupation' is interpreted and understood.[16]

The floors of the shelters, where Koori groups once lived, are as significant as any markings on the walls. But of course the floors have little to offer in the way of visual display.

Therefore the tourism literature concentrates on the walls. When it was realized that some of the art could not be reproduced clearly in a photograph, people complained of an inferior product. In 1990 the Victorian Archaeological Survey relayed these concerns to the Tourist Commission.[17] 'Poorly viewable' art resulted in 'considerable dissatisfaction', and led to 'graffiti on suitable surfaces around and above the shelter'. The report recognized that while the 'Camp of the Emu's Foot' was a significant site of occupation, it should be closed to the public because it was 'not appropriate for promotion as an art site'.

On visiting the shelters one is struck by the high wire cages which protect both the sites and the art from vandals and over-zealous tourists. The cages are of course necessary, as damage occurs if sites are visited without supervision. But the cages are themselves both artefact and metaphor, representing the invasive nature of the tourist and European culture – which has often used cages to 'protect' Kooris. A similar metaphor may apply to the vandalizing of sites. The painted-over artwork represents attempts to erase Koori culture from view. In the past, white 'pioneers' attempted this erasure by murdering Aboriginal people to satisfy their hunger for land. Today many in the western district aim to eradicate Koori culture by either denying the Aborigine's present existence or simply mourning the fictional 'passing of the Aborigine'.

NAMING AND KNOWLEDGE

Piper carries a pair of handcuffs slung round him as one [blackfellow] must be taken prisoner for the sake of obtaining native names of the places.

'The Journal of Granville William Chetwynd Stapylton'[18]

In his spatial history of Australia, *The Road to Botany Bay*, Paul Carter has written of 'how little value our culture attaches to names'. This is because 'we', feeling imperially secure, and ignorant of the presence of another culture and history, see 'not a historical space' that may be contested, and may contain multiple histories, but a 'historical fact . . . as if it was always there'.[19] The cultures of indigenous people are relegated to 'prehistory' and the 'ancient', allowing only for meta-historical myths, located outside the boundaries of 'historical facts', which support imperial domination. As Chris Healy has stated, 'true knowledge of the past was knowledge of white Australia and reserved for white Australians.'[20] The Koori history of the western district which was also 'restored' through the naming project displaced the 'true knowledge' of Australian history.

To name spaces is to 'name histories' and also to create them. The colonial naming project in nineteenth-century Australia represents imperial ownership, and a 'reality' that the country both belonged to and was a white Australia. But this sense of security evaporates when this history of colonial domination is challenged by an attempt to restore earlier histories through the names of spaces which form part of the historical narrative. When British explorers attached names to captured landscapes they legitimated the theft of land for their governments who 'owned' the names. Indigenous names themselves do not constitute a threat to white Australia. Houses, streets, suburbs and whole cities have indigenous names. This cultural appropriation represents imperial possession and the quaintness of the 'native', but does not recognize an indigenous history or possible indigenous ownership. Nor is it of *absolute* importance that Koori peoples' daily existence and culture be legitimated with indigenous place names. The suburbs of Fitzroy and Redfern, in Melbourne and Sydney respectively, have historically been associated with strong urban Koori communities.

It is when names are restored to recognize earlier histories and cultures that the threat to ownership occurs. A history of dominance, achieved through violence and theft, passively and amnesically becomes the history of a 'nation'. To acknowledge the history of indigenous people creates insecurity, paranoia, even hysteria. It 'wipes out over one hundred and fifty years of [British] history' and 'takes away that heritage'.[21] Existing names are 'recommended for consignment to the scrapheap of history'.[22] The features themselves can actually vanish: 'Ayers Rock [Uluru] is no longer'; 'GRAMPIANS, ARE THEY GONE?'; 'Familiar places or land- marks . . . would disappear from the map.'[23]

Opponents of the Grampians/Gariwerd name restoration eulog- ized the nineteenth-century 'pioneers' who had 'developed the land using nothing but their bare hands and crude farm implements'.[24] One opponent asked of the indigenous peoples' relationship to the land: 'Did they strive to explore, to overcome danger, to improve their lot?' His answer: 'I don't know. There's no record. Who cares?'[25] Even when their presence was recognized, the present Koori community in the western district was often regarded as lacking their own culture. J. R. of Murtoa rejected the suggestion that the Kooris had 'some sort of culture', adding 'It's too late for all this nonsense.'[26] M. W. of Phillip Island asked:

How many Western District Aborigines are there anyway? And what have they contributed to the progress of the area over the last fifty years or so? I'd guess, not many and not much.[27]

Philip Lienert of Horsham, in a letter to the *Wimmera Mail-Times*, argued for the need to put a contact history of 'murder, theft, rape, cruelty and ignorance' into its proper perspective: 'At what time in the world's history has one group of people not done that to another group?' He claimed that the indigenous people of Australia were fortunate that they had been colonized by a civilized race: 'If Great Britain had not colonized Australia then someone else would have – and what would have been the fate of the Aborigines then?'[28] The *Hamilton Spectator* urged Crabb to 'leave history as it stands'.[29] By this the newspaper meant a dominant history that not only ignored Koori history, but also only selectively remembered the 'pioneer' history of the area.

Control of the Australian landscape is vital to the settler psyche. The victors' histories are those of absence: of *terra nullius*. In order to uphold the lie of an 'empty land', Europeans have either denied the indigenous people's presence, or completely devalued its cultures. These hegemonic histories take possession of others' histories to silence, manipulate and 'deform' them.[30] The challenge from indigenous people to confront these imperialist fictions displaces 'the seamless normality [of] a triumphal national history'.[31]

These histories may not be presented in the pages of a conventional text (although they often are). They are evoked in the media and on film and in political discussion of 'Aboriginal issues'. Many of these debates centre on the relationship of peoples to land. In Perth, the Swan River Fringe Dwellers, Nyoongar people, waged a struggle against developers and the state Labor government over the erection of a recreation centre on the Old Brewery site on the Swan River.[32] They attempted to protect a sacred dreaming track, formed by Waugal, a serpent who created many of the landscape features in the area, including the river. Although the developers and government had difficulty accepting the Nyoongar belief in a 'giant snake', they also tried to appropriate this creation story for their own purposes. The original designs for the redevelopment included a 100-metre-long 'polychrome brick Waugal path'. Steve Mickler has called this 'a colonialist disdain for the fallen "noble savage"', the urban ' "half-caste" '.[33] The simplest way to deny groups such as the Swan River Fringe Dwellers a right to their sacred land is to deny their existence as indigenous people. If such a denial fails, some opponents revert to the *terra nullius* myth. There was opposition to the Uluru [Ayers Rock] name restoration on the grounds that the area had been unoccupied by 'tribes of the desert . . . for centuries', with the exception of 'nomadic hunters' who visited 'in prolonged wet seasons'.[34]

Europeans continue to 'make' and 'unmake' indigenous people. When they attempt to claim rights to land, or to the bodies of their ancestors, they are separated from an 'ancient past'. Mickler believes that, as the appreciation (and possession) of Aboriginal art has increased, so too has 'the intensity of the denigration of practised or "lived" Aboriginal culture'.[35] This form of racism relates to what Renato Rosaldo has termed 'imperialist nostalgia', which makes racial domination appear 'innocent and pure'.[36] Having altered or destroyed the culture of the 'Other', the colonizers then appropriate it for their own gain, or even mourn its passing, while at the same time concealing their 'own complicity with often brutal domination'.

Historically, Europeans expected to witness the eradication of indigenous peoples, and Australian governments have attempted to erase the identity of indigenous people by physical genocide and policies of cultural 'assimilation'. Despite their failure, 'imperialist nostalgia' is everywhere. The passing of an ancient culture is both lamented and celebrated. The collection of art, for example, can serve as evidence of the superiority of the imperialist culture, while allowing its owners the gratification of appreciating the 'beauty' in objects from a past time. James Clifford has noted the Western preference for collectibles that are from an 'ancient (preferably vanished) civilization'.[37] For mourning to occur 'innocently and purely', without opposition, the possessed and commodified culture must be certified dead.

MAPPING HISTORIES

As much as guns and warships, maps have been the weapons of imperialism.

J. B. Hartley, 'Maps, knowledge and power'[38]

We should fully recognize what nineteenth-century explorers and 'pioneers' accomplished in Victoria's western district. In 1836 Major Thomas Mitchell passed through the land of the Jardwadjali people around the mountain range that he named the Grampians. During this search for exploitable land, Mitchell claimed he was exploring a *terra nullius* – an empty land – despite having contact with local indigenous people, some of whom his party murdered. Mitchell wrote:

> It was evident that the reign of solitude in these beautiful vales was near a close; a reflection which, in my mind, often sweetened the toils and inconveniences of travelling through such houseless regions.[39]

He described the country he saw as 'resembling a nobleman's park', and as an 'Eden' awaiting 'the immediate reception of civilized man'.[40] Its 'primitive' inhabitants would be swept aside in order to add to the wealth and power of the British empire. Mitchell's second-in-command, Granville William Chetwynd Stapylton, saw the area as an 'El Dorado' which would be 'at present worth sixty millions to the Exchequer of England', and hopefully result in 'a good fat grant' for the 'discoverers'.[41]

Mitchell was a surveyor, taking control of the land by charting it on a map. By naming features, he placed a symbolic British flag on each of them. The land was ordered and labelled, becoming a colonial possession. His cartography and favourable reports to the British government resulted in an immediate grab for land by Europeans. He anticipated that his expedition would lead to the exploitation of 'those natural advantages [of the land], certain to become at no distant date, of vast importance to new people'.[42]

Although the land had been occupied for thousands of years, Mitchell was able to map a 'socially empty space'.[43] Elizabeth Ferrier has written that 'mapping determines the way landscape has been conceived'; it is described as an 'unfolded map'.[44] This is a powerful metaphor. The land that was possessed could literally be held in the hands of the invading colonizers. When Mitchell mapped his 'Australia Felix' he gave the land a new history – a British history. His maps conceal the histories of the indigenous people. Such is the power of cartography.

Opponents of the Gariwerd name restoration regarded the project as an insult to Mitchell's 'memory and tenacity'.[45] And although the Koori Tourism Unit's submission highlighted the fact that Mitchell had only conferred ten of the forty-four European names at issue, it also said that 'Mitchell should be credited with advocating the retention of Aboriginal place-names', and had often done so: 'I have always', he had written, 'gladly adopted Aboriginal names.' Crabb, quoting this passage from Mitchell's diary, 'said the explorer went to great lengths to use Koori words when he named landscape features'.[16]

The indigenous groups of the Gariwerd area followed Mitchell's party as it moved across the mountain range, but made little contact with him. Mitchell sometimes left the main party and 'explored' ahead with a smaller group, leaving Stapylton in charge. When visited by indigenous peoples, Stapylton recorded: 'I wish to detain them if possible until the Surveyor-General returns, for by them we may obtain a great deal of knowledge of the intervening country.'[17] Piper, a 'black' from New South Wales who accompanied the party, carried the handcuffs that would capture the local peoples and hence their names. But Stapylton sometimes had trouble attracting visitors:

> Blackfellows shot at and wounded today by one of the men in the bush. The native shipped his spear and was accordingly very properly fired at. Now to war with these gentry I suppose. They are encamped around us tonight. Tomorrow we will give them a benefit if they don't keep off.[48]

Stapylton entered comments in his diary in reference to the peoples whose place names he wanted to possess: 'Their hollow resembles precisely the cry of some wild beast, which in fact it is.'[49] On one occasion he disturbed a family and took great pleasure in the fear he instilled in them: 'these devils will always run if you give them the time.'[50] This is the man after whom Mitchell named Mt Stapylton. The Victorian Place Names Committee, apparently on aesthetic grounds, refused to restore the name of Gunigalg to the mountain.

In May 1836, north of what is now the Murray River, Mitchell's party had clashed with indigenous groups. Mitchell decided to take action 'in a war which not my party, but these savages had virtually commenced'. He set up an 'ambuscade' in order to surprise 'the vast body of blacks' that had been tracking the party. Realizing that Mitchell's men were waiting for them, the group ran toward 'their citadel, the river'. Without waiting for an order from Mitchell, his men ran after the 'blacks', shooting them as they attempted to escape across the river. Mitchell later reported that seven had been shot. He accepted fully the decision of his men to chase and kill, 'for the result was the permanent deliverance of the party from imminent danger'. Mitchell commemorated the killings by conferring a name upon the site:

> I gave to the little hill which witnessed this overthrow of our enemies, and was to us the harbinger of peace and tranquillity, the name of Mt Dispersion.[51]

The massacre created enough 'ripples' to delay Mitchell's knighthood.[52] To ensure that his place in history is remembered, though, there are some fifty memorial cairns dotted along a commemorative track bearing his name.[53] This celebration of a 'great explorer' buries the dead and their histories. As Chilla Bulbeck has shown, most Australian monuments to pioneer history 'avoid the sore spot of race relations'.[54]

Mitchell's exploration of the western district of Victoria had been pre-empted by the land-hungry Henty brothers, who occupied land at Portland Bay in 1834.[55] The way to gain free title to land was to exploit it vigorously. A claim was established by 'occupying it with sheep grazed in flocks from 500 to 1,000 head, each flock in the care of a shepherd'.[56] This had a devastating effect on the indigenous population. When the Chief Protector of Aborigines, G. A. Robinson, arrived in Portland in May 1841, he discovered that only 'two of the tribe who once inhabited the country of the Convincing Ground are still alive'.[57]

Robinson's tour of the western district uncovered large-scale murder by the European squatters, as well as Koori resistance. At Portland the Police Magistrate, Mr Blair, stated that the 'natives' of a 'tribe' that had killed a squatter and his shepherd 'should be exterminated'. He would 'shoot the whole tribe' if the murderer was not 'delivered up'. Two days later, one of the Henty brothers informed Robinson that 'the settlers were dropping them'. Blair, who was present, 'replied he hoped so', and added that 'he had no power to restrain the settlers from shooting the women and children'. At the Fitzroy River near Portland, a Mr Pilleau informed Robinson that 'the settlers encouraged their men to shoot the natives', and 'that for every white man killed twenty blacks were shot'. Robinson commented in his journal that the settlers spoke of

> dropping the natives as if they were speaking of dropping cows. Indeed, the doctrine is being promulgated that they are not human, or hardly so and thereby inculcating the principle that killing them is no murder. [58]

At the Tulloh property near Gariwerd, Robinson 'saw the corpse of a native on four sticks', apparently used as bait to lure and kill emus. Robinson despaired at 'the heartless manner in which Charles Winter and his ruffians [reacted to] the barbarous murder of this man'. Tulloh told Robinson that he and eight other men had previously gone to the Grampians 'in quest of blacks'. They found a child, laid it near the fire, and Robinson recorded 'roasted it or, to use his [Tulloch's] qualified expression, burnt it'. They also found a 'fine little boy', who bit one of the men who had abducted him. 'The ruffian then kicked the child to death.' A week later, following yet another attack on a native camp near Mt Sturgeon, Robinson could only state the obvious: '[this] would not be allowed in civilized society.'[59]

More than a century later, on 15 October 1991, Crabb announced the Place Names Committee's decision on the Gariwerd name restoration. Forty-nine place-name restorations were accepted, fifteen were rejected and four required further investigation.[60] Most of the accepted names were given dual Koori/English names. The Koori Tourism Unit had publicly accepted this position during negotiations at least a year earlier: 'We have no objection so long as the Koori name goes first.'[61] But this did not happen. The National Park was officially known as The Grampians (Gariwerd). The Koori name was therefore linguistically subordinated, 'handcuffed' in parentheses.

The local Member for Lowan, Bill McGrath, promised that the names would be 'thrown out . . . as soon as the Opposition was returned to Government'.[62] (And true to its word, the removal of Gariwerd from the official name of the park was one of the first pieces of legislation passed by the Victorian Liberal Government following its election in 1992.) Bob Stone, now Stawell's Mayor, said that 'you won't have anyone around here using the names.' He believed that the signs would most likely be torn down, adding 'I wouldn't do it myself, as much as I'd like to.' Geoff Clark of Brambuk, on the other hand, felt that on its own the name restoration was 'a poor attempt at some form of social justice', and would only amount to something of substance when 'the concept of land ownership [and] recognition of our cultural heritage within this particular area is recognized'.[63]

The name restoration may be a beginning or an end. The tourist dollar chases the 'niche market'. The market may one day target a western district town as a heritage-style theme park – perhaps Stawell, which has a gold-mining history, will be selected to fulfil this role. Its citizens may then become artefacts, performing behind colonial façades, stuck in a local version of Peter Carey's 'American Dreams'.[64] But if the market moves away from 'dreamtime legends', the money may as well. Koori culture is not a commodity. It must be interpreted in an educative fashion by those who live it – Koori people. To assist in this process, the Koori names of landscapes in the region need to be fully restored, not presented in a tokenistic fashion, or as a 'dead tongue'.[65]

The first publication to promote the newly named Grampians (Gariwerd) National Park claimed: 'There's a place in Victoria where time seems to have stood still. A place of dreamtime legends.' The booklet tells of the Kooris, who 'roamed' the area before European exploration, the arrival of Mitchell, then the squatters, 'the farmers, the foresters, and the miners'.[66] It asks tourists to visit Brambuk Living Cultural Centre, or possibly the 'Grand Canyon . . . Fallen Giant . . . Whale's Mouth . . . Jaws of Death'. Visitors to the Park can experience 'the same panoramic views Major Mitchell marvelled at in 1836. Nothing has changed.'

But some things have changed. On 3 June 1992 Australia's High Court ended the charade of *terra nullius* in its 'Mabo' decision, which legally recognized the 'ownership' of Murray Islands in the Torres Strait by the Meriam people. It decided that they were entitled 'against the whole world, to possession, occupation, use and enjoyment of the lands of the Murray Islands',[67] in their ability to show an ongoing occupation of their country, and the continued practice of laws and customs based on tradition. Although the ramifications of the decisions are yet to be fully tested on the mainland, and any 'reading' of the legal situation is speculative at best, it is unlikely that Koori communities in Victoria will gain from the decision. Although two justices stated that 'the acts and events by which that dispossession in legal theory has carried into practical effect constitute the darkest aspect of the history of this nation',[68] the decision also means that 'when the tide of history has washed away any real acknowledgment of traditional law . . . native title has ceased.'[69] Therefore, perversely, indigenous communities who have had their lifestyles most disrupted, and who have lost their land, are least likely to receive full and proper justice.

Race relations in post-Mabo Australia are dominated by a public rhetoric of reconciliation and self-determination, despite periodic 'throw-back' statements supporting past failures such as Australia's policy of Aboriginal assimilation.[70] The Gariwerd/Grampians name restoration project was a test of white Australia's ability to reconcile its own past, some of which it had attempted to erase from historical memory. The people of the western district had invested so much in a history of 'white mythologies' that a challenge to it questioned the basis of their collective and individual identities. Faced with an alternative history, both their own and that of Koori people, their reaction was one of fear and anxiety. The project itself was, in addition to being an exploitative one, a symbolic venture (at best). Although the concept of indigenous land rights entered into, or indirectly influenced opposition to the name restoration, it was never a central issue of the controversy. In the 1990s it is vital that the past collective histories of black and white Australia be acknowledged and understood. Reconciliation is not possible in Australia, and nor is the expression of mature national identity, unless white Australia is prepared to 'reopen the old wounds, so they can heal' and accept histories that 'relinquish their amnesia'.[71]

NOTES

1 Koori refers to Aboriginal Australians living in south-eastern Australia.
2 Melbourne *Sun*, 27 March 1989.
3 See Koori Tourism Unit Files – Media File. All Koori Tourism Unit Files (henceforth referred to as KTUF) are held by the Victorian Tourism Unit, Melbourne.
4 KTUF 9/7/76/3.
5 *Stawell Times-News*, 31 Mar. 1989.
6 Geoff Clark, Chairperson Brambuk Incorporated, 29 Mar. 1989, KTUF 9/7/76/3.
7 *Wimmera Mail-Times*, 16 Oct. 1991.
8 This petition and the following letters are held in the KTUF 9/7/76/3.
9 *Wimmera Mail-Times*, 20 June 1990.
10 *Portland Observer*, 9 July 1990.
11 KTUF 12/2/6/3, 10 Oct. 1990
12 KTUF 9/7/76/3, 10 May 1989.
13 KTUF 12/2/6/3.
14 KTUF 12/2/6/2; *Tourism and the Grampians Region*, Melbourne, Victorian Tourism Commission, 1990, p. 18.
15 Interview with Ian Clark, 21 Oct. 1991.
16 Koori Oral History Program, Museum of Victoria, Grampians Visit, 1 June 1989, Tape 46.
17 See *Tourism and the Grampians*.
18 28 July 1836, 'The Journal of Granville William Chetwynd Stapylton', in L. O'Brien and M. H. Douglas (eds), *The Natural History of Western Victoria*, Canberra, Australian Institute of Agricultural Science, 1974, p. 95.

19 Paul Carter, *The Road to Botany Bay*, London, Faber & Faber, 1987, pp. 2 and xiv.
20 Chris Healy, '"We Know Your Mob Now": Histories and their Cultures', *Meanjin*, no. 3, 1990, p. 512.
21 R. S. of Stawell, 7 Apr. 1989, in KTUF 9/7/76/3.
22 *Hamilton Spectator*, 22 Dec. 1990.
23 B. G. of Horsham, 28 March 1989, in KTUF 12/2/6/3; *Boort and Quambatook Standard-Times*, 29 May 1990; *Portland Observer*, 4 July 1990.
24 P. N. Griffin, in *Stawell Mail-Times* (cutting, n.d.).
25 *Melbourne Sun*, 19 Apr. 1989.
26 KTUF 9/7/76/3, 10 Apr. 1989.
27 KTUF 9/7/76/3, 18 Dec. 1990.
28 *Wimmera Mail-Times*, 22 June 1990.
29 *Hamilton Spectator*, 13 May 1990.
30 Janet Abu-Lughod, 'On the remaking of history: How to reinvent the past', in B. Kruger and P. Mariani (eds), *Remaking History*, Seattle, Bay Press, 1989, p. 118.
31 Healy, '"We Know Your Mob"', p. 512.
32 *Melbourne Age*, 27 May 1991.
33 Steve Mickler, 'The Battle for Goonininup', *Arena*, no. 96, 1991. The Western Australian Government purchased the land in 1985.
34 Don Petersons, *Melbourne Sun*, 15 Oct. 1991.
35 Mickler, 'The Battle', p. 74.
36 Renato Rosaldo, 'Imperialist Nostalgia', *Representations*, no. 26, Spring 1989, pp. 107–22.
37 James Clifford, *The Predicament of Culture*, Cambridge, Mass., Harvard University Press, 1988, p. 222.
38 J. B. Hartley 'Maps, knowledge, and power', in D. Cosgrove and S. Daniels (eds), *The Iconography of Landscape*, Cambridge, Cambridge University Press, 1988, p. 282.
39 Major T. L. Mitchell, *Three Expeditions into the Interior of Eastern Australia*, Adelaide, Australiana Facsimile Editions, Libraries Board of South Australia, 1965, vol. 1, p. 174.
40 Mitchell, *Three Expeditions*, p. 171.
41 Stapylton, 'Journal', p. 99.
42 Mitchell, *Three Expeditions*, p. 171.
43 See Hartley, 'Maps, Knowledge, Power'.
44 Elizabeth Ferrier, 'Mapping Power and Contemporary Cultural Theory', in *Antithesis*, vol. 4, no. 1, 1990, p. 41.
45 D. S. of Bentleigh, 30 March 1989, in KTUF 9/7/76/3.
46 Warnambool *Standard*,1 Dec. 1990.
47 Stapylton, 'Journal', p. 87.
48 Stapylton, 'Journal', p. 95.
49 Stapylton, 'Journal', p. 100.
50 Stapylton, 'Journal', p. 105.
51 Mitchell, *Three Expeditions*, p. 104.
52 Manning Clark, 'Major Mitchell and Australia Felix', in Manning Clark et al., *Australia Felix*, Dunkeld, Dunkeld and District Historical Museum, 1987, p. 79.

53 Clark, 'Major Mitchell', p. 76.
54 Chilla Bulbeck, 'Aborigines, Memorials and the History of the Frontier', in J. Rickard and P. Spearritt (eds), *Packaging the Past: Public Histories*, Melbourne, Melbourne University Press, 1991, p. 170.
55 M. F. Christie, *Aborigines in Colonial Victoria 1935–86*, Melbourne, Melbourne University Press, 1979, p. 24.
56 L. P. Peel, 'The First Hundred Years of Agricultural Development in Western Victoria', in O'Brien and Douglas (eds), *Natural History of Victoria*.
57 'Journals of G. A. Robinson – May to August 1841', *Records of the Victorian Archaeological Survey*, vol. 11, Oct. 1980, p. 15.
58 'Journals of Robinson', pp. 15–43.
59 'Journals of Robinson', pp. 77–87.
60 *Wimmera Mail-Times*, 16 Oct. 1991.
61 *Ballarat Courier*, 20 Oct. 1990.
62 *Ararat Adviser*, 17 Oct. 1991.
63 *Vox Populi*, SBS Television, 28 Oct. 1991.
64 Peter Carey, 'American Dreams' in *The Fat Man in History*, University of Queensland Press, St Lucia, 1988.
65 Melbourne *Herald*, 31 May 1990: 'Dead Tongue Sparks Hot Words in the Grampians'.
66 *The Grampian (Gariwerd)*, Victorian Tourism Commission, Melbourne, 1991, p. 3.
67 *The Australian*, 3 June 1992.
68 Melbourne *Age*, 4 June 1992.
69 *The Australian*, 3 June 1992.
70 For example, the Emeritus Professor of History at The University of Melbourne, Geoffrey Blainey, stated that 'the future of Aborigines is as Australians, not Aborigines', Melbourne *Age*, 21 Aug. 1993.
71 Thomas Butler, 'Memory: A Mixed Blessing', in T. Butler (ed.), *Memory: History, Culture and the Mind*, Oxford, Basil Blackwell, 1989, p. 25.

BIBLIOGRAPHY

Abu-Lughod, J., 'On the remaking of history: How to reinvent the past', in B. Kruger and P. Mariani (eds), *Remaking History*, Seattle, Bay Press, 1989.
Butler, T. (ed), *Memory: History, Culture and the Mind*, Oxford, Basil Blackwell, 1989.
Carter, P., *The Road to Botany Bay*, London, Faber & Faber, 1987.
Clifford, J., *The Predicament of Culture*, Cambridge, Mass., Harvard University Press, 1988.
Ferrier, E., 'Mapping Power and Contemporary Cultural Theory', in *Antithesis*, vol. 4, no. 1, 1990.
Hartley, J. B., 'Maps, knowledge, and power', in D. Cosgrove and S. Daniels (eds), *The Iconography of Landscape*, Cambridge, Cambridge University Press, 1988.
Healy, C., ' "We Know Your Mob Now": Histories and their Cultures', *Meanjin*, no. 3, 1990.

'Journals of G. A. Robinson – May to August 1841', *Records of the Victorian Archaeological Survey*, vol. 11, October 1980.

'The Journal of Granville William Chetwynd Stapylton', in L. O'Brien and M. H. Douglas (eds), *The Natural History of Western Victoria*, Canberra, Australian Institute of Agricultural Science, 1974.

Mickler, S., 'The Battle for Goonininup', *Arena*, no. 96, 1991.

Mitchell, T. L., *Three Expeditions into the interior of Eastern Australia*, Adelaide, Australiana Facsimile Editions, no. 18, Libraries Board of South Australia, 1965, 2 vols.

Rosaldo, R. 'Imperialist Nostalgia', *Representations*, no. 26, Spring 1989.

Part III

BORDERS, BOUNDARIES, OPEN SPACES

12

MARTHA HAS NO LAND
The tragedy of identity in
The Marabi Dance

Abner Nyamende

The story of Martha in Modikwe Dikobe's *The Marabi Dance* (1973) takes us back to the Johannesburg of the 1930s and 1940s, where black people come to look for wealth and opportunity, together with the hordes of others who have been drawn like a magnet to the Golden City. Doornfontein, the urban space in which the novel opens, is a section of Johannesburg, characterized by broken families, fatherless children and squalid, overcrowded dwellings.

The narrative traces the life of Martha Mabongo from the time of her premature removal together with the black members of her community from Doornfontein, to the newly built South Western Townships (SOWETO). The crossing in consciousness between the urban and rural space is a constant feature of the novel, and an early marker of this is the stress on the rural longings of Martha's parents, the first generation of city-dwellers. Thus the parents look forward to a proper bride-price for their daughter, and hope that they will obtain the cattle required as bride-price if she marries her cousin, Sephai, who hails from the rural areas. To their dismay, however, they discover that Martha is already pregnant from her relationship with George, the pianist who plays the wild and joyous music of marabi for the urban dancers of Doornfontein.

The tragic circumstances discussed in this essay centre around the spacial significance of Doornfontein. For Martha it represents domestic space, since it is the only 'home' she knows in her life. Yet the style of life among the black members of her community suggests a temporariness similar to that of a prisoner-of-war camp. Martha becomes involved in what can be termed an unresolved dialogue between urban and rural space. What is crucial for her, is that she must make an urgent decision about her true identity before she loses it altogether. Should she see herself against the background of rural space, and as someone only temporarily in the city? Or alternatively, should she define herself in the light of the squalour materializing as No. 26 Staib Street, Doornfontein and its immediate environment, which represents all that she has of an urban experience? As Martha fights to assert her true identity, her struggle brings her closer to the domain of truth – the truth that her space has been invaded and utilized. She has no land that she can call her own and which can give her the identity she requires.

Martha's deprivation of space mirrors that of the novelist Dikobe himself, who seems to lament the erasure of existences in places like Sophiatown, Doornfontein and other black urban places. The physical erasure of such existences has affected abstract values and states of being, and crucially, Dikobe implies, it has affected the individual's self-identity.

Dikobe's personal tragedy can be seen in the following light: although he seems to identify with the community of Doornfontein, that community has long dispersed and can only be reassembled through the story of Martha. Dikobe's loss is also that of many other South Africans who have experienced forced removals. In fact people who identify themselves with Doornfontein or Sophiatown in Johannesburg, or with District Six in Cape Town and other sites of forced removal have, lately, raised their voices quite strongly at meetings, cultural come-togethers, talkshops and other such gatherings emphasizing their former identity. Writers like Richard Rive, (and to a lesser extent Alex la Guma) who put District Six at the centre of their work, have given a permanent identity to these sites and to those who have inhabited them. Similarly the poet Don Mattera's autobiographical *Memory is the Weapon* (1987) revives the pride of belonging to Sophiatown long after the people of that place were removed. For many of these people the complete restoration of that identity seems to be the one salvation in their lives, and there is hope, perhaps faith in the hope, that such redemption will ultimately be realized. For the people of District Six, that hope recently expressed itself in the formation of a District Six Committee. Their cry for a reclamation of District Six is presently as strong as if the dwellers were removed only yesterday and not over forty years ago, when the Nationalist Party put its urban segregation policies into effect through enforcing the 1953 Group Areas Act.

The Marabi Dance therefore becomes a story of a lost identity and a vanished space. Doornfontein, the place 'where Martha grew up' holds this identity. K. Sole and E. Koch make the following comment:

> *The Marabi Dance* is based around the young woman Martha in order to allow Dikobe to focus on the home and family life of lower class black people where women predominate. In the main, he deals with Martha's search for identity as she is attracted to Marabi on the one hand and desires respectability on the other.[1]

Dikobe actually focuses on people who may even be regarded as lower-than-lower-class, and who may at best be seen as the dregs of society, people who, even among the dwellers of Doornfontein, are looked down upon and despised. That they are black people simply aggravates matters for them, but that they are severely deprived lends them the transparent identity shared among all those who feature somewhere below any standard classification of any society, people who are sacrificed on the altar of progress and development.

As Martha is born and grows up in Doornfontein we expect her to be closely attached to that environment. Although she stands out as a leading character, at the same time her existence in the story is important only in so far as it highlights the collective experience of the background characters, both female and male. Her portrayal by Dikobe aptly fits with Robert July's observation on the depiction of modernity in African literature:

> Each work presents a major character and a number of lesser figures whose lives are made by the world they live in, and whom we can see as authentic modern Africans presenting the rich detail of internal mental stress, external physical action, and environmental force whose tensions balance to form these particular African personalities.[2]

Martha's own personal dilemma is recognized only to the point where it reflects the plight of the people around her, who in turn expand to encompass all those urban dwellers who find themselves with neither land nor property. Hofmeyr sums up this plight of the landless Doornfontein community thus:

> history of land dispossession, to most characters in *The Marabi Dance*, is something only vaguely remembered; to Martha it is

totally alien. For her the only reality is an urban one, but dispossession makes clear why urbanization is permanent. A return to a rural existence is out of the question for most or others like Sephai must seek work in town to pay poll-taxes.[3]

Thus Martha is brought up within a heterogeneous community and hybrid culture; and her very 'home' is 'also a home to more than twenty other people'. She is immersed in the squalor of a poverty-stricken section of Johannesburg, but almost as if by intuition she senses that her identity is somewhat different from that of a country girl. Her difficulties facing up to her true identity arise mainly because, as a child of once-rural parents, she sometimes feels that she should inherit elements of an identity from her own people, including more traditional African ways. What she tries to do is seek common trends that bind together a volatile community. Although the western influence of city life is quite dominant, the people of Doornfontein are not fully absorbed into the rhythm of western exist-ence. They are in any case made to keep to their own section of town where they practise a medley of traditional systems of 'order'.

All the characters in this peculiarly South African urban space experience the general suffering caused by poorly paid jobs and the absence of good opportunities. In the circumstances in which they live possession of property seems to be out of the question. Even the marabi dance itself, a popular social activity in Doornfontein, is viewed as a dance party for persons of 'low type' and for those derogatorily called 'malala-pipe' – who huddle in drainpipes at night, 'homeless ruffian children'. Martha, therefore, finds herself at a crossroads with a number of options to choose from in deciding her future. The rural life appears to offer her a chance to possess land and stock, but to achieve this she would have to give up her present identity as an urban child; the urban life secures her true identity as she sees it, but offers her no security of a place of abode, no living space to call her own. Rural life appears to offer her a promise of a husband and a decent community to live in; urban life surrenders her to the power of an unreliable and unprincipled boyfriend as well as the woes of a downtrodden segment of society.

Martha as an individual rejects the identity of a country girl which her parents try to impose upon her. It appears as though the social environment that has shaped and influenced Martha's personality also lends her true identity. Dorothy Driver explains this sense of identity drawing on the language of Derrida thus:

'Self' is constructed in dialectic with others or another: one cannot see oneself in the absence of projections from the world around one. What the self is awaits its determination by or from those outside the self, those who say 'me' to me, or who constitute the self for which I strive.[4]

George is singled out as someone for Martha to look up to, but unfortunately for her he changes into an irresponsible and ruthless youth. She does not have a simple choice to make as her own parents, who hold fast to the memory of the absent rural space, insist on her following the path of country people. Her mother insists on the unquestionable right of the parents to enforce the identity of their child upon her. She declares:

Do you think I have given birth to you for nothing? If you don't listen to what your father and mother tell you, you must get out of our house.[5]

Quite ironically, the 'father' and 'mother' Ma-Mabongo refers to in the third person here possess no home of their own, something that would stand as a base to support a family unit. Martha can hardly be blamed for holding their 'advice' in suspicion. Nevertheless, to ensure that she claims unquestioned control over the child by virtue of her being a parent, Ma-Mabongo expresses her distaste for her daughter's manners thus, 'I wish God had denied me children'.

What matters most to Martha, however, is not that she seeks her roots in an unknown rural environment but that she asserts her identity as an urban black. We cannot help but admire her when, to achieve the latter, she resists even her own parents' influence, thereby daring to face, single-handed, her present predicament as a dispossessed urban black. Defending her right to receive singing lessons from Samson she retorts to her mother:

I won't keep quiet to see myself turned into a country girl who is forced to leave school early and work in the white people's kitchen![6]

It seems as though the novelist is making a point about the justification of Martha's resistance to any effort to link her birth to a life in the rural areas. We might even be alarmed that Martha seems bent on denying herself an opportunity to possess her own share of the land, but then what is implied is that such a piece of land would, in the wider context of black dispossession, fail to give her the identity she yearns for. July also observes the inclination by metropolitan African novelists to mark the distinctive modernity of 'the African city with its way of life, its physical appearance and its values so different from those of the traditional villages'. He shows a lack of any sense of the African city as itself a gendered space, although, interestingly, he identifies certain 'forces' that, according to him, 'have shaped the African city dweller, making him in turn equally different from his country cousin'.[7] Regarding the African urban social setting July has this to say:

> At one extreme is the unselfconscious amorality of the gangsters, implicit in their actions and, of course, never articulated. The middle ground is occupied by the ordinary citizen – decent, hard working, vaguely aware that his life lacks something but unable to understand what it is and how to go about getting it. The younger people, hopelessly unable as they are to deal with their lives, and encumbered with values which only a lunatic might find of service, at least do have some conscious standards and the warped courage to live by them.[8]

Martha, in terms of her youth, represents the last category in July's analysis. As part of the alienated segment of the urban society in South Africa, however, her attempts to assert her true identity reveal an even more 'warped' identity on her part. Hers is a continuously negative process of development within a community that continues to generate warped perceptions of the individual and his or her home ground. It could be for this reason that the social resistance which Martha and her people stand for, their defining for themselves of a new urban lifestyle, becomes the central virtue of her moral rights.

An interesting section in *The Marabi Dance* reflects a number of characters who can be regarded as a cross-section of the Doornfontein community, all of them attending to matters of custom or of spiritual importance: the Mabongo couple is discussing Martha's marriage to Sephai; the Indian family is making its devotions to Allah; and old Mapena, as he recalls the rain ceremonies of the past, goes outside and, after studying the heavens, predicts rain. Martha also 'gazes into the sky', but she is not reported to read anything there. For her all that seems to have any meaning is the Molefe Yard and its surroundings, the rickshaws and the dusty road. Perhaps to vindicate Mapena's prediction or in answer to the rickshaw man's prayer for rain, the rain does indeed fall. Traditionally, rain represents relief from the suffering, here represented by the hot and dusty day, but rain also requires land if its blessing is to be felt. Thus old Mapena's complaint is a just pointer to the absent land when he says, 'The gods have answered our prayers and now we are engulfed in this yard'.[9] Their fervent appeal to the gods for rain returns almost as an indictment against them, for having lost the land upon which the rain – the blessings from the gods – should fall. Just after this, the horror of the curse upon the landless victims looms menacingly before July Mabongo as the following extract suggests:

> Martha's father, guided by the carbide light of his cycle, splashed through the yard and waded his way ankle deep through the pool of muddy water. It took him all his strength to pull his feet and boots out of the slush. One of the lavatories had overflowed and the excrement and urine mixed freely with the mud and water. The stench polluted the air which had been purified by the rain. A tin of skokiaan which had been dug into the ground, to conceal it from the police, lay uncovered and threw a yellow circle of colour, and the whole yard smelled of bread and yeast. Mabongo stumbled further until he reached the gate. 'Morena! If this is how we live, then God, suffer us all to die.'[10]

The confusing social set-up of Doornfontein becomes crystallized in Martha's own personal experience of life and shapes her entire personality. Rejecting Sephai, the country fellow, she openly tells her mother, 'I was born in town. I don't know the laws of the people at home and Sephai is not a boy like the town ones'. In one of her songs she complains that her lover has left her 'in the land of slavery', by which she means, ironically enough, the place that is her own birth-right, the urban space where she wishes to belong.[11]

Martha takes up the grim option to pioneer her own way as an urban black. Her decision condemns her to a bleak future, a future well-defined by what she says about herself: 'I have from childhood to womanhood lived in the slums.' All the examples she can possibly follow are not those of the illustrious leaders she might hope for but a bunch of downtrodden people who only exist from day to day almost under a perpetual emergency situation of a poverty-stricken refugee camp – or a neglected concentration camp. As they are shifted from one place to another each environment seems to clasp them firmly and to give them a ready made form of identity – very much like the chameleon Martha watches on the doorstep of a match-box house that is her new home in Soweto's Orlando town-ship.[12] Martha and her people have to accept the lack of permanence that dominates the way of life that is imposed upon them by society.

The circumstances of Martha's 'home' reflect dire deprivation and much uncertainty, but Martha is so conditioned to her tragic circumstances that she seems almost oblivious to the extent of her own suffering, as the following passage demonstrates:

> Whilst she was washing outside Moipone lighted the primus stove and brewed tea. The 'house' where the Mabongo family lived was not more than 15 by 20 feet. In summer the mealies were cooked outside and some of the household goods of little value were kept outside in the yard. Martha had slept in the same room as her parents from babyhood to womanhood and felt little inconvenience, except when she had visitors. She did not complain.[13]

Martha's calm is constantly challenged by the prospect of having to make a choice between the background in which she has been brought up and that of the rural people. Yet both options promise her no change in social status: she will continue to be regarded as a common street girl and later as a simple township woman in the urban environment, while a life as Sephai's wife in the rural areas can only offer her the status of a severely deprived and neglected existence in the backwaters of the land. Her mother, however, tries to sharpen her desire for marriage by a false suggestion that life in the rural areas could be very smooth. She says,

> 'Ah! you talk about cattle! Two kraals full! They milk, and give to the pigs. Other people just come and milk some of the cattle for themselves and in exchange for the milk give their children to look after the cattle. They are rich my child. If he marries you, you won't want to come to town any more.'[14]

Her account of the wealth of the rural people is an exaggeration which also reflects a silent regret on her part at the loss of the values that she seems to have forfeited together with her dispossession of land. One cannot help but wonder how the Mabongo family would handle their wealth in stock at No. 26 Staib Street, Doornfontein, if Sephai did pay his *bogadi* (bride stock). Admittedly, ownership of stock is highly valued by Africans, but then it presupposes ownership of land.

Martha's decision to reject Sephai and to face up to the

consequences of her pregnancy and her desertion by George is sub-limated in verse form towards the end of the story, in a language that almost epitomizes her. Here the child features as a symbol of hope and victory. More than that the speaker, who is clearly a woman and probably Martha, declares, 'This child will be my mother and father'.[15] This is a clear indication that although Martha is herself the forerunner of the urban black society she is not a leader, but looks up to the oncoming generation and expects them to offer leadership. It is also quite significant that right from the start Martha guards and protects the identity of her child. While Ma-Mapena insists that the child shall be called 'Ndala', Martha silently deplores the name as an 'old-fashioned' name suitable only for a 'farm boy'. She calls him Sonnyboy, a name that embodies the grim but vibrant and defiantly urban life of the marabi dancers. The name is derived from a Marabi song, 'Climb up on my knee, Sonnyboy/ You are only three, Sonnyboy/ There's no way of saying, there's no way of mourning ...' It is quite clear that besides Martha's bitter experience the child has no other form of heritage. The only redeeming factor in his life is provided by the leadership role he is expected to play. He is also expected to operate from a 'home' which is nothing more than a rented municipal box-house.

Sonnyboy's heritage is not measured by an estate, just as Martha's own heritage after the death of her mother is simply a package of suffering and bitterness. Instead, those accused by the writer of holding Martha's share of the land are said to receive her person in addition as their legacy from her mother, Mathloare, as the novelist points out with deep sarcasm:

> Ma-Mabongo died in the hospital a few days after being admitted. She died poor but she left a legacy for the white people in that her daughter remain a servant to them, a nanny, housekeeper, cook, even to the extent of opening and closing the gates for the master's car.[16]

Much irony is also suggested when Mathloare's dead body is compared to a 'Pharoah's tomb', which, though still rich in history and cultural artefacts of the past, only represents the feeble claim of its occupant to the last few cubic metres of ground that was once part of the Pharoah's kingdom many centuries ago. Her only (prophetic) prayer however gives a warning that her offspring may still retrieve the rest of the kingdom as she says, 'God help my child to give birth. The child will take my place.'[17]

The rescuing factor for Martha is that, unlike her parents, she turns round to face the circumstances that assail her and keep her under constant pressure. Indeed, like the 'bull-fighter' she claims to be, she manages to change her attitude towards her own pregnancy. While Mathloare dies of heart failure and July takes himself off to the army, Martha indomitably faces her fate by adopting an aggressive stance against the circumstances that contribute to the grimness of her background, instead of making the mere effort to survive that we see with the other women. The birth of her child marks the beginning of her new determination. Dikobe claims that, 'Martha did not curse her 'sin' when she became pregnant. ' "This child is going to work for me".'[18] We end the story with a feeling that Martha is determined finally to reclaim her land, mainly through the actions of her progeny.

NOTES

1 K. Sole and E. Koch, '*The Marabi Dance*: A Working Class Novel?', in M. Trump (ed.), *Rendering Things Visible: Essays on South African Literary Culture*, Johannesburg, Ravan, 1990, p. 214.

2 Robert July, 'The African Personality in the African Novel', in U. Beier (ed.), *Introduction to African Literature*, London, Longman, 1967, p. 218.

3 Isabel Hofmeyr, '*The Marabi Dance*', *Africa Perspective*, no. 6, 1977, p. 3.

4 Dorothy Driver, 'M'a-Ngoana O Tsoare Thpa ka Bohaleng – The Child's Mother Grabs the Sharp End of the Knife: Women as Mothers, Women as Writers', in Martin Trump (ed.), *Rendering Things Visible: Essays on South African Literary Culture*, Johannesburg, Ravan 1990, p. 232.

5 Modike Dikobe, *The Marabi Dance*, p. 28.

6 Dikobe, *Marabi Dance*, p. 27.

7 July, 'African Personality', p. 221.

8 July, 'African Personality', p. 220.

9 Dikobe, *Marabi Dance*, p. 31.

10 Dikobe, *Marabi Dance*, p. 32.

11 Dikobe, *Marabi Dance*, pp. 67, 44.

12 Dikobe, *Marabi Dance*, p. 108.

13 Dikobe, *Marabi Dance*, p. 66.

14 Dikobe, *Marabi Dance*, p. 67.

15 Dikobe, *Marabi Dance*, p. 99.

16 Dikobe, *Marabi Dance*, p. 92.

17 Dikobe, *Marabi Dance*, p. 93.

18 Dikobe, *Marabi Dance*, p. 73.

BIBLIOGRAPHY

Coplan, D., *In Township Tonight: South Africa's Black City Music and Theatre*, Johannesburg, Ravan Press, 1985.

Dikobe, M., *The Marabi Dance*, (first pub. 1973), London, Heinemann, 1977.

Driver, D., 'M'a-Ngoana O Tsoare Thipa ka Bohaleng – The Child's Mother Grabs the Sharp End of the Knife: Women as Mothers, Women as Writers' in M. Trump (ed.), *Rendering Things Visible: Essays on South African Literary Culture*, Johannesburg, Ravan, 1990.

Hofmeyr, I., '*The Marabi Dance*', *Africa Perspective*, no. 6, 1977, pp. 1–11.

July, R., 'The African Personality in the African Novel', in U. Beier (ed.), *Introduction to African Literature*, London, Longman, 1967, pp. 218–32.

Mattera, D., *Memory is the Weapon*, Johannesburg, Ravan Press, 1987.

Sole, K. and Koch, E., '*The Marabi Dance*: A Working Class Novel?' in M. Trump (ed.), *Rendering Things Visible: Essays on South African Literary Culture*, Johannesburg, Ravan, 1990, pp. 205–24.

13

SPACES OF THE 'OTHER'
Planning for cultural diversity in Western Sydney

Sophie Watson

Such assignations of social difference – where difference is
neither One nor the Other but *something else besides, in-between* –
find their agency in a form of the 'future' where the past is not
originary, where the present is not simply transitory. It is, if I
may stretch a point, an interstitial future, that emerges *in-between*
the claims of the past and the needs of the present.

H. Bhabha, *The Location of Culture*[1]

Nearly thirty years after the demise of the racist White Australia
policy, Sydney has become a visibly multicultural city. An article in
the *Sydney Morning Herald* on 4 February 1995 entitled 'Orient
Express' tells us that Sydney has reinvented itself as Australia's first
truly Eurasian metropolis. The United Nations conference on global
diversity to be hosted in Sydney, will, it is said, be an opportunity to
show off multiculturalism as practised peacefully in the city. This is a
far cry from the headlines of the same newspaper commenting on
Australia's first political assassination in the most multicultural area
of Sydney on 5 September 1994. Here the fear, not substantiated,
was that the murder had been carried out by one of the Asian gangs:

Cabramatta is the fulfilment of our migration dream and
its nightmarish conclusion . . . An amalgam of poverty and
prosperity, marked by high rise flats with laundry-draped
balconies, it is a dazzling collision between Australian
suburban ugliness and South East Asian big-city garishness.[2]

And a headline two days later proclaimed: 'Australia – paying the price for lax migration laws'.[3]

There is no one truth as to the success or otherwise of multi-cultural Australia, but simply many discourses on multiculturalism. This chapter seeks to elucidate how predominantly British planning theory and practice remains located in a modernist framework which disavows difference, and how this has serious implications in the context of the colonial and post-colonial societies – in this instance, Australia – into which it has been imported. I will focus on the contestation of public spaces in Sydney by non-Anglo migrants rather than by Aboriginal people, since despite the similarities in their respective battles for space, there are also many differences: to conflate the two groups would do justice to neither. In Australia the imported British planning system paid no attention to Aboriginal culture and practices and in many cases has been, and continues to be, part of the very decimation of indigenous culture. More recent non-Anglo migration has also contributed to the erosion of Aboriginal culture as well as itself being moulded by, and into, the dominant Anglo-Australian culture that these migrants encountered, although usually with much less disastrous effects.

REGULATING PUBLIC SPACE

Within the modernist ideal, public spaces in cities are the places where people are able to engage in a whole range of activities; in doing so, however, they are expected to abide by dominant norms and codes of behaviour. Planners play a crucial role in the micro-politics of power which circumscribe the uses of public space. In South African cities, for instance, urban planning has been used explicitly as a tool of control and repression – although such forceful monitoring of public space is the exception, rather than the rule, in the modernist cities of the First World.[4] Rather than relying primarily on overt authority and force to regulate behaviour, the public spaces of the modernist city have been regulated in subtler and apparently non-coercive ways. For most of the time, implicit and assumed shared beliefs, which have been constructed over decades and are only rarely policed, circumscribe non-normative practices within the city. These collective beliefs are culturally, historically and temporally specific: the use of public space allowed in one country or culture may not be allowed in another.

The culture of public spaces which is encountered in Australian cities does not constitute a fixed set of practices, notions and processes. Non-Anglo migrant cultures and the dominant Anglo-Australian cultures produce each other at every point of intersection, including that relating to public space. Culture is continually contested. As K. Anderson and Fay Gale have written: 'In direct and indirect ways, both wilful and unintentional, people construct environments, regions and places.'[5] In the case of culturally differentiated uses of space, there are multiple sites of power where different interests are constructed. What is interesting is how what is viewed as permissible usage of public spaces changes both over time and within spaces. There is often an assumption that certain public uses of space have existed since time immemorial, rather than recognizing that the rules governing Anglo-Australian public spaces are the outcomes of particular historical processes of 'civilization'.[6] Those making the laws or regulations have a tendency to forget the value judgements or assumptions that are imbued in almost every piece of legislation that is passed. For non-Anglo migrants to Australia, the various forms of circumscription are often mysterious and difficult to fathom or discover.

Western Sydney

Sydney is increasingly defined as a global city, a cosmopolitan city, a city which can be compared with other exciting, even post-modern, cities.[7] As with all cities, there is no one Sydney: there are countless Sydneys, both real and imaginary.[8] In this chapter, and in recognition of the inherent complexities and fragmentation of any bounded area, one large part of Sydney – Western Sydney, where over half of Sydney's total population of around four million now live – will be considered as a whole. This is an area which is characterized by lack of services and resources, urban sprawl, high unemployment, a low level of amenities and little architectural or environmental distinction. Such characterization ignores the heterogeneity of the area in many ways, including its ethnic diversity. Yet the common urban form and development, the planning policies and the responses to ethnic difference justify treating Western Sydney as a definable area here.

Sydney is a city of considerable cultural diversity. Nearly 50 per cent of the city's inhabitants are from first or second generation non-English speaking backgrounds; in 1991, one in four of the total Australian population was born overseas. The British had invaded and settled Australia during the eighteenth, nineteenth and early twentieth centuries; and in 1945, 98 per cent of the Australian population were of British origin. But in the years following the Second World War, there were successive waves of migration from Northern, Southern and Eastern Europe. In the initial post-war period, the Australian government was concerned to meet the growing demands by industry for labour, with an immigration policy which would not overly disrupt the homogeneity of the population. Migrants with fair complexions were favoured because they were believed to be easier to assimilate.

By the mid-1960s the White Australia Policy, which had been in place since the Immigration Restriction Act of 1901, and was aimed at excluding non-white immigrants, had broken down. Changes in immigration policy in the 1970s and 1980s, whereby large numbers of political refugees were admitted, and significant numbers entered under the family reunion programme, led to a growing number of migrants from countries where there were often major cultural and religious differences from those of the Australian population as a whole. These more recent migrant groups were more visibly different and included migrants from Asia and Latin America. This pattern of migration has continued into the 1990s with people from Asia forming a large proportion of the migrants to Australia, although overall more migrants continue to come from Britain than from any other single nation.

What is striking, though, about the migrant intake into Australia is the number of countries from which people come and hence the diversity of cultures that arise. This is reflected in Fairfield, a suburb of Western Sydney, where council brochures are printed in ten languages. Any stereotyping of migrants to Australia is therefore absurd. People not only come from different countries, they also come from different economic backgrounds, religions, cultural traditions, from rural and urban areas and so on. Despite the massive influx of migrants, planning policies in the outer suburbs where many of these migrants live have tended to ignore ethnic diversity and assume Anglo-Australian needs and customs.

Planning in Outer Sydney – an Anglo modernist framework

Planning in outer Sydney, as in many Western cities, reflects a modernist imperative and Enlightenment ideals. Inherent in its project is the notion that cities can be made better, that outcomes are knowable, that order and rationality should replace chaos and irrationality. The planner is situated as the knowing subject who imposes 'his' vision on the unknowing object/s. Although 'he' operates within a network of power relations where those who are planned for have multiple forms of resistance at their disposal – from community participation or organization to defying the regulations – the ultimate sanctions rest in 'his' hands. A development or activity can be refused permission.

In modernist discourse the grand visions of the planners and the 'master plans' they devised were also constructed according to the notion of a homogeneous population. Cultural, racial or gendered/sexed differences were not only not recognized, they have also tended to be subsumed under the generics of individuals or households. Enlightenment notions of the common good are thus protected by positioning the needs of those that are 'Other' (than the white bourgeois male) outside planning considerations.[9] The Australian planning system which derived from Britain has rested on this model, with associated assumptions about what individuals or collections of individuals did. Further, the 'public or common good' also assumes a notion of community. This political ideal of community implies unity and subsumes difference.[10] In this discourse, social homogeneity is seen as a good thing and cultural diversity is not to be encouraged because there is no sense in which it is regarded as making a positive contribution to 'the public good'. A liberal democratic perspective of the state underpinned the planning ethos, where the state was supposed to respond to and mediate the diverse interests of the population. Therefore, it is assumed that there is a public whose interests, which can be met, are knowable and known, homogeneous, and exist in a prior and coherent form to be represented by planners.

Australia's planning system grafted British ideas of city form and housing onto cities which had developed in a fairly random market-led fashion through the late nineteenth and early twentieth centuries. Within this colonial context, Australia's Aboriginal population and Aboriginal ways of life were either ignored or eradicated. Given that the vast majority of migrants have come from Britain, the influence of Anglo norms and values on the development of the suburbs and the housing produced is neither surprising nor contentious. An Anglo-Australian city form developed, in part as a response to what was seen to be lacking in the 'home country'.

There was little visible resistance to this type of urban planning since it appeared to satisfy many peoples' needs.

In recent decades, multiculturalism has been on the political agenda, and though not central to planning discourses it has begun to have an impact on public policy in Australia[11]. It can be argued that multiculturalism in modernist discourse has been a homogenizing strategy which has defined and created limits within which acceptable difference is permitted. Multiculturalism was a reaction to an earlier homogenizing strategy – that of assimilation – which attempted to minimize difference through defining the dominant Anglo culture as the norm which would envelop and embrace other cultures under its umbrella. Within this discourse migrants would, after a certain period of time, become Australianized and part of the mainstream.

MULTICULTURAL SPACE

Edward Said has written that 'culture is a system of discriminations and evaluations . . . it also means that culture is a system of exclusions'.[12] The strategies through which non-Anglo cultures are asserted may take a number of forms, depending on the strength of the group and its class, gender and age composition: these strategies range from those that are overt and confrontational, to those that are covert and quiet. Where communities are fragmented and powerless their potential for resistance will be clearly less. A critical mass of people collaborating with each other will have greater political clout, especially those with financial means. In this respect, the Hong Kong Chinese and the Koreans have made a much greater visible impact on the built environment of the Australian suburbs than the Chileans, for example.[13] The local government response, and demographic and cultural practices within any given community, also play a part in these assertions of cultural difference. Older women of non-Anglo origin, for instance, will find it harder to counter dominant cultural norms than their sons and grandsons who, as younger men, may feel more confident to act. On the other hand, Muslim women in purdah, screened from the sight of men and strangers, will be treated by Anglo-Australian culture as very different from women from other religious and cultural groups.

The built environment of Sydney bears some marks of cultural difference in its housing and public spaces, although the overriding visible impact, particularly in the outer suburban areas, is one of an urban homogeneity. Planning discourses and practices have so far been little affected by multicultural debates, although some changes to planning regulations have occurred in some localities to accommodate cultural differences. For example, there is a trend in many migrant groups, particularly those from South-East Asia, to establish small industries that are based in their homes. These tend to be perceived as a nuisance by neighbours and are treated with hostility. Fairfield has confronted the problem by setting standards for such activities, hence combating their negative impact without disallowing their practice. Similarly, the preference amongst some migrants to live in extended households has been accommodated by local government allowing dual occupancy on a single urban site.

Almost all migrants to Australia share a history of some displacement or dissatisfaction with their place of origin; and in many cases, they share more turbulent or violent histories of exclusion, terror or poverty which have precipitated migration and diaspora. They also share a desire to represent and locate themselves in their new place of residence. Part of this process is finding a space within Australian urban life. Many migrants have preconceived notions as to what this actually means, although Australian identity is continually contested, rearticulated and reproduced. As Homi Bhabha puts it: 'it is in the emergence of the interstices – the overlap and displacement of domains of difference – that the intersubjective and collective experiences of *nationness*, community interest, or cultural values are negotiated.' He then asks the question:

> How do strategies of representation or empowerment come to be formulated in the competing claims of communities where, despite shared histories of deprivation and discrimination, the exchange of values, meanings and priorities may not always be collaborative and dialogical, but may be profoundly antagonistic, conflictual and even incommensurable?[14]

That this is a complex and problematic process is well illustrated in the built environment. Cultural difference can be perceived as a threat or as emblematic of the exotic 'Other'. In Sydney it seems that where cultural differences in the built form or use of space have been perceived as exotic by local residents and planners, there appears to have been less resistance to the non-traditional uses of public space – and even some encouragement to use these as a tourist site. Where different uses have been constructed as a threat to local dominant styles, norms or patterns of social interaction and cultural life, then discourses of resistance and racism have been more often deployed. The boundary between these two perceptions of cultural difference as either exotic or threatening can shift over time and space.

By far the most contentious cultural practices involving public spaces in Sydney suburbs have been in the religious sphere. One pattern in the 1980s was for Muslim or Hindu communities to acquire a site on which a residential dwelling, and possibly an outbuilding or warehouse, were situated, and then convert the buildings to a mosque or temple. This use would lead local residents to complain to the local council about traffic and noise, particularly on festival days. In most cases, planning officers then visited the site and informed the group that it could no longer be used as a mosque or temple unless certain regulations were complied with. The lack of adequate space for parking, for instance, legitimated requests that the group apply for another site.

A great deal of conflict arose during the processes of selecting sites for mosques and temples. Council officers often suggested sites on open land away from residential areas. The transformation of existing residential or commercial buildings into places of worship was contentious for several reasons. The architectural forms of the mosque or temple are distinct, and these buildings are used for social as well as religious purposes. With poor public transport in Western Sydney, parking and noise impact become issues for local residents. As recently as the late 1980s local politicians who opposed Hindu or Muslim places of worship were not embarrassed to express racist attitudes: 'the temple will not be an asset. There are no Vietnamese people living there. You are hoping to put in a complete foreign body in anticipation of people coming to use it'.[15] The body metaphor is interesting here – with Anglo-Australia as the pure body seen to be in danger of contamination.

On some occasions, building permits were refused simply because they were different, and represented the 'Other'. An increase in the height of a mosque spire was refused 'on the grounds that it was likely to spoil the amenity of the area'. The council report stated that 'the visual privacy of adjoining properties would be reduced. It is out of character with the surrounding areas and the height is considered to be excessive'.[16] There were no similar cases where a Christian church tower had not been permitted.

In 1991 a Greek bishop submitted an application for a private chapel on his property. The local council objected saying it was too close to the house and that its 'design was not in keeping with the area'. New plans were submitted and fifty-nine objections were received, mostly concerning crowds, noise and traffic. Some residents also complained that 'the fence is not in keeping with the area and that trees have been cleared and a track cut through the land'. This was followed by claims that the bishop was not an authentic bishop of the Greek Orthodox Church. The local council then deferred its decision until they received a statutory declaration that the chapel would only be for private use; it was alleged that the aldermen were 'fence sitting to avoid being labelled racist'. Eventually, permission for the private chapel was granted on the condition that the bishop provided a letter of intent. It had been recognized by the local council that if he was not permitted to build a private chapel, then this constituted an infringement of the right to religious freedom and could be taken to the Anti-Discrimination Board. One alderman shouted during the debate, 'I'll stand here and say Germans are better than bloody Greeks.'[17]

In cases such as these outlined above, planning norms are invoked to neutralize objections which often derive from a different source than mere urban development and usage. Other contested cultural sites in Western Sydney have been social clubs, particularly senior citizens' groups, where long use of public community centres is seen to denote ownership. In one case, a group of Anglo-Australian senior citizens felt that it was legitimate to keep a local club for their exclusive use. Their president stated that: 'Last year the Spanish senior citizens began using our rooms, and wish to use the inside toilets. This is not possible without allowing access to our private lounge room, the heart of our organization, which contains all our records, private furniture and other material'.[18] Once again, a metaphor of the body as sacred was evoked. This is an interesting illustration of how seemingly public space is reconstituted as private.

In the outlying Western Sydney suburb of Penrith, an Ethiopian group wanted to develop a house into a community centre and hall to provide a link 'between the two cultures the migrants straddle'. According to the local newspaper, this plan was 'causing some heartburn among neighbouring residents worried about their rural ambience'. Twenty residents attended the council's planning and works committee. One neighbour,

> a poultry farmer, said his chickens had been literally scared to death by the noise from a (fundraising) disco and cars and this

211

would threaten his livelihood. Another resident said that it did not fit into a rural area even though the zoning allowed it, and a third said it was out of character with the area.[19]

In this same area, there are large numbers of clubs – such as the Returned Services Leagues Clubs – serving the Anglo-Australian community, but these do not evoke an equivalent hostile response.

Yet, where the non-Anglo migrant use of public space can be construed as exotic there appears to have been much less resistance from the Anglo-Australian community and from planners. The Vietnamese shopping centre of Cabramatta in Fairfield provides a well-known example. Here, Chinese dragons guard a mall where signs and symbols of ancient China are interspersed with Asian shops and restaurants, and people come and go, sit around, play music and pass the time of day. The shopping centre has also developed into a tourist site for Sydneysiders from the inner city and the more prosperous North Shore, who come to experience a slice of the exotic and partake of an Asian 'dim sum' breakfast on the week-end. In 1992 more than a million visitors, mainly from elsewhere in Sydney, made the trip to Cabramatta, which now bills itself as the space 'where the East meets West'.[20]

The exceptional commercial success and cultural integration of the Cabramatta shopping centre has not been achieved without controversy, even over the choice of its name of Freedom Plaza. The symbols that have been deployed to construct Chinese identity and to evoke China, are those of ancient Chinese culture ossified in time. Chinese culture is therefore being reinvented and reconstituted by myths and symbols which have been superseded and changed in the very places from which they originate. As time has passed, Cabramatta has shifted from being perceived as a threat (its earlier derisive epithet was Vietnamatta), as a cultural invasion, and as alien, to representing an exotic place and a tourist attraction where income can be generated. There are some parallels here with the reception of migrant writing in Australia. As Sneja Gunew puts it:

> Multiculturalism becomes too often an effective process of recuperation whereby diverse cultures are returned homogenized as folkloric spectacle . . . In this formulation, multiculturalism functions to amalgamate and spuriously to unify nationalism and culture into a depoliticized multimedia event.[21]

Most of the formal recreation areas in the suburbs of Western Sydney are given over to traditional sporting fields. These spaces are not conducive to more informal uses, including walking, sitting around, bowls, volley ball and other games. The environment is often barren with few areas that are shaded by trees and pleasant to sit in. In contrast, recreational activities in many of the countries from which non-Anglo migrants come, such as badminton and chess, would traditionally be played informally in the town square. In Western Sydney, there are few public spaces for these types of activities. It is rare to find a landscaped piazza, places to sit or tables to sit by.

The homogeneity of the Australian outer suburbs constrains the expression of difference. David Sibley makes a related argument about public space in Europe, although in his case the 'Other' are Gypsies:

> Spaces which are homogeneous or uniform, from which non-conforming groups or activities have been expelled or have been kept out through the maintenance of strong boundaries, can be termed pure in the sense that they are free from polluting elements and the purification of space is a process by which power is exercised over space and social groups. The significance of such purified spaces in the construction of the 'other' is basically that difference is more visible than it would be in an area of mixed land use and social diversity.[22]

This tale of contested sites in Western Sydney illustrates the tensions and conflicts inherent in non-Anglo migrants representing themselves symbolically and literally in Australian suburban spaces. It is a story with which Aboriginal Australians are only too familiar.

PLANNING FOR DIVERSITY AND RETHINKING PUBLIC SPACE

The notion of planning for a 'multiple public' may be one approach to planning in a post-colonial and multicultural environment.[23] B. Hooper argues for a planning theory and practice that must become decentralized and radically democratic, while R. Beauregard suggests that planners need to address more directly social and cultural conflicts within society.[24] If we recognize that cities are important as places of dreams and fantasies as well as in constructing our identities, then spaces, places and buildings need to be created which feed the imagination and where different, alternative or marginal identities can flourish.[25] Planners certainly need to have visions, but not visions that are set in stone. As Hans Westerman has pointed out, 'a singular vision, no matter how persuasive and pertinent at the time, can become an impediment in the long term'.[26] But whose vision will create the city, and how do visions of urban planning allow for diversity and change? How can the cultural use of public space be resisted and re-formed into a new shape? Planning has to break out from its rational, comprehensive strait-jacket and formulate new possibilities.

The planner needs to find ways of acknowledging ambiguity and the possibility of surprise in city spaces. Richard Sennett suggests the planner should

> think in terms of what makes for a narrative beginning . . . Time begins to do the work of giving places character when the places are not used as they were meant to be . . . For the person who engages in this unanticipated use, something 'begins' in the narrative sense.[27]

This means creating spaces which are flexible – with 'weak borders rather than strong walls'. One way of approaching this is to reduce fixed zoning as much as possible, and to create spaces whose construction is simple enough to permit constant alteration. Much of the character of an urban space derives from its being a site of resistance and contestation – a site that matters to people. So planners need to be involved in moments of cultural contestation as they arise, and not be afraid to support the non-traditional uses or views of marginal groups. The planning process has to allow for the unseen, the spontaneous and the unpredictable. Urban planning should be as much about dreams and fantasy as about meeting 'technical' objectives.

This means engaging with new forms of democracy which address notions of difference and power.[28] In the context of South African cities, for example, this requires the recognition that urban space has been mobilized in constituting differences within the framework of exclusion and repression.[29] Mechanisms to allow for a state of flux as well as addressing the ebbs and flows of power need to be incorporated into the planning process. The uncomfortable relationship between the state and the market will have to be more forcefully confronted, rather than allowing the market to dictate terms. Public spaces have, in recent years, become increasingly privatized. More and more spaces within the modernist Australian city exclude both the poor and non-Anglo people, and thus create enclaves for a wealthy minority.

But if cultural difference and different spaces in the city are to be celebrated, then the question becomes how will this be possible without producing P. Marcuse's quartered cities or cities of walls, or cities of ghettos, or M. Davies's fortress cities where public spaces are characterized by segregation, surveillance and exclusion?[30] If planners are to embrace the post-modern or late modern world, a world of fragmentation and diversity, as well as a world of global powers, mobile national and international vested interests, then planning theory and practice will have to unbutton its modernist strait-jacket. This does not necessarily imply an abandonment of Enlightenment ideals in the sense that planning inevitably has to engage with some notion of the 'public good'. But this notion has to be rethought to recognize notions of difference, power and flexibility.

NOTES

1 H. Bhabha, *The Location of Culture*, London, Routledge, 1994, p. 219.
2 *Sydney Morning Herald*, 7 Sept. 1994, p. 8.
3 *Sydney Morning Herald*, 9 Sept. 1994, p. 5.
4 See A. Mabin, 'On the Problems and Prospects of Overcoming Segregation and Fragmentation in Southern Africa's Cities in a Postmodern Era', in S. Watson and K. Gibson (eds), *Postmodern Cities and Spaces*, Oxford, Basil Blackwell, 1995.
5 K. Anderson and F. Gale (eds), *Inventing Places*, Melbourne, Longman Cheshire, 1992, p. 4.
6 See R. Sennett, *The Conscience of the Eye*, New York, Knopf, 1990.
7 See Watson and Gibson, *Postmodern Cities*.
8 See, for instance, D. Modjeska (ed.), *Inner Cities: Australian Women's Memory of Place*, Melbourne, Penguin, 1989.
9 B. Hooper, 'Split at the Roots: A Critique of the Philosophical and Political Sources of Modern Planning Doctrine', *Frontiers* vol. XIII, no. 1, 1992, pp. 45–80.
10 See I. Young, 'The Ideal of Community and the Politics of Difference', in L. Nicholson (ed.), *Feminism/Postmodernism*, London, Routledge, 1990.
11 M. Kalantzis, 'Ethnicity meets Gender meets Class in Australia', in S. Watson (ed.), *Playing the State*, London, Verso, 1990.
12 E. Said, *The World, the Text and the Critic*, London, Faber, 1984, p. 11.
13 *Sydney Morning Herald*, 3 May 1993, p. 38.
14 Bhabha, *Location of Culture*, p. 2.
15 *Fairfield Advance*, 3 Mar. 1987, p. 4.
16 *Fairfield Advance*, 21 Nov. 1989, p. 11.
17 *Penrith Press*, 16 Apr.–23 Apr. 1991.

18 *Fairfield Advance*, 18 Aug. 1987, p. 6.
19 *Penrith Press*, 2 Oct. 1990, p. 7.
20 *Telegraph Mirror*, 2 Mar. 1993, p. 5.
21 S. Gunew, 'PMT (Postmodernist Tensions): Reading for (multi) cultural difference', in Gunew, S. and Longley, K., (eds), *Striking Chords: Multicultural Literary Interpretations*, Sydney, Allen & Unwin, 1992.
22 D. Sibley, 'Outsiders in Society and Space', in Anderson and Gale, *Inventing Places*, p. 114.
23 Hooper, 'Split at the Roots', p. 72.
24 R. Beauregard, 'Between Modernity and Postmodernity: The Ambiguous Position of US Planning', *Environment and Planning D: Society and Space*, 1989, no. 7, pp. 381–96.
25 S. Watson 'Cities of Dreams and fantasy: Social Planning in a Postmodern Era', in R. Freestone (ed.), *Cities of Hope: Urban Planning, Traffic and Environmental Management in the Nineties*, Sydney, Federation Press, 1993.
26 H. Westerman, 'Visions for Housing', *Urban Futures Journal*, vol. 1, 1991, pp. 1–9.
27 Sennett, *The Conscience of the Eye*, p. 196.
28 For instance, see Young, 'The Ideal of Community', in E. Laclau and C. Mouffe, *Hegemony and Socialist Strategy*, London, Verso, 1984.
29 A. Mabin, 'On the Problems and prospects of overcoming Segregation and fragmentation in Southern Africa's Cities in a Postmodern Era', in Watson and Gibson, *Postmodern Cities*, pp. 187–99.
30 P. Marcuse, 'Not Chaos but Walls: Postmodernism and The Partitioned City', in Watson and Gibson, *Postmodern Cities*, pp. 243–54; M. Davies, *City of Quartz*, Verso, London, 1990.

BIBLIOGRAPHY

Anderson, K., and Gale, F. (eds), *Inventing Places*, Melbourne, Longman Cheshire, 1992.

Beauregard, R., 'Between Modernity and Postmodernity: The Ambiguous Position of US Planning', *Environment and Planning D: Society and Space*, 1989, vol. 7, pp. 381-96.

Bhabha, H., *The Location of Culture*, London, Routledge, 1994.

Davies, M., *City of Quartz*, London, Verso, 1990.

Hooper, B., 'Split at the Roots: A Critique of the Philosophical and Political Sources of Modern Planning Doctrine', *Frontiers*, vol. XIII, no. 1, 1992, pp. 45-80.

Kalantzis, M., 'Ethnicity meets Gender meets Class in Australia' , in S. Watson, (ed.), *Playing the State*, London, Verso, 1990.

Laclau, E., and Mouffe, C., *Hegemony and Socialist Strategy*, London, Verso, 1984.

Mabin, A., 'On the Problems and Prospects of Overcoming Segregation and Fragmentation in Southern Africa's Cities in a Postmodern Era', in S. Watson and K. Gibson (eds), *Postmodern Cities and Spaces*, Oxford, Basil Blackwell, 1995.

Marcuse, P., 'Not Chaos but Walls: Postmodernism and The Partitioned City', in S. Watson and K. Gibson (eds.), *Postmodern Cities and Spaces*, Oxford, Basil Blackwell, 1995.

Sennett R., *The Conscience of the Eye*, New York, Knopf, 1990.

Sibley, D., 'Outsiders in Society and Space', in K. Anderson and F. Gale (eds), *Inventing Places*, Melbourne, Longman Cheshire, 1992.

Watson, S., 'Cities of Dreams and fantasy: Social Planning in a Postmodern Era' in R. Freestone (ed.), *Cities of Hope: Urban Planning, Traffic and Environmental Management in the Nineties*, Sydney, Federation Press, 1993.

Watson, S., and Gibson, K. (eds), *Postmodern Cities and Spaces*, Oxford, Basil Blackwell, 1995

Westerman, H., 'Visions for Housing', *Urban Futures Journal*, 1991, vol. 1, pp. 1–9.

Young, I., 'The Ideal of Community and the Politics of Difference' in L. Nicholson (ed.), *Feminism/Postmodernism*, London, Routledge, 1990.

14

FLATNESS AND FANTASY
Representations of the land in two recent South African novels

Sarah Nuttall

Historically, the land in white English South African fiction has raised hermeneutic questions: how to read it and how to find a language to speak about it. J. M. Coetzee, in his book *White Writing*, has described how landscape writing from the turn of the century until the 1960s either continued to adopt a European lens through which to view African landscape or announced its failure to 'track' the land, the refusal of the land to 'emerge into meaningfulness as a landscape of signs'.[1] After the 1960s, the question of adopting an African nationality increasingly confronted whites, and relationships to the land gave way to more overtly political concerns.[2]

In two recent novels by South African writers, the land is once again a central subject, explored as a deposit of myths and memories, a topography invoked by Afrikaner nationalism and white masculinity to give their ruling ideas a 'natural' form. Both Damon Galgut, in his novel *The Beautiful Screaming of Pigs*,[3] and Elleke Boehmer, in *An Immaculate Figure*,[4] address the political and gendered myth-making to which the land has been subjected, showing it to be caught in a set of contemporary white, and largely male, fantasies. Both novels (published in 1992 and 1993 respectively) were written on the cusp of profound political change in South Africa, with the imminent creation of a 'new land' and its transformed political and topographical power lines.

Galgut reformulates earlier liberal responses to the land which have related to questions of ownership and belonging, while Boehmer, with a different emphasis, depicts contemporary versions

219

of the African romance tradition of H. Rider Haggard and John Buchan. What it has meant to own the land in the apartheid context has been notoriously difficult to interpret. While whites have had legal ownership of land, dispossessed blacks have challenged the legitimacy of such 'ownership'. In the case of desert-land, or vast open tracts of land, in which much of Galgut's book is set, the notion of ownership, though largely a political question, is nevertheless elusive. The terms, that is, on which such land can be 'owned', or which constitute 'ownership', can be difficult to determine. Galgut's text raises the question, too, of what it means to 'belong' to the land, and how far a sense of belonging relates to a sense of being 'owned' by the land. Afrikaners, who took the South African land by conquest, and practised an illegitimate form of 'ownership' in the view of the majority, nevertheless have asserted a sense of belonging in the land; more than an instrumentalist view of the land, they have asserted a relationship to the land for its own sake. As Galgut's protagonist Patrick struggles to define his relation to the land, the complexity of such questions of ownership and belonging is explored, though not necessarily resolved, in the text.

Galgut depicts a masculine and militarist 'taking of the land', which borrows its phraseology from that other hallmark of masculine conquest, 'taking a woman'. Patrick, in this understatedly gay novel, seeks to distance himself from this form of masculinity, and to refuse any such appropriative ownership of the land. Yet, although Patrick's gay consciousness affords him some distance on the heterosexual gendering of the land as 'woman', an alternative relation to the land is largely left open in the text. Galgut displays a concern, too, with writerly spaces, the ways in which the Southern land he inhabits can shape fictional form, and institute a version of fictional belonging, and the way writing can create a spaciousness for questions of male identity and national belonging in this context.

In what is in some ways a more contained novel, Boehmer depicts a male abuse of a feminized land. Her protagonist Rosandra, in her lack of awareness, her passivity and her acceptance of a submissive femininity, is shown to be at least partially complicit in this process however. Boehmer's portrayal of an instrumentalist abuse of the land by apartheid's proponents is suggestive of current ecological debates in which the land is accorded an agency of its own. She hints, too, at the possibility of a non-instrumentalist 'woman's' view of the land. Both writers, then, are concerned with ways in which the Southern African land has been gendered and with how to begin to clear a space, both political and fictional, for a different relationship to the land. Both, as we shall see, are concerned with the crossing of borders, not only as national signifiers which mark off the apartheid régime from 'freer states', but as internal markers of potential insight and change. These are indicative of the historical moment in which the texts were written, of the desire to break new imaginative ground as the first signs of political transformation seem imminent. I turn to a more detailed analysis of these two texts below, in which I consider the uses made of notions of ownership and belonging, of flatness and emptiness, and of fantasies of the African land.

THE BEAUTIFUL SCREAMING OF PIGS

Much of Galgut's novel is set on the South African–Namibian border, and it is a book about crossings, literal and emotional journeys over borders and frontiers. Patrick, the protagonist, has served on the border as a soldier in the South African Defence Force. Obedient rather than patriotic, his service has been demanded of him, as a comrade-in-arms, by the racist régime. 'The border' is as much political boundary as frontline of a marauding masculinity, and throughout the novel, appropriation of the land, and its harnessing to a nationalist vocabulary, lies close to a cult of masculinity. Patrick's grandfather was an Afrikaans farmer whose murmurings about '*Die land*' [this land] recall the words of the Republic's national anthem, 'Ons land Suid-Afrika' [Our land South Africa].[5] Patrick's father and his brother, Malcolm, go on hunting weekends in 'the swamps',[6] appropriating the African land with their guns, occupying the plundering explorer narrative which lies at the heart of the colonial romance story.

If this is one part of Patrick's inheritance, another derives from his mother, with whom he is left behind during these hunting weekends. For her, a relationship with Africa invokes a crisis of identity, and leads to a tale of liberal agonistics. She seeks, but fails, to belong to the African land: 'Displaced, lacking a past, she was nevertheless African: a creation of this misshapen continent. Though she yearned to belong, she had no idea of where. She dug for her roots in the rock.'[7] Patrick shares with his mother a sense of 'dislocation',[8] yet will come to be more self-aware in his attempt to work out his political, national and sexual identities.

'Emptiness', in Galgut's novel, is both a condition of the land and the mark of a destructive masculinist military universe, whose primitivist underpinnings are exposed in the isolation of the border outpost. The way Galgut draws the landscape into his writing, finding in it a reflection of his own condition but also turning the topography back on his superiors, accusing them of their one-dimensional masculinity, marks it out from other stories, such as those in the 1987 collection *Forces Favourites*,[9] which have addressed the experience of the South African military and the isolation and alienation which has resulted for the protagonists. On the border, Patrick meets Lappies, a man who cannot catch a rugby ball, and who 'trembles' beside him when Patrick shoots a SWAPO (South West African People's Organization) soldier who would otherwise have shot him.[10] Patrick and Lappies meet on the boundary of an acceptable masculinity, and on guard the night after the skirmish, they stop, at the darkest corner of the camp, and come together: 'We fumbled with buttons, we slung down our guns . . . Standing pressed together, the continent about us, we took each other in hand . . . It was an act of revenge, undertaken in pain: against men, who had made the world flat.'[11] Their complex act of love is an act against the great 'hissing nullity' of the land, and its conquering men.

Galgut's novel differs from the stories in *Forces Favourites*, and indeed from those which deal with military themes in *The Invisible Ghetto: Lesbian and Gay Writing from South Africa*,[12] through his portrayal of the 'other side', the so-called 'enemy'. In so doing, he deconstructs a border which continues to prevail – the perpetuation of a focus on white males – in the stories in the above collections.[13] Patrick's accounts of his time as a South African soldier are interspersed with a trip made to SWAPO headquarters in Namibia on the eve of the country's independence. He is accompanying his mother on a visit to her SWAPO-activist lover Godfrey. The journey is sexually charged by the purpose of the visit, only added to by the erotic combination of speed and space. Crossing the border, too, is crossing into a 'new land', beyond the bounds of the apartheid state into a country poised to win democracy in the first non-racial elections. The car leaves the border post 'backfiring in rapture' as they enter what is in part the imaginary space of a different kind of South Africa.[14]

Patrick and his mother find Godfrey preparing for the funeral of Andrew Lovell, a white underground SWAPO activist who has been killed. The funeral is to be combined with an eve-of-elections rally. Patrick sees in Lovell his 'other, impossible self',[15] a freedom fighter dedicated to the 'struggle', a man he could have shot on the border.

When Godfrey calls Patrick 'comrade' he is partly 'in love' with the image of solidarity and brotherhood it invokes, yet he senses how fragile it is.

Godfrey (and to a lesser extent the dead Andrew) represents a different political and nationalist claim to the land. The war he is fighting is one against forced removals, and the atrocities of the South African army in the country. 'You have no nation . . . you're so . . . neurotic',[16] he says to Patrick, talking of both him and his mother, and whites like them. Retrieving the land for its rightful owners is the legitimate claim that drives his rhetoric. But Godfrey's African nationalism is also strongly masculinist, marauding in its own way: from his massive dark chest hangs a medallion of a bullet hole plated in gold; parting the air like a ship, swigging his coffee, hitting Patrick hard on the shoulder, and beating Patrick's mother in their bedroom, he exudes more 'heat',[17] Patrick thinks, than his father ever did. Godfrey is one of a set of masculine figures, and fighters for the land, against whom Patrick has to try to determine his own male identity.

If at first it seemed as though Godfrey could bestow on Patrick's mother his 'redeeming desire',[18] securing for her access to the African land and an African identity, it soon becomes clear that he can no more provide a 'home' and a sense of belonging for her than her former husband did. Existing on the margins of male action, she becomes increasingly incidental in Godfrey's life. Patrick, by contrast, dissociates himself from the masculinist culture of both sides of the colonial frontier, even while exploring the attractions of liberation politics and activism. It is interesting to compare this with a story by Brent Meersman in *The Invisible Ghetto*, in which the object of the gay protagonist's desire and fantasy is a highly masculine white military man who had escaped the army and arrived at the protagonist's farm. Unlike Galgut's story, white machismo is incorporated within a gay sexual ethic. But if it is the exploration of a problematic and often violent masculinity that marks out Galgut's story from others of its type, the distance Patrick observes from the male figures he sets up is also a reflection of a wider inner alienation. A desolation begins in Patrick until he feels that the land itself has entered into him ('the whispering bush, seething with air, was merely a part of my mind');[19] later, he feels that there is 'too much desert' in him.[20]

Patrick's dislocation is expressed through a complex relation to the land which, in the last part of the book, turns from political and gendered readings to a more existentialist or metaphysical relation, recalling the preoccupations of earlier white writers. In the final funeral scene, Patrick feels that the land cannot be contained by those who are there, but itself contains – cannot be owned, but owns. As he helps with the preparations for the funeral/rally, he sees the tenuousness of the political process which is taking place: election posters hang askew on poles, shreds of pamphlets fly about. 'Whirling and turning in eddies of heat, the detritus of liberation kept moving.'[21] The markers of liberation are fragile impositions on the landscape. The people gathered become inanimate objects fused with the geometrical shapes of the land: curved dunes make a natural basin and people fill the base of the arena 'like a liquid'; bodies grouped together make a line across a curve.[22] Patrick, at first identifying with the arcs of song which begin to rise, and which represent a claim of new ownership, soon feels the frailty not only of his own belonging, but the collective frailty of those gathered there:

> Years of war and ideology had converged on this land. All the laws and guns and blood for this – rocks, sand and air. Barren, omnipotent, emptiness waited beneath us. When we had gone this arid earth would remain.[23]

The notion of an ancient land, seemingly oblivious to political struggles for liberation, potentially evokes an important issue about the elusiveness of human 'ownership' of such land. Yet it also has a distancing effect on a more political reading of the land, which at other points the text so clearly offers. At the moment when Patrick witnesses the coming of political liberation, there is a displacement into the language of metaphysics. At the moment of political trans-formation, there is a lack perceived. We might perhaps read this 'lack' in the Lacanian sense of a subject permanently divided against itself. The epiphany is not so much the political change itself but the emergence of other forms of consciousness.

It is at this stage in the story that Patrick reveals his writerly self. Looking over the pamphlet about Andrew Lovell which has been prepared for the funeral, Patrick notices all the typographical and grammatical errors, and feels that the accompanying posters, with their cramped message of 'Go Well', are 'somehow unfinished'.[24] His concern with language, and its potential for making and carrying meaning, is a writerly concern and expresses a writerly distance. Just as the Namibian land seems to expand beyond the claim of political ownership, so, for Patrick, writerly space seems to extend beyond the immediacies of political struggles and nationalist claiming. Thus the meaning of Patrick's relation to the land is enacted in a series of displacements which are political, metaphysical and writerly. Although the ethical need for political change, including the way in which the land has been gendered, has dominated the narrative, political liberation has the effect of opening up other ways of seeing, other kinds of meaning. For the white writer this can be both liberating and dangerous, for it can easily represent, even in an apparently democratic consciousness, a resistance to the loss of white power. It may be this double-bind which causes Patrick to leave the funeral/liberation rally, running up the side of the desert bowl, and down the other side, 'convoluted, involuted, bent on' himself.[25]

Australian scholar Ross Gibson has written of three phases in white Australian responses to the land: in the first, it is seen as an emblem of 'preternatural incomprehensibility'; in the second, stories of 'heroic failure' are created, stories 'required by postcolonial society to help it make its peace, conditionally, with the continent it could not defeat'; in a third and current phase the landscape is treated 'not as an obstacle to be subdued, nor as something unapproachably sublime, but as something to be learned from, something respectable rather than awesome'.[26] Not only is this consistent with the wisdom informing traditional Aboriginal land-culture but with environmentalist debates which accord respect, historical agency and, as Simon Schama has observed, 'the kind of creative unpredictability conventionally reserved for human actors', to the land.[27] This third phase, Gibson says, implies a 'subjective immersion in place'. Patrick's response to the South African land is a complex amalgam which is much harder to trace. He, too, resists an appropriative vision of the land, yet a 'subjective immersion in place' is highly tenuous for Patrick. Moreover, stories which explore, in a way quite different from anywhere else, places and their powers, how boundaries emerge and are articulated, spatio-political domains, what boundedness is, and how power moves from and into the land – still have to take up their place in a text like Galgut's and in a new South African political context.

AN IMMACULATE FIGURE

The heroine of *An Immaculate Figure* is a young white South African woman, apparently vacuous, gliding over the surface of things, registering little or giving nothing away. In her unselfconscious and fuzzy vision, Africa is 'big, hot and intense',[28] and is predominantly a continent of beaches. Rosandra lives in a world where men rather than women act upon the land, and the men she accompanies conquer and reshape the African land according to their own desires and fantasies, just as they appropriate and act upon her own body. Her 'uncle' Bass (based on the figure of Mike Hoare, the South African mercenary who attempted a coup of the Seychelles in 1980), is 'a man of Africa' and 'prepared to fight for it'.[29] Bass wants 'a kingdom', 'a palace in the tropical bush and a first-class hit squad to . . . defend it'; a 'bit of Africa', where Rosandra can be queen.[30]

Later, Rosandra is spotted by Thony, who is out looking for 'unspoilt beauties'[31] and is a man who 'collects beauty only to damage it'.[32] He is the owner of 'Star Palace', and a thinly veiled Sol Kerzner, the South African entrepreneur who created Sun City in the homeland of Bophuthatswana. For Thony, women and land are mutually reinforcing possessions: 'I used to imagine having this woman, this beautiful woman beside me, someone who would stand for everything the place would mean to me.'[33] While Bass is something of a 'comic-book' hero, Thony's life reminds Rosandra of sagas and suspense stories. As Martin Hall argues, the Kerzner-type hotel and theme park take the old appeal of the popular romance, and the ideology of colonialism upon which it was based, into the extravagant multi-media environment of late capitalism.[34] Kerzner's creations draw, as their master narrative, on the lost worlds of the Queen of Sheba and Prester John, mythologized in Haggard's *King Solomon's Mines* and Buchan's *Prester John*, Stephen Spielberg's *Indiana Jones* and Wilbur Smith's *Sunbird*, and which continue to structure the cultural politics of Africa.

Thony's fantasies for his kingdom include slides, fountains, whirlpools, spinning baths and water chutes created out of drought-lands: as Hall wryly remarks of Kerzner himself, 'he is an alchemist, someone who can bring water to the dry land of Bophuthatswana, someone who can turn an age-old dream into hard cash.'[35] They are based on a mutilation of the land, and a pirating of its resources, a dimension which Boehmer makes vivid: in the river bed, 'forced and crumpled' clods of earth collapse into dust underfoot. A group of boulders is 'scraped to a shine', 'scabs' of parched mud lie about, and the earth looks 'in pain'.[36] Thony pursues a brutally instrumentalist approach to the land. Rosandra's responses, however, amount only in the most muted way to an alternative, 'woman's' view, based on respect for the land. Indeed, her 'deadpan' response is reappropriated by Thony,[37] who finds it makes her look sexy. Boehmer once again explores both Rosandra's implication in a white male abuse of the land and the smallness of the space from which an alternative response can be mounted.

Boehmer makes the connection between the land and the woman's body explicit when she describes a birthmark which Rosandra has on her stomach as 'the Antarctic continent'.[38] Rosandra sees the birthmark as something she should try to hide, a threat to the translucent femininity which Bass and Thony seek, a 'malignancy' inside her,[39] and an 'internal bleed'.[40] But Ahmed, a freedom fighter whom she later meets, describes it as her 'little hidden blackness'.[41] With its obvious political overtones, Ahmed's comment acts as an invitation to identify with the cause of black liberation, the fight for a democratic right to the land; to take sides, declare her allegiances and to act. Rosandra is given 'a border and a way out':[42] she has left Thony and the border she crosses as she drives out of South Africa 'cut across her path . . . it worked . . . to free her again'.[43] But Rosandra persists in not acting, in not making a choice, and in doing so becomes increasingly implicated in the actions which take place around her. Although she drives Ahmed and a group of anti-apartheid activists on 'missions' into South Africa, she fails to make connections, based on information she has, which could have saved their lives. Given a chance to participate in their struggle for the land of their birth, she opts out again, and her failure to act becomes a form of guilt. Thus while male appropriation of the South African land is marked on her woman's body, Rosandra does not take up the fight to resist this, nor the system of white domination within which it is implicated.

Rosandra tells her story to Jem, a childhood friend who has long been in love with her. Jem has his own story of the South African land to tell: 'I felt the land. I felt it in my bones. The size, the breadth of it, so much sky to breathe in . . . I wanted to stay part of it, I wanted to be in it. So I went to the army.'[44] But Jem's story, he feels, can't compete with Rosandra's: 'infected' by fantasy,[45] her tales of Africa and its men (learned from the men themselves who have fancied themselves as figures of African romance) have a dramatic appeal he can't match.

These, then, are the stories in which, as Boehmer would have it, the land has been caught in white South African imaginations: the romances of Haggard are realized in the perversions of late-apartheid white culture, and a 'love of the land' comes to be translated into soldiering in the South African Defence Force. Flying from Africa to Europe, Rosandra looks down at the land below. She can, finally, neither know, nor see, nor feel, what is there:

> But Africa wasn't much to look at, grubby yellow mainly, whereas she imagined stark contrasts, jungle green, sapphire lakes, a bright Sahara, conical mountains, Bass's images. This is where we live, she told herself, that is our Africa. But it was too far away to feel anything much.[46]

In both Galgut's and Boehmer's work, the Southern African land continues to be caught in masculinist, militarist ideologies which depend on violence and oppression. In Galgut's book black nationalism, though pursuing a legitimate claim to the land, nevertheless displays the similar masculinist underpinnings to those of the South African military. 'Woman' as sign, and a largely male-constructed ideology of femininity, continue to be the means through which such relations to the land are negotiated. For Galgut, however, a series of discourses about the land displace one another as he attempts to reach into an identity which is at once democratic white, gay, existentialist and writerly. For Boehmer, white South African representations themselves have been 'infected' by fantasies of the African land derived from a romance tradition of writing. Both writers try to clear a space beyond an appropriative ownership of the land, a space for a different relation, one which might institute a less exclusivist sense of belonging. In each work this is a very different process, with different implications, yet we might say that in each, such a space remains, as yet, largely unformed and uncertain.

NOTES

1 J. M. Coetzee, *White Writing: On the Culture of Letters in South Africa*, Sandton, Radix, 1988, p. 9.
2 Coetzee, *White Writing*, p. 8.
3 Damon Galgut, *The Beautiful Screaming of Pigs*, London, Abacus, 1992.
4 Elleke Boehmer, *An Immaculate Figure*, London, Bloomsbury, 1993.
5 Galgut, *Beautiful Screaming*, p. 32.
6 Galgut, *Beautiful Screaming*, p. 14.
7 Galgut, *Beautiful Screaming*, p. 46.
8 Galgut, *Beautiful Screaming*, p. 116.
9 *Forces Favourites* (anonymous editors), Emmarentia, Taurus, 1987.
10 Galgut, *Beautiful Screaming*, p. 75.
11 Galgut, *Beautiful Screaming*, p. 76.
12 *The Invisible Ghetto: Lesbian and Gay Writing From South Africa*, ed. Matthew

Krouse, Johannesburg, COSAW, 1993.
13 Hein Willemse, review of *Forces Favourites*, *Journal of Southern African Studies*, vol. 16, no. 2, June 1990, p. 382.
14 Galgut, *Beautiful Screaming*, p. 39.
15 Galgut, *Beautiful Screaming*, p. 140.
16 Galgut, *Beautiful Screaming*, p. 134.
17 Galgut, *Beautiful Screaming*, p. 136.
18 Galgut, *Beautiful Screaming*, p. 46.
19 Galgut, *Beautiful Screaming*, p. 113.
20 Galgut, *Beautiful Screaming*, p. 160.
21 Galgut, *Beautiful Screaming*, p. 62.
22 Galgut, *Beautiful Screaming*, pp. 149–50.
23 Galgut, *Beautiful Screaming*, p. 155.
24 Galgut, *Beautiful Screaming*, p. 81.
25 Galgut, *Beautiful Screaming*, p. 159.
26 Ross Gibson, *South of the West: Postcolonialism and the Narrative Construction of Australia*, Bloomington and Indianapolis, Indiana University Press, 1992, pp. 16–17.
27 Simon Schama, *Landscape and Memory*, London, Harper Collins, 1995, p. 13.
28 Boehmer, *Immaculate Figure*, p. 230.
29 Boehmer, *Immaculate Figure*, p. 4.
30 Boehmer, *Immaculate Figure*, p. 25.
31 Boehmer, *Immaculate Figure*, p. 106.
32 Boehmer, *Immaculate Figure*, p. 136.
33 Boehmer, *Immaculate Figure*, p. 105.
34 Martin Hall, 'The Legend of the Lost City; Or, The Man with the Golden Balls' (forthcoming in *Journal of Southern African Studies*).
35 Hall, 'The Legend of the Lost City', p. 54.
36 Boehmer, *Immaculate Figure*, p. 109.
37 Boehmer, *Immaculate Figure*, p. 108.
38 Boehmer, *Immaculate Figure*, p. 140.
39 Boehmer, *Immaculate Figure*.
40 Boehmer, *Immaculate Figure*, p. 148.
41 Boehmer, *Immaculate Figure*, p. 212.
42 Boehmer, *Immaculate Figure*, p. 188.
43 Boehmer, *Immaculate Figure*.
44 Boehmer, *Immaculate Figure*, p. 183.
45 Boehmer, *Immaculate Figure*, p. 12.
46 Boehmer, *Immaculate Figure*, p. 127.

BIBLIOGRAPHY

Boehmer, E., *An Immaculate Figure*, London, Bloomsbury, 1993.
Coetzee, J. M., *White Writing: On the Culture of Letters in South Africa*, Sandton, Radix, 1988.
Forces Favourites, (anonymous editors), Emmarentia, Taurus, 1987.
Galgut, D., *The Beautiful Screaming of Pigs*, London, Abacus, 1992.

229

Gibson, R., *South of the West: Postcolonialism and the Narrative Construction of Australia*, Bloomington and Indianapolis, Indiana University Press, 1992.

Haarhof, D., *The Wild South-West: Frontier Myths and Metaphors in Literature Set in Namibia, 1760–1988*, Johannesburg, Witwatersrand University Press, 1991.

Hall, M., 'The Legend of the Lost City; Or, the Man with the Golden Balls' (forthcoming in *Journal of Southern African Studies*).

Krouse, M., (ed.), *The Invisible Ghetto: Lesbian and Gay Writing from South Africa*, Johannesburg, COSAW, 1993.

Schama, S., *Landscape and Memory*, London, Harper Collins, 1995.

Willemse, H., review of *Forces Favourites* in *Journal of Southern African Studies*, vol. 16, no. 2, June 1990.

15

DRUM MAGAZINE (1951–9) AND THE SPATIAL CONFIGURATIONS OF GENDER

Dorothy Driver

Drum magazine is crucial in South African literary and cultural history.[1] Its short stories are frequently reprinted, and its political exposés remain models of investigative journalism. Embracing a modernity apparently yearned for by the rapidly growing black urban population of the time, *Drum*'s circulation rose steadily through the 1950s, letters poured in from readers, and its journalists were emulated and adored. Although both Lewis Nkosi and Ezekiel Mphahlele have stressed the constraint the magazine placed on writers, because of its 'ready-made plots',[2] *Drum* ran regular short story competitions and in other ways gave space to a group of writers who made up what has since been called a South African literary renaissance:[3] Alex la Guma, Can Themba, Nat Nakasa, Richard Rive, Bloke Modisane, Casey Motsisi, Todd Matshikiza, Arthur Maimane and Peter Clarke, besides Mphahlele and Nkosi themselves. For these black writers, the magazine offered a vehicle that was part training ground and part enabling community. It offered quite the reverse for women. Only two black South African women published books written in English in the 1960s – Noni Jabavu and Bessie Head – and both did so from outside the country. Moreover, as the threatening manifestations of the 'nice-time girl' in Head's *A Question of Power* tell us and as her recently resurrected early work, *The Cardinals*, suggests, Head survived as a writer in spite of *Drum*.

Besides the short stories, literary competitions and investigative journalism, *Drum*'s monthly issues included essays on boxing, jazz, gangsters, businessmen, beauty queens, and housewives. It also ran beauty contests, beauty columns and advice columns, and published advertisements for skin-lightening creams, hair-straightening treatments, blood-purifying tablets, correspondence colleges, and the plethora of domestic items that were meant to make up urban life. Gender was deeply implicated in the modernizing process. As part of its general promulgation of a black middle-class within the context of the massive urbanization of the time, the magazine had an interest in constructing consumer desires and forging an ideology of domesticity through the aggressive demarcation of masculine and feminine spheres. *Drum* engaged in a process of psychic resettlement, from country to city, from 'Africa' to 'Europe', across the threshold into a nuclear family and 'home'. Some of the implications of this resettlement, for both women and men, provide the focal point for this essay.

Among the numerous analyses and reminiscences of *Drum* magazine,[4] none see it in relation to black South African literature written by women, and very few even refer to gender.[5] Yet *Drum* gives invaluable insight into the ways in which rural patriarchal structures were giving way to urban forms, as well as into the ways in which women's voices were silenced and a set of 'feminine' voices constructed in their place. It also shows, more generally, how gender was being reshaped as part of the rapid and large-scale processes of urbanization in the mid-twentieth century. Not only was *Drum*'s so-called 'vibrancy' constructed at women's expense, but the magazine's shift from rural 'past' to urban 'present' was negotiated largely by means of belittling and damaging misrepresentations of women.

Drum's domestic ideal bore virtually no relation to material reality. For instance, its demarcation of a certain kind of home as the 'proper place' for modern black South African women and as economically accessible to the men who wished to marry them, ignored the crippling conditions of apartheid, which forced both women and men to work long hours for very little pay. Moreover, *Drum* reshaped and in other ways adjusted women's bodies in order to confirm, in the eye of the beholder, the modern 'male gaze'. Femininity was being made to fit a certain space, but it was always also threatening to exceed that space: contradictorily, then, in a state of 'nervous condition',[6] *Drum* writers sometimes celebrated femininity as a force that might work *against* the very ideology of domesticity that the magazine was using to contain it.

For many black South Africans during the first half of the twentieth century, gender was in a marked state of flux, mostly because of

232

rapid urbanization. During the 1940s, and particularly during the period of post-war industrial expansion, Africans flocked to the cities, with the African population of Johannesburg and the surrounding Reef area increasing substantially by the end of the decade. Migrant labour among men had already caused a massive disproportion between the sexes, in both the rural and urban areas, but in the 1940s and 1950s increasing numbers of women left the reserves, although not enough to balance the sexes. *Drum* reported four men to one woman in the Johannesburg area, and, in the Reef's mining communities, an even higher disproportion: in Springs, for instance, it was seven to one.[7] Community and family structures were in disarray.

In the face of this social confusion, *Drum* magazine blandly reproduced European and American constructions of gender as part of an overall ideology of romantic love. This was not romantic love in the courtly tradition, but a modern form of romantic love within an ideology of domesticity, aiming for the establishment of a consumer-oriented nuclear family, headed by the husband and father and hospitable to female authority in only its most carefully controlled domestic forms. Gender constructions were both imposed *on* and negotiated *in* the magazine. The magazine was part of a signifying system whereby patriarchy manfully reasserted itself in the face of the destabilization of its traditional rural form, but it also necessarily acknowledged women's increasing power, even as it tried to exploit and contain this power.

During the 1950s, 'modern' black men and women were being positioned in a set of contradictory ways. While the South African government was busy with its policies of 'Bantu retribalization' and 'separate development', consumer interests – as evidenced in *Drum* – were promoting a 'universal' figure with 'universal' desires: shiny pots, fresh armpits, tidy houses, polished shoes. Migrant labour, the pass system, urban influx control and single-sex hostel life were destabilizing the family, while Christian and humanist groups were preaching its cohesion. Although the extended family had become all the more important in the absence of other forms of social security for black South Africans, Western influences were promoting the nuclear family instead.

Moreover, as already suggested, black urban women were inevitably working women, yet the developing ideology of domesticity forged an ideal distinction between the public and social as a masculine sphere and the private and domestic as the feminine sphere. These contradictory social prescriptions were written into *Drum* magazine in fascinating ways. What is of particular concern to me is the way *Drum*'s move from rural 'past' to urban 'present', from 'tradition' to 'modernity', was negotiated by means of the represent-ation of women: woman as 'sign'.[8]

Drum's shift of focus from the 'traditional' rural to urban modern-ity took place very suddenly, with a change of editors at the end of 1951. Among its more blatant modernizing gestures were the replacement of features on the value of mother's milk with advertise-ments for milk substitutes, and the use of the 'cover-girl', a figure passively positioned by the male gaze. Most importantly, 'Dolly Drum' made her entrance, nominally in the form of a monthly column, 'Ask Dolly', and imagistically in the form of the single woman out to have – and to offer – a 'nice-time' in the city. The very first features on 'cover-girl' women gave background sociolog-ical and biographical detail. These very quickly disappeared, however, and features began to withhold the kind of information which – for female readers – might work against the idea of a dream life being lived. Similarly, for its male readers, features withheld material which might undercut the idea that women would only achieve fulfilment in the presence of male desire.

In the advertisements, the beauty pages, the 'agony' columns and letters, the feature articles, and the short stories, *Drum* established gender in its Western configuration. In April 1952, after *Drum*'s circulation soared following a courageous piece of investigative journalism by Henry Nxumalo, this newly authorized 'Mr Drum' moved through Johannesburg streets in quest of 'the ideal of African glamour'. *Drum*'s first beauty competition, in March 1952, had been for 'Miss (or Mr) Africa', since a number of male readers had clam-oured to enter. But in the beauty competition advertised the following year, *Drum* took care to say, 'So, ladies – and not you gentlemen – send in your photos now!' Thus was gender being defined. Advertisements for skin-lightening creams, hair-straight-ening lotions and competitions around the three 'vital statistics' defined the modern African woman's body as an idealized European or American look-alike. Pond's Vanishing Cream promised that blackness itself, like dirt, would vanish.

After the photograph of the 'most popular pin-up girl', Priscilla Mtimkulu, first appeared in *Drum*, she was said to have received thirty proposals of marriage within a fortnight. And so it is that one of *Drum*'s women readers sends in the following letter:

Greetings to you, Mr DRUM,
I am one of the girls who read DRUM every month and I am not
satisfied to see other girl on the covers. And please Mr DRUM help
me to be a cover girl too and one thing is this Mr DRUM I am the
Kit who does not have her father and Mother, and I am suffering
about Mr Wrong. I can't get Mr Right, and please Mr DRUM I
wish one of our readers can help me to get Mr Right, because I
don't want to be Miss M — for ever, no marriage.
    So now we pray
    Our father and mother who are in town hallowed be thy name
    C— M—
    Amen.[9]

If town had become heaven, *Drum* was now God-the-father who
took the place of customary patriarchal structures.

As 'the director of desire' (Rene Girard's term), *Drum* presented
itself as if it owned its models, made jokes about the journalists
'beauty editing' all night, teased readers about *their* possible (sexual)
possession of *Drum*'s women, and liked to broadcast the fact that its
models, besides being continually 'proposed to', were fought over
and even abducted by gang members for days at a time. *Drum* also
suggested that domestic commodities were the features of the new
'bride price'. A famous jazz singer and model posed in the kitchen:
'I'm just crazy about cooking . . . I guess the guy who'll marry me
will be satisfied if he can find me a kitchen.'[10]

Although the rules for 'getting' a woman were in fact quite
different — economic success, and in its absence, rape — men who
wished to be worthy partners of the new woman were told to obey
the precepts of a romantic tradition propagated largely by the
columnist 'Dolly Drum', who was, in fact, 'a worried syndicate of
men'. Anthony Sampson, *Drum*'s first major editor, reports the
following conversation between the male journalists on one of the
days the column was being written:

'Here's someone in Orlando who wants a second wife.'
'Tell him he can't love two women at once.'
'Why not? I can.'[11]

Despite the name, 'Dolly Drum' was in fact a contrapuntal 'feminine' voice, a voice produced partially or even largely by male journalists in the name of the ideology of domesticity and romantic love.
Similarly, the South African short stories *Drum* published in the

1950s under women's signatures, under the names Rita Sefora, Joan Mokwena, and Doris Sello, were in fact not written by women.[12]

Thus the place of the 'feminine' in the magazine was particularly complex. 'Dolly Drum' delivered to the public a set of modern urban precepts which the men did not themselves believe but which represented the world they felt should be passed on through *Drum*. Promiscuous, rural and 'uncivilized' male attitudes were thus deflected through the male-constructed 'feminine' voice of modern, 'civilized' urban Africans – men and women. Reminders of a wilder sexuality ('Why not? I can') were retained: a virile masculine force which received its confirmation not from the columnist 'Dolly Drum' but from her alter ego: the 'other' women placed outside the modern, civilized, nuclear home. Yet for the purposes of *Drum*'s domesticating theme, sexual desire in women (as opposed to 'love') was evil, a 'poison' that might seep into the family, as in Joan Mokwena's 'My Husband was a Flirt'. Women's uncontrolled passion was even associated with tribalism in Can Themba's 'Mob Passion'.[13]

Drum's representation of housewives, sportswomen, and political women always emphasized their femininity, and involved a characteristic mixture of idealization, anxiety and contempt. Writing about Lilian Ngoyi when she was president of the African National Congress Women's League, Ezekiel Mphahlele described her as 'tough granite on the outside, but soft and compassionate deep down in her' in a trope which smoothly reproduced the woman's body in terms of conventional space-gender dichotomies. Ngoyi's voice was less easily managed. Quoting a member of the audience – 'She almost rocks men out of their pants when she speaks' – Mphahlele added: 'She can toss an audience on her little finger, [and] get men grunting with shame and a feeling of smallness.'[14] In an essay on women's hockey in 1957, the little finger became a 'big stick', wielded with energy and strength by the women players, who were also said to wear out the male referees by the end of the game, as if the real contest were between them and the women.

The author Casey Motsisi referred twice in a short space of time to the fact that the women could play a game once reserved for men, *and* do all 'their womanly chores at home'. He also took care to feminize their bodies: 'I asked one cutie whether they padded themselves as a precaution against injury. "No," she panted at me. "Everything we've got is our own".'[15] During the game the women, or 'girls' as Motsisi generally called them, still behaved with 'masculinity', as on

a 'battlefield', or were 'tigerish hellcats', mad women neither masculine nor feminine. But after the game the women became, in
Motsisi's words, 'well, FEMALES! Combs, lipstick, powder puffs,
feeding bottles, babies, husbands, boyfriends'; a 'magical' transformation, as Motsisi let slip, for this change happened 'as they walked
towards the dressing room' (my emphasis), as if Motsisi's litany, and
not the actual use of 'powder puffs', was all that was required to
transform these unnatural beings into the most natural of things,
'wisp[s] of cloud'.[16] Writing – 'the big stick' – remained in male
hands after all. Similarly, in an essay on women playing softball,
Motsisi had the male coaches 'put their arms round an otherwise
reluctant belle as they show the curvaceous Miss how to hold a bat'.[17]

In *Drum*'s representation of jazz singers, however, a different
spatial gender configuration opened up. Here, the process of eroticization sometimes seemed to allow desire to pass back and forth
between 'subject' and 'object', threatening to disturb the hierarchy
maintained so carefully at other times. Dorothy Masuka, as
described by Todd Matshikiza, had a dress whose wide stripes
seemed to run 'down her whole body, neck to hem. Round her
curves. Under the belt round her cute waist. Into the men's eyes.
Yes, man!'[18] She too had eyes, 'bedroom eyes' and 'goo-goo eyes'
used so successfully that you would think she wanted every man
around (this is 'most exciting'). Of course, in *Drum*'s standard pattern
of promise and denial, the essay went on as follows: But 'those eyes
gents ... those eyes are as fully booked as the December train': not to
a large number of passengers, as one might expect from the simile
and the context it is given, but to one man in particular: 'Mister
Simon Petto', who had two shops, two butchers, two cars and 'lots of
dough'.[19]

According to *Drum*'s representation, authority in the urban world
was invested, nominally, in the male head of the family, rather than
in the patriarch whose power was linked to that of the chief in a
mutually reinforcing relationship. But at the same time this modern
male authority was under continual threat. It promoted a *false*
ideology of separate male and female spheres despite the reality that
urban African wives were not confined to the domestic realm but
were economically and politically active. *Drum* was also misleading in
its (male) reproduction of domestic, female authority regarding
courtship, monogamy and family life – urging men to be home for
mealtimes, to help in hanging out the washing, having tea. Yet at the
same time, women's domestic authority was seen as a threat.

How did *Drum* manage this double contestation? By means of the discursive abuse of powerful women, on the one hand, and an abiding contempt for the norms of romantic love and domesticity, on the other hand. Thus, even while being glorified in terms of the domestic ideal, housewives were said to do nothing but 'yak, yak, yak' all day.[20] Through a set of gestures ranging from domestication to eroticization, intelligent, active and energetic women were returned to subjection: put back in the narrowness of domesticity or physically recast as self-conscious and sometimes even slightly ludicrous feminine bodies. Yet the voices and eyes of female jazz singers kept offering something one might call subjectivity, figured in some cases as 'promiscuity', which, like male polygamy, signified the opposite of modern domestic love.

However 'exciting' it may have seemed, this untamed female sexuality was also seen as dangerous to men, for it spelled the loss not just of patriarchal authority but of any masculinity which found its power in spatial separation and sexual control. Nevertheless, in a fascinating move, it came for a moment to represent a politically useful force, as shown in Can Themba's presentation of Dolly Rathebe, top model, film star and jazz singer.[21] While Rathebe is quoted as saying that she likes men to be men, and deplores women who wear slacks, she is spoken of in terms that confuse the gender categories of the masculine and feminine. She is a tomboy, which (complicatedly) is glossed as 'fond of boys'; she sings gruffly in a voice that is also 'husky, furry', kindling dreams of 'torrid love and wanton abandon'; she uses the stage 'as if she were a boxer in a ring'. Gender is not stabilized, and a different and wilder kind of femininity is produced than the 'wisps of cloud' Motsisi managed to conjure up in his re-vision of skilful sportswomen. Rathebe is presented uncontradictorily as the desiring subject: 'She wanted men at her feet'; she stopped seeing one of her lovers because 'you can't harness a race-horse with a mule'; and, unlike so many other women represented in *Drum*, is said to have fought successfully against an attempted abduction. She would not settle down – 'marriage was utterly unnecessary' – and was particularly appreciated for her refusal to be a domestic servant or factory-worker, which is glossed as 'work . . . for a white man'. As a singer of jazz, giving out 'the pounding rhythm that interpreted township jazz so well', and thus identified with 'all Africa', Rathebe gave her audience songs of township life which spoke about their own class and race positions.

In black America, jazz had become the signifier of an energy that had not been harnessed by white authority. Jazz replaced tribal music in *Drum* magazine when the magazine moved into its modern phase, but it also signified a space where a vision of Africa might persist: an Africa which refused the enforced separation between rural past and urban present and the policies of Bantu retribalization being pursued by the white government. Through jazz, 'Africa' moved to the city; 'Africa' infused the present. By the end of the 1950s, jazz became contained within a European space. *Drum* spoke sarcastically of the way it was now listened to by white South Africans, in halls where you got a 'nasty look' if you so much as tapped your foot on the floor. Dolly Rathebe took her audience back to an earlier time when jazz shows were held at the Bantu Men's Social Centre, where 'men were men in those days and did not want to dance with women'.

Jazz was an antidote to romantic love, which was first formulated in *Drum* as a means of liberation from traditional rural patriarchy and as an entry into modernity but then came to ensnare men instead. This new world of domesticated desire kept men not only in psychological thrall to the 'feminine' voice but also in financial debt as they strove to 'earn' modern women, thus intensifying the oppression experienced under apartheid. Like jazz, a quite different form of female sexuality entered *Drum*'s pages, active rather than passive, wild rather than tame, promiscuous rather than domestic, black rather than white – in dialogue (sometimes) with male sexuality rather than subordinated and owned. This femininity was associated with an 'other' world which combined the rural and urban, the 'past' and the 'present'. In two ways, then, this 'other' femininity worked against European domination, for it not only reproduced Africanness but also maintained it as part of the urban present. Powerful as it was, it could not be permitted to transform itself into something 'un-African', something which might transgress the spatial separations deemed necessary for masculinity and femininity and thus go to work against black men as well: 'men were men in those days and did not want to dance with women.' Dancing with women, in couples, would bring African men into the romantic, domestic and European space, a world dominated by women and whites.

For a moment, it seems, a different space had started opening up in *Drum* magazine: a different relation between men and women, a different relation between the urban present and the rural past, and even, perhaps, a different dialogue between 'black' and 'white'. But

Drum, mistrusting itself in its state of 'nervous condition', turned back on its own gestures of liberation from the categories of gender and race. And then, from the 1960s into the 1980s, with the development of Black Consciousness, *Drum* would be misread (Harold Bloom's term) as nothing more than a 'non-white' or 'assimilationist' gesture, and women's subjectivity would take a less interesting turn, compelled once again to take a subordinate position rather than to emerge in a voice of its own. In 1990 Christine Qunta, for instance, was able to claim, 'I take the view that we are Africans before we are women',[22] as if racial identity obliterated gender difference, as if a subjectivity specific to African femininity did not after all exist.

NOTES

Note: The financial assistance of the Centre for Science Development (HSRC, South Africa) towards this research is hereby acknowledged. Opinions expressed and conclusions arrived at are those of the author and are not necessarily to be attributed to the Centre for Science Development.

1 *Drum* was established in 1950 and is still published: this study refers to the years 1951–9.
2 Lewis Nkosi, 'African Fiction: Part I: South Africa: Protest', *Africa Report*, no. 7, Oct. 1962, p. 3; see also Ezekiel Mphahlele, *Down Second Avenue*, London, Faber & Faber, 1959, p. 188.
3 See N. W. Visser, 'South Africa: The Renaissance that Failed', *Journal of Commonwealth Literature*, vol. 9, no. 1, 1976, pp. 42–57.
4 For published accounts of *Drum*, see Anthony Sampson, *Drum: A Venture into the New Africa*, London, Collins, 1956; Tom Hopkinson, *In the Fiery Continent*, London, Victor Gollancz, 1972; Michael Chapman, 'More Than Telling a Story: *Drum* and its Significance in Black South African Writing', in M. Chapman (ed.), *The Drum Decade: Stories from the 1950s*, Pietermaritzburg, University of Natal Press, 1989; Mike Nicol, *A Good-Looking Corpse*, London, Secker and Warburg, 1991; Rob Nixon, 'Harlem, Hollywood, and the Sophiatown Renaissance', in *Homelands, Harlem and Hollywood: South African Culture and the World Beyond*, New York and London, Routledge, 1994.
5 Nicol, *A Good-Looking Corpse*, has a chapter entitled 'Love and Hot Dames', pp. 143–5; See Dorothy Driver, 'Woman and Nature, Women as Objects of Exchange: Towards a Feminist Analysis of South African Literature,' in Michael Chapman, Colin Gardner, and Es'kia Mphahlele (eds) *Perspectives on South African English Literature*, Johannesburg, Donker, 1992, pp. 454–74.
6 See Tsitsi Dangarembga, *Nervous Conditions*, London, The Women's Press, 1988.
7 For population figures, see Tom Lodge, *Black Politics in South Africa since 1945*, London, Longman, 1983, pp. 11–12; and Deborah Posel, *The*

Making of Apartheid 1948–1961: Conflict and Compromise, Oxford, Clarendon Press, 1991.

8 See Elizabeth Cowie, 'Woman as Sign', *m/f*, vol. 1, no. 1, 1978.

9 Reprinted in Hopkinson, *Into the Fiery Continent*, p. 359.

10 *Drum*, Dec. 1954, p. 26.

11 Sampson, *Drum: A Venture*, p. 122.

12 Although the stories sometimes read like Can Themba's, Arthur Maimane has told me that he himself wrote at least two and perhaps all three of them. Ironically, the story by Doris Sello was reprinted in Annemarie van Niekerk's recent anthology of women writers: *Raising the Blinds: A Century of South African Women's Stories*, Johannesburg, Ad Donker, 1990.

13 *Drum*, Apr. 1953.

14 *Drum*, Mar. 1956, pp. 63-5.

15 *Drum*, Oct. 1957, p. 31.

16 *Drum*, Oct. 1957, pp. 29-31

17 *Drum*, Sept. 1955, p. 73.

18 *Drum*, Jan. 1955, p. 35.

19 *Drum*, Jan. 1955, p. 39

20 See, for instance, *Drum*, Mar., 1953, pp. 17–19; Oct. 1956, p. 63.

21 The essays are reprinted in Essop Patel (ed.), *The World of Can Themba*, Johannesburg, Ravan, 1985.

22 Christine Qunta, *Tribute*, Aug. 1990, p. 44.

BIBLIOGRAPHY

Brown, D. M., 'The Anthology as Reliquary: *Ten Years of Staffrider* and *The Drum Decade*', *Current Writing*, vol. 1, no. 1, 1989, pp. 3–21.

Chapman, M., 'More Than Telling a Story: *Drum* and its Significance in Black South African Writing', in M. Chapman (ed.), *The Drum Decade: Stories from the 1950s*, Pietermaritzburg, University of Natal Press, 1989, pp. 183–232.

Coplan, D., *In Township Tonight!: South Africa's Black City Music and Theatre*, Johannesburg, Ravan, 1985.

Cowie, E., 'Woman as Sign', *m/f*, vol. 1, no. 1, 1978.

Dangarembga, T., *Nervous Conditions*, London, The Women's Press, 1988.

Driver, D., 'Woman and Nature, Women as Objects of Exchange: Towards a Feminist Analysis of South African Literature', in M. Chapman, C. Gardner, and E. Mphahlele (eds), *Perspectives on South African English Literature*, Johannesburg, Donker, 1992, pp. 454–74.

Lodge, T., *Black Politics in South Africa since 1945*, London, Longman, 1983.

Mphahlele, E., *Down Second Avenue*, London, Faber & Faber, 1959.

Ndebele, N., 'The Ethics of Intellectual Combat', *Current Writing*, vol. 1, no. 1, 1989, pp. 21–35.

Nicol, M., *A Good-Looking Corpse*, London, Secker and Warburg, 1991.

Nixon, R., *Homelands, Harlem and Hollywood: South African Culture and the World Beyond*, New York and London, Routledge, 1994.

Nkosi, L., 'The Fabulous Decade: The Fifties', in *Home and Exile and Other*

Selections, (2nd edn), London, Longman, 1983, pp. 3–24.

Patel, E. (ed.), *The World of Can Themba*, Johannesburg, Ravan, 1985.

Posel, D., *The Making of Apartheid 1948–1961: Conflict and Compromise*, Oxford, Clarendon Press, 1991.

Sampson, A., *Drum: A Venture into the New Africa*, London, Collins, 1956.

Sole, Kelwyn. 'Class, Continuity and Change in Black South African Literature, 1948–1960', in B. Bozzoli (ed.), *Labour, Townships and Protest: Studies in the Social History of the Witwatersrand*, Johannesburg, Ravan, 1979.

Visser, N.W. 'South Africa: The Renaissance that Failed', *Journal of Commonwealth Literature*, 1976, vol. 9, no. 1, pp. 42-57.

16

RURAL TRANSNATIONALISM
Bessie Head's southern spaces

Rob Nixon

Among the host of black South African authors exiled by apartheid, Bessie Head alone chose to situate the bulk of her oeuvre in her adopted locale. The work of most of the literary exiles – Bloke Modisane, Lewis Nkosi, Es'kia Mphahlele, Alex La Guma, Dennis Brutus et al. – reveals few attachments to the alien present, focusing obsessively on the imaginative recuperation of a South Africa that is past and elsewhere. Almost all of these exiles wrote at a great physical distance from South Africa, having put oceans and continents between themselves and apartheid. Head's circumstances and approach proved wholly different.

As a single mother and a refugee, she faced a constrained set of options. She could not avail herself of the standard literary routes from South Africa to the Northern hemisphere and merely moved, in her words, 'one door away from South Africa'.[1] Consequently, she achieved a perspective of proximate exile in which cross-cultural differences were offset by the significant spatial and cultural continuities which were contingent on her remaining in the South.

Most of South Africa's specifically literary exiles headed for those venerable magnets for bohemian diasporas – London, Paris, New York, Chicago, and Berlin. Unlike the literary set, however, most of the non-literary refugees and exiles from apartheid crossed over into neighbouring countries, where they remained vulnerable to the predations of South Africa's regional imperial designs. For them, exile was principally a rural, not a metropolitan, plight. Thus, while Head was totally estranged from the dominant traditions of South

243

African literary exile, her preoccupation with rural, regional experience brought her closer to the presiding traditions of South African exile *per se*.

Head's rural transnationalism began as an affliction, which she appropriated as an allegiance. After crossing the border into the frontline state of Botswana in 1964, she became a pawn in a chess-game between that country and South Africa. The Botswana government, fearing South African military intervention if the exile community expanded, refused to grant her permanent status. So for fifteen years as a refugee, she had to report weekly to the police. As pressures mounted, she began to fear that the Batswana might certify her as insane in order to deport her to South Africa where she would be forced to re-enact her mother's institutional history.[2] The abuse dispensed first by the South African, then by the Botswanan, state seeded her growing scepticism toward the grand narratives of national politics. She was equally suspicious, however, of the category of national literatures and resisted attempts to reduce her to either a South African or a Botswanan phenomenon. She projected herself, instead, as a Southern African writer, someone whose writing was profoundly informed by the partial continuities that linked the two adjoining national spaces.

If Head's regional transnationalism began as a symptom of her viciously administered life, it was one of her singular achievements to transform that regionalism into a groundbreaking literary vision. Almost all her writings are set in a Botswanan village and accumulatively they convey a powerful sense of the ceaseless border crossings of imperialists, missionaries, refugees, migrant workers, prostitutes, school children, teachers, and armies that score Southern Africa as a region.

Like her identification with the region, Head's growing allegiance to the village of Serowe never lost its comparative edge. The complexities of this affiliation are most manifest in *Serowe: Village of the Rain Wind*, Head's oral history that appeared in 1981, five years before her death in 1986 at the age of forty-nine. *Village of the Rain Wind* offers the fullest account of her sedulous efforts to cultivate ancestry and community, dramatizing, in the process, her reliance on the village and the Southern African region as complementary sites of affiliation, spaces that offset her estrangement from national and Pan Africanist identities.

From the perspective of Head's relentlessly disrupted life, the Botswanan village held a particular restorative promise. For, like most of Botswana, Serowe's history was unrepresentative of the history of Southern Africa in that it had remained relatively un-trammelled by colonial conquest. The depth of Botswana's mineral wealth was only exposed in the 1960s and 1970s and, as a mostly desert region lacking a coastline, the land contained few enticements for Europeans. Over the course of five hundred years, Portuguese, Dutch, British, French, and British explorers and colonists had remade the face of South Africa, whereas Bechuanaland (as Botswana was previously called) had been a British colony for a mere eighty years prior to independence, and even then, had only been lightly colonized. Throughout Africa, there has been a correlation between the scale of European settlement and the blood-iness of decolonization – witness the wars in Kenya, Algeria, Zimbabwe, Mozambique, Angola and South Africa. By such standards, Botswana had experienced a peaceful and sheltered twentieth century, a point not lost on Head as she sought a refuge from the psychic and bureaucratic violence that had marked her life.

Yet Head found it difficult to identify with Botswana at large. Instead, she focused her ambitions on Serowe, an isolated village of 33,000 inhabitants where daily life was criss-crossed with indigenous traditions, some of them pre-dating the colonial irruptions into the subcontinent. Head was encouraged in her idealism by Serowe's exiguous contact with colonialism: even among the poorest folk she recognized a resilient self-respect that she felt was far more difficult to sustain under the conditions of South African apartheid.

Head's determination to win greater social acceptance was boosted by her experimentation in the late 1970s with a change of genre. Compared to the solitude of composing a novel (she had by then written *When Rainclouds Gather*, *A Question of Power* and *Maru*), Head's research for an oral history forced upon her a greater intim-acy with the village. The process of interviewing some one hundred inhabitants about their collective history became integral to her efforts to gain entry into the community through the gates of the past. Arguably, in a village where only a fraction of the population could read English, oral history allowed Head to enact her assimilat-ion to a degree that the novel form never permitted.

Head's approach to Serowe's history is redolent of Walter Benjamin's insistence that 'To articulate the past historically does not mean to recognize it "the way it really was". It means to seize hold of a memory as it flashes up at a moment of danger.'[3] Emerging in the mid-1970s from her cycles of high inner distress, racial rejection, psychological breakdown, confinement in a Botswanan mental asylum, and the strange solipsistic creativity of *A Question of Power*, Head saw local history not least as a mechanism for survival. She once remarked that 'a sense of history was totally absent in me', an observation that is susceptible to layered readings.[4] Serowe promised Head a redeeming alternative to the threatening histories to which she had been exposed: familial blankness, a predestined female history of atonement for a transgressive life, and systematic racial conquest.

Head's later writings suggest that she came to view the governing forms of historical narration as symptoms and agents of colonial violence. Looking back on her South African education, she recognized how she had been denied any sense of history as a flexible resource – indeed, as anything other than an incontestable record of loss and obliteration.[5] If black South Africans laboured beneath a tradition of triumphalist colonial historiography, colonialism's marginal interest in Botswana had produced a quite contrary legacy of partisan, expansive silences, as if villages like Serowe had proved so deficient in significant event as to defeat all attempts at historical rendition. As Head observed sardonically of Serowe: 'There isn't anything in this village that an historian might care to write about. Dr Livingstone passed this way, they might say.'[6]

In *Village of the Rain Wind*, Head sought to offset this neglect without merely reacting to it. Struggling to piece together a rich but diffuse interview with a 104-year-old man, she articulated her motives for connecting with a tradition that

> had kept no written record of [its] searches, enquiries and philosophical anguish. All that was written of this period by white historians trod rough-shod over their history dismissing it as 'petty, tribal wars', . . . It had seemed more important that a black man should be known as a 'good boy' or a 'bad boy' and hurry up and down with the suitcases of his master, who was creating 'real' history.[7]

With this in mind, she disturbs external, colonial standards of what constitutes event, concluding wryly:'I decided to record the irrelevant.'[8]

Village of the Rain Wind thus takes shape as a remedial project that allows Head to fortify and diversify Serowe's oral records of its past while simultaneously endowing herself with a surrogate genealogy.[9]

The result is a eulogy to Serowe's past that doubles as an orphan's act of affiliation.

To take up a genre of collective memory is to intervene in the parameters of group identity. All her life, Head had experienced the partialities of such collectivities from a position of exclusion. It is significant, therefore, that her efforts to influence the boundaries of Serowe through historical form stress the porousness of the village's identity, its long record of accommodating migrants, refugees, and strangers. *Village of the Rain Wind* is animated by Head's desire to chart, within Serowe's (and the Bamangwato people's) history, precedents for the values she herself upholds.[10] The history that Head fashions assumes a form that implicitly favours her claim to belong. Much of *Village of the Rain Wind*'s fascination flows from her evident investment in figures reminiscent of aspects of her own condition: the traditional story-tellers, single mothers, and illegitimate children; the refugees from nineteenth-century Matabele conflicts, from the Anglo-Boer War, and from apartheid's pass laws, all of whom sought sanctuary in Serowe; the educated women straddling awkward divides; the village leaders who, despatched across the border for their schooling, had adapted childhood memories of urban South Africa to their rural Botswanan lives. Given Head's history as an *apatride extraordinaire* and a champion of the 'Masarwa' cause, she understandably reserves a special curiosity for those outsiders whose partial absorption into the Bamangwato people has altered the course of the culture while furnishing them with a compensatory sense of home.

Head plainly relishes an exchange with the venerable 'traditional historian,' Ramosamo Kebonang, whose commentary on the fraught question of origins testifies to Serowe's record of incorporation:

> 'O tswa kae?' ('Where's your original home?')
> 'South Africa,' I said.
> 'Well, that's all right,' Ramosamo said kindly. 'What we like is for all foreigners to accept themselves as Mongwato and stay peacefully with us. This custom started from the time of our King Khama. King Khama used to be the lover of foreigners, both black and white. In the case of black people we have very large village wards in Serowe of foreign tribes. It came about that we cannot easily trace who is a foreigner these days. They have added to the Bamangwato tribe and all talk Setswana.'[11]

If the presiding tone of *Village of the Rain Wind* is one of pride in a community which – to a degree unimaginable under apartheid – could set the terms for the conduct of its own affairs, Head's cross-cultural heritage fractures her mostly celebratory voice. The apprentice insider's claim to a slice of Bamangwato dignity remains edged with a sense of remorse that black South Africans had been denied such historical possibilities and had enjoyed so little respite from dancing the colonial-anti-colonial two-step.

The regional perspective of Head's oral history makes it manifest that Serowe's regenerative traditions of cultural syncretism are not equally available to all cultures under all circumstances. Head implies that such flexibility requires, over and above open-mindedness, historical good fortune. Serowe's Bamangwato people had been largely exempt from the deforming pressures of reacting against the impositions of colonial history, colonial values, and colonial institutions. They were thus better able to develop an easygoing eclecticism – even towards white culture – that would have been inconceivable across most of Southern Africa. Head's memories of colonial brutality in South Africa thus provide the implicit backdrop for her amazement at one interlocutor's enthusiasm for aspects of white culture: 'Serowe may be the only village in Southern Africa where a black man can say with immense dignity: "I like some of the things the white man brought, like iron bolts." '[12]

Head's stance on syncretism has implications for contemporary debates on multiculturalism as she seldom loses sight of relations of power. Her approach suggests that the relative security of an indigenous culture – and, by extension, its territorial integrity – is often crucial to whether the cultural meld proves threatening or enabling. As Head once remarked, in Serowe every new idea 'is absorbed and transformed until it emerges somewhere along the line as 'our traditional custom'. Everything is touched by 'our traditional custom' – British Imperialism, English, Independence, new educational methods, progress, and foreigners. It all belongs.'[13] But Serowe's customary accommodations arose out of the security of its peripheral and relatively fleeting subjection to colonialism, a heritage that allowed it to accommodate difference in a manner that could express, not disavow, its identity.

Such was Head's determination to belong that we can read *Village of the Rain Wind*, by turns, as a celebration of Serowe's record of cross-cultural accommodation and as a romantic projection of the author's yearnings. One senses the huge allure for Head of the idea of a society that secures its identity through flexible continuities of custom and territory rather than through the imposition of ethnic criteria. She thus projects Serowe as a space that promises the possibility of a subnational identity and, through its connections beyond Botswana, a transnational one. But despite her growing veneration for Serowe – replete with flourishes of romanticism – there are evident limits to Head's readiness to idealize the village whose rejection had once stung her. One hears echoes of a very personal vexation when she exposes those moments in the village history where clan ructions, failures of justice, and crimping traditions inhibited its openness to change.

Ideally, *Village of the Rain Wind* should be read alongside *The Collector of Treasures*, the superb volume of short stories which is an offshoot of Head's research for the oral history. Between them, the two books convey her keen enjoyment of the freedom – so rare among South African writers – to engage with social issues that bypass binary forms of racial conflict. One detects in Head an anxiety that racial domination, through its power to compel protest, may continue to preoccupy black forms of self-definition, preventing them from setting more independent imaginative co-ordinates.[14]

Certainly, the distance that Head put between herself and national liberation politics is sometimes cited as evidence of the apolitical character of her work.[15] So, too, is her preoccupation with the 'ordinary,' a word that runs like a mantra through her work, acquiring an almost philosophical force. Her commitment to redeeming the ordinary was seen by some as commitment of the wrong, apolitical kind. Yet, what one finds in *Maru, Tales of Tenderness and Power, Serowe: Village of the Rain Wind*, and, above all, in *The Collector of Treasures*, is her gift for rediscovering the turbulent power-plays within those expanses of rural society which, from an urban perspective, may appear becalmed, bland, uneventful, immutable, and inconsequential to 'real' politics.

Head's most affecting prose arises from her quickness to redeem the irrelevant, the common, the ordinary and, in the etymological sense of 'earthly', the mundane. Given her background, ordinariness appeared not as something which she could take for granted but as an exhausting, improbable attainment. Head's animation by the ordinary was partly a reaction against the tremendous violence of South Africa which had fallen, like a dead hand, across her imagination. In fleeing apartheid, she rejected both the imaginative priority of such extraordinary violence and the functionalist imperatives of most South African literature, both of which she rejected as dehumanizing.[16] Like Njabulo Ndebele (see his short stories in *Fools*),[17] if for somewhat different reasons, she broke with the literary tradition of the titanic clash, often staged between characters who are little more than ciphers representing self-evident moral extremes.

Head is the only black South African writer – writing in English – to have grown up in the city and to have transformed herself into a rural writer, in her case by crossing over into a frontline state. (Indeed, aside from the very different case of John Berger, no contemporary writer has travelled as dramatically as Head against the prevailing flow from country to city, by settling permanently in a foreign, adopted peasant community, and producing a body of fiction grounded in oral traditions.) Head's reversal of the norm has sometimes encouraged the perception of her as a literary misfit rather than as a writer who anticipated the need to counter-balance South African literature's fixation with male, urban space and with realms of spectacular conflict rather than the 'small' pressures of daily survival.

In her literary concerns and her life alike, Head pushed against the prevailing currents of black South African literary culture which flowed from country to city. Indeed, not just in literature, but in film, music, and theatre, this urban drift had produced a vast body of culture around the motif popularly known as 'Jim comes to Jo'burg'. Head's reversal of this tradition matters because it helps redress the unequal balance of urban and rural experience in the literature. It also initiates a second form of redress, one which even Njabulo Ndebele, in his role of critic rather than creative writer, fails to address. He urges a return to rural themes, yet declines to consider a crucial connection between the imaginative construction of urban and rural spaces and gender.[18] For there is an inextricable link between South African literature's amnesia towards rural space and its amnesia toward the experience of women, a point that Dorothy Driver stresses in her article in this volume (see pp. 231–42). Virtually without exception, and cutting across the genres of novel, theatre and film it is the generic 'Jim' who bends his way towards Jo'burg. This is broadly true regardless of whether his creators be black, like Peter Abrahams (in his novel *Mine Boy*) and Percy Mtwa (in the play *Bopha!*) or white, in for instance Lionel Rogosin's classic film *Come Back Africa* and Alan Paton's *Cry, the Beloved Country*. This state of affairs results partly from gendered inequities in literacy. It stems, too, from black women's profoundly restricted access to leisure and institutional support for their writing.[19] Yet the predominance of male urban experience is also to some degree a consequence of the geography of apartheid, whereby disproportionately large numbers of women were consigned to the impoverished bantustans.

Over the past fifteen years, the lives of such rural women have begun to trickle into the literature through works such as Lauretta Ngcobo's *And They Didn't Die*, Miriam Tlali's collection of short stories, *Mihloti*, Elsa Joubert's *Poppie Nongena*, and also through the stories of Gcina Mhlope, her play, *Have You Seen Zandile?*, and the performance poetry of Nise Malange. Yet in many ways the most impressive precursor for such writing was Head's 1977 volume, *The Collector of Treasures*.[20] This may seem an unlikely claim, as Head's stories are set, not in an impoverished rural bantustan, but in a Botswanan village. Despite this cross-border displacement, however, Head conveys the cadences of rural women's lives in a manner that challenges, with unprecedented force, many of the conventional silences in South African literature.

While the dereliction of her women is less acute than that ordinarily endured in the bantustans, many of Head's concerns assume a direct, transnational relevance and resonate directly with South African rural experience. Her stories are preoccupied with epidemic family breakdown, with gendered relations to the land, with tensions between peasant women's agricultural authority and their subordination to local patriarchy, and with women's crimped sense of economic and social mobility. But Head is equally engaged by the plasticity of tradition and by the intrepid women who flex its frontiers: the village's first prostitute who challenges received views on the sexual double standard and marriage ('Life'); the abused women who become husband-murderers ('The Collector of Treasures'); and the woman who conducts a clandestine affair with the village priest and advocates that post-menopausal women should take young lovers ('The Special One'). Herself born from the inconceivable, Head seems particularly drawn to women who press the limits of what is locally imaginable.

Collectively, the stories testify to Head's readiness to transfigure oral into written narrative form rather than attempting the doomed task of replicating oral features in writing. Thus, *The Collector of Treasures* stands as an invaluable antecedent for much of what Ndebele in his critical essays has advocated: it is a singular instance of a writer allowing the experience of rural space both formal and thematic weight.

Although Head never returned to South Africa, she spoke of herself as having 'performed a peculiar shuttling movement between two lands'.[21] That phrase is best understood in the light of her intimation that, while drawn to the comparative tranquillity and 'ordinariness' of Botswanan life, imaginatively she remained too violent for her surroundings.[22] Thus, the cross-border split between sensibility and subject matter helps account for the transnational feel to *The Collector of Treasures*. This spatial shuttling had profound implications for the development of her historical imagination. For Head moved from brute 'colonialism of a special type' under apartheid, to what, on her arrival in 1964, was the mild colonialism of the British protectorate of Bechuanaland, colonialism so muted that it had left many of the country's pre-colonial traditions relatively intact. Then, from 1966 onwards, Head lived through Bechuanaland's transformation into Botswana, a post-colonial state in official argot, yet one that continued to fall under the long shadow of South African regional imperialism.[23] The sense of Head's passage through versions of the pre-colonial, colonial, and post-colonial eras ensures that her later writing offers rare commentary on the porous, ambiguous frontlines among national and historical divides. This quality heightens the perception in both *Serowe: Village of the Rain Wind* and *The Collector of Treasures* of her work as an iconoclastic act of geographical and historical bridging.

Head's work was apt to project a degree of social acceptance which, in her life, she knew only as a wavering prospect. Such determined optimism quietened in her fiction the cadences of desolation that distinguished her letters. If, to the last, Head's integration into Serowe on paper remained somewhat ahead of her integration in daily life, she at least acquired there a degree of allegiance and acceptance unimaginable in her early years in Botswana from the mid-1960s through to the early 1970s. Moreover, she had engineered for herself a spread of commitments that spanned writing as a vocation, the village, the Southern African region, and those rural women who sought a greater share of Botswana's perceived cultural and economic life.

Thus through her sharp redefinitions and refocusing of rural space Head exposed a cluster of amnesias in Southern African writing and yielded a greatly expanded sense of its prospects. Indeed, perhaps more than any other writer, she has drawn attention to the possibility of a Southern African literature that is more than the sum of the region's various national literatures. Head was unable to settle into a vision of the nation as a 'natural' space on the basis of which she could lodge 'natural' claims. Instead, she recognized the nation as a contingent and laboriously fabricated site, subject to all manner of violent reinvention. It was her angularity to the nation that encouraged Head to recognize other lines of geographical, historical, and cultural connection that nationalism typically obscures. Thus her writing gives voice to the distinctive experiences of refugees and other embattled itinerants whose lives are often circumscribed less by nation-space than by a shuttling rural transnationalism.

NOTES

1 Bessie Head, 'Preface to Witchcraft', in *A Woman Alone*, Craig MacKenzie (ed.), Portsmouth, Heinemann, p. 27.
2 Letter dated 27 November 1965, in R. Vigne (ed.), *A Gesture of Belonging: Letters from Bessie Head, 1965–1979*, Heinemann African Writers Series, Heinemann, 1991, p. 14.
3 Walter Benjamin, *Illuminations*, trans. Harry Zohn, 1970, reprinted. London, Fontana-Collins, 1973, p. 258.
4 Head, *A Woman Alone*, p. 66.
5 See, for example, *A Woman Alone*, pp. 79–82, 65–72.
6 Head, *A Woman Alone*, p. 30.
7 Bessie Head, *Serowe: Village of the Rain Wind*, London, Heinemann, 1981, p. 67.
8 Head, *Serowe*, p. 67.
9 Head, *Serowe*, p. xii.
10 Serowe is the capital of the Bamangwato people, who have traditionally inhabited the north-east of Botswana. The Bamangwato are a subgroup of the Batswana.
11 Head, *Serowe*, p. 68.
12 Head, *Serowe*, p. 70.
13 Head, *A Woman Alone*, p. 70.
14 This can be compared with Elizabeth's account, in *A Question of Power*, of why she left South Africa: 'there wasn't any kind of social evolution beyond that [hatred], there wasn't any lift to the heart, just this vehement vicious struggle between two sets of people with different looks.' See Bessie Head, *A Question of Power*, 1974, reprinted London, Heinemann, 1986, p. 19.
15 See, for example, Lewis Nkosi's, insistence that Head 'is not a political novelist in any sense that we can recognize'. Lewis Nkosi, *Tasks and Masks*, Harlow, Longman, 1981, p. 100.
16 Head, *A Woman Alone*, p. 67.
17 Njabulo Ndebele, *Fools and Other Stories*, Harlow, Longman, 1984.
18 Njabulo Ndebele, *Rediscovery of the Ordinary: Essays on South African Literature and Culture*, Johannesburg, COSAW, 1991.
19 According to one researcher, of 140 black South African writers publishing in English between 1920 and 1988, only seven were women.

See Cherry Clayton, *Women and Writing in South Africa*, Johannesburg, Heinemann, 1989, p. 1.

20 Head once described *The Collector of Treasures* as her 'resumé of 13 years of living entirely in village life.' Quoted in Charlotte Bruner, 'Bessie Head: Shock and Loss' in *African Literature Association Bulletin*, vol. 12, Spring 1986, p. 42.

21 Head, *A Woman Alone*, p. 67.

22 Head, *A Woman Alone*, pp. 101–2.

23 For an inclusive critique of the implications of post-colonialism, see Anne McClintock, 'The Angel of Progress: Pitfalls of the Term "Post-colonialism" ' in *Imperial Leather: Race and Gender in the Colonial Contest*, New York, Routledge, 1995.

BIBLIOGRAPHY

Abrahams, P., *Mine Boy*, London, Heinemann African Writers Series, 1954.

Benjamin, W., *Illuminations*, trans. Harry Zohn, 1970, reprinted London, Fontana-Collins, 1973.

Clayton, C., *Women and Writing in South Africa*, Johannesburg, Heinemann, 1989.

Head, B., *A Question of Power* (1974), reprinted London, Heinemann African Writers Series, 1986.

Head, B., *The Collector of Treasures and Other Stories*, London, Heinemann African Writers Series, 1980.

Head, B., *Serowe: Village of the Rainwind*, London, Heinemann African Writers Series, 1981.

Head, B., 'Foreword to Sol Plaatje, *Native Life in South Africa*', Cape Town, David Phillip, 1984.

Head, B., *A Woman Alone*, Portsmouth, New Hampshire, Heinemann, 1992.

Lazarus, N., *Resistance in Postcolonial African Fiction: The Novels of Ayi Kwei Armah*, New Haven, Yale University Press, 1990.

McClintock, A., 'The Angel of Progress: Pitfalls of the Term 'Post-colonialism', in McClintock, *Imperial Leather: Race and Gender in the Colonial Conquest*, Routledge, New York, 1995.

Mhlophe, G., *Have You Seen Zandile?*, Braamfontein, Skotaville, 1988.

Mtwa, P., '*Bopha!*', in Duma Ndlovu (ed.), *Woza Afrika! An Anthology of South African Plays*, New York, George Braziller, 1986.

Nkosi, L., *Tasks and Masks*, Harlow, Longman, 1981.

Vigne, R., (ed.), *A Gesture of Belonging: Letters from Bessie Head, 1965–1979*, London, Heinemann African Writers series, Heinemann, 1991.

INDEX